The New Economics of the Less Developed Countries

Other Titles in This Series

Westview Special Studies in Social, Political, and Economic Development

The Political Economy of the Less Developed Countries: Changing Perceptions in North-South Bargaining
edited by Nake M. Kamrany

After a quarter-century of experimentation with economic development in the poorer countries, the disarray, and in some cases the calamitous results, are so obvious that a fresh look at and reexamination of traditional assumptions, methodologies, theories, and policies is needed. The contributors to this volume explore--with supporting theoretical frameworks and empirical evidence--the new perceptions concerning the development of the poor countries, providing clear and sophisticated treatments of North-South bargaining, commodity power, indexation, the theory of power and the international distribution of rights and resources, and the effectiveness of international organizations as vehicles for conflict resolution. The authors discuss the position and prospects of the non-oil-producing, less developed countries, focusing on measurements of the quality of life in these countries, growth and income distribution policies, and the effectiveness of public expenditures to enhance social welfare.

Nake M. Kamrany is professor of economics and director of the Program in Productivity and Technology at the University of Southern California. He has held faculty and research positions with M.I.T., Stanford Research Institute, the World Bank, and U.C.L.A., and has conducted research on the economic development and technology of twenty countries.

The New Economics of the Less Developed Countries

Changing Perceptions in the North-South Dialogue

edited by Nake M. Kamrany

Routledge
Taylor & Francis Group

LONDON AND NEW YORK

First published 1978 by Westview Press

Published 2019 by Routledge
52 Vanderbilt Avenue, New York, NY 10017
2 Park Square, Milton Park, Abingdon, Oxon OX14 4RN

Routledge is an imprint of the Taylor & Francis Group, an informa business

Library of Congress Cataloging in Publication Data
Main entry under title:
    The new economics of the less developed countries.
    (Westview special studies in social, political,
and economic development)
    1. Underdeveloped areas--Addresses, essays, lectures.
2. International economic relations--Addresses,
essays, lectures. I. Kamrany, Nake M., 1934–
HC59.7.N39   330.9'172'4   77-14602

ISBN 13: 978-0-367-29434-2 (hbk)

ISBN 13: 978-0--36730980-0 (pbk)

TABLE OF CONTENTS

FOREWORD

The North-South dialogue represents a global issue
to fight world poverty -- which is indeed a perennial
concern of our times and a major challenge to the inge-
nuity of mankind. Although the issue of poverty has
been with us since Adam and Eve, its present intensity
and magnitude is unparalleled. It is further magnified
by the realization that millions of peoples have been
able to break out of poverty while a majority of the
world inhabitants are still caught in its vicious circle.
While the issue has been discussed, debated, and acted
upon, there is no evidence of a deep commitment and a
genuine universal resolve to eradicate it. For one reason
or another, the human race so far has failed to come to
grips with it. The issue has been postponed and, as a
result, it has become more complex over time. There is
indeed a need to revolutionize our perceptions of the
issue of world poverty and transform our understanding
of it.

This volume represents a modest step toward an attempt to objectively explore the various dimensions of
the issue of poverty by a group of scholars representing
varied backgrounds. The papers for this volume were
either invited or selected competitively. Moreover,
the authors discussed their findings in a Conference on
Major International Economic Issues, which was held at
the University of Southern California during December
15-17, 1976. The papers cogently address the various
dimensions of our perceptions of poverty -- both in terms
of theories and empirical observations with resultant
policy implications. Historical coverage is minimal.
This work is addressed to the policymakers in the national
and international organizations, universities at the
undergraduate and graduate levels, and concerned citizens.

I am grateful to my students and colleagues at USC
and MIT for encouraging me to undertake the task of addressing the issue of poverty by drawing upon the collective wisdom and participation of several scholars. In
particular, I am grateful to the members of the Monday
lunch seminars of the Harvard Center for International
Development which were held under the chairmanship of
Professor Lester Gordon. Those meetings were a major
source of inspiration for me. I am also grateful to my

colleagues at MIT, especially the research staff of the Center for Policy Alternatives for the stimulating environment. Special thanks are due to Professor Charles Kindleberger of MIT who provided guidance and moral support. Likewise, I am indeed grateful to Professor Richard Day, Chairman of the Department of Economics at USC, for fully endorsing my concern and providing hospitality to the participating group. Faculty members of the Economics Department at USC provided encouragment and several participated in this endeavor, including Richard Day, John Niedercorn, A. Morgner, S.D. Pollard, John Elliott, and Jeff Nugent. Mr. John Nilles, Director of the Office of Interdisciplinary Program Development at USC provided the necessary staff and administrative support. Dr. Henry Birnbaum, Special Assistant to President Hubbard for International Programs, provided stimulating insight and exchanges which helped me along with the overall development of this framework.

I am indeed grateful to Janna Wong and Gayle Brady for their relentless support to all aspects of this effort, including administrative, secretarial, coordination and production efforts.

My greatest gratitude is to the authors of this volume. They undertook this major task entirely on their own without grant support for their research, travel, and related expenses. Moreover, they maintained an unfailing cooperative attitude to many of my demands for revisions, presentations, deadlines, and all the pulls and pushes that are necessary as part of putting together such a volume. I am hopeful that the readers of this volume will share with me the admiration that I hold for the contributors of this volume. To the extent that these papers hopefully will contribute to our perceptions of the issue of global poverty and help us toward a better understanding of some of the fundamental resolutions, we owe a major debt of gratitude to the contributors.

Nake M. Kamrany
Pacific Palisades
California
July, 1977

THE AUTHORS

DAGOBERT L. BRITO received his Ph.D. from Rice
University in 1970. He is a Professor of Economics
and Political Science at Ohio State University. His
publications include: Mathematical Models of Arms Con-
trol, 1977; "A Dynamic Model of an Armaments Race,"
International Economics Review, 1972; "Stability and
Control of the Money Supply," Quarterly Journal of
Economics, 1974.

NICHOLAS G. CARTER is currently Chief of the Comparative Analysis and Projections Division at the World
Bank. He received his B.A. in Economics from Harvard
University (1958), and his M.S. (1960) and Ph.D. (1970)
from M.I.T. His doctoral dissertation was, "On the Use
of a Non-Linear Criterion Function in Development Pro-
gramming Models, 1967." Other publications include:
"A New Look at the Sandee Model," The Theory of Optimal
Economic Growth, MIT Press, 1967; "A Macro Economic
Model of Jamaica, 1959-66," Social and Economic Studies,
1970; "Foreign Assistance and Development Performance,
1960-70," American Economic Review, 1973.

JOHN E. ELLIOTT is a Professor of Economics at the
University of Southern California. He received his
Ph.D. from Harvard University in 1956. His fields are
Economic Theory, History of Economic Thought, Compara-
tive Economic Systems. He is currently involved in re-
search in the following areas: Marx's Socialism in the
Context of his Typology of Economic Systems; Marx and
Schumpeter on Capitalism's Creative Destruction; Marx
on Economic Systems. His publications include: "Pro-
fessor Roberts' Marx: On Alienation and Economic Systems,"
Journal of Economic Issues, September 1975; "Marx and
Contemporary Theories of Socialism," History of Political
Economy, Summer 1976; "Marx Resurrected: The Transformation and Socialization of Capitalism," Bulletin of the
Association for Comparative Economic Studies, Summer
1976; Comparative Economic Systems, Prentice-Hall, Englewood Cliffs, 1973; Comparative Philosophies in American
Political Economics, Goodyear, 1975.

MICHELE FRATIANNI was born in Firenze, Italy in 1941, and was educated in Italy and in the United States. He is an Associate Professor at the Graduate School of Business at Indiana University and has been a visiting professor at the Katholieke Universiteit de Leuven. He is currently on leave as an advisor to the European Community in Bruxelles. He has written extensively in economics journals and books.

NAKE M. KAMRANY of Kabul, Afghanistan, is a Professor of Economics and the Director of the Program in Productivity and Technology at the University of Southern California. He has previously held faculty and research positions with M.I.T., Stanford Research Institute, the World Bank, and U.C.L.A. He has carried out research in economic development and technology on 20 countries and has over 100 publications in these fields. His main fields of interest are: Economics of Technology; Economic Development, Economic Systems and Interdisciplinary Research. His publications include: "International Economic Reform," 1976; "The Three Vicious Circles of Underdevelopment: The Sahel-Sudan Case of West Africa," Socio-Economic Planning Sciences, IX:3, 1975; "Technology: Measuring the Socio-Economic Impact of Manufacturing Automation," Socio-Economic Planning Sciences, VIII:5, 1974; Technology, Productivity and Public Policy: A National Needs Analysis (with John Elliott), Center for Policy Alternatives, Massachusetts Institute of Technology (CPA/WP-75-11), 1975; "U.S. Productivity and Foreign Trade," National Inquiry into Productivity in the Durable Goods Industry, National Science Foundation, 1972; "A Long-Range Plan Defining Alternative Strategies for the Development of the Sahel-Sudan Zones," Center for Policy Alternatives, Massachusetts Institute of Technology, 1974. His books in progress include: Economics of Technology and Contemporary Economic Issues.

MICHAEL D. INTRILIGATOR received his Ph.D. in Economics at M.I.T. in 1963 and joined the faculty of the Department of Economics at U.C.L.A., where he is now a Professor of Economics. He teaches upper division and graduate level courses in economic theory, mathematical economics, and econometrics, and he has won Distinguished Teaching Awards for both graduate teaching (1966) and undergraduate teaching (1976). The theory and applications of quantitative economics, including mathematical economic theory and econometrics and their applications to health economics, strategy and arms control, and industrial organization, form the major research interests of Intriligator. Among his several books in these areas are Mathematical Optimization and Economic Theory, Prentice-Hall, 1971 (also translated into Spanish and Russian); Econometric Models, Techniques, and Applications, Prentice-Hall and North-Holland, 1978; A Forecasting and Policy Simulation Model of the Health Care Sector: The HRRC Prototype Microeconometric Model (with Donald E. Yett, Leonard Drabek, and Larry J. Kimbell), Lexington Books, 1978; and Strategy in a Missile War, UCLA Security Studies Project, 1967. He is also Editor of Frontiers of Quantitative Economics, North-Holland, 1971; Vol. II, 1974; Vol. III, 1977; and Co-Editor (with Kenneth J. Arrow) of the Handbook of Mathematical Economics, North-Holland, 1978. His numerous professional articles have appeared in virtually every major economics journal. Among other professional activities, Intriligator is Co-Editor (with Christopher Bliss) of the North-Holland Series, "Advanced Textbooks in Economics"; Associate Editor, Journal of Interdisciplinary Modeling and Simulation, and International Journal of Applied Analysis; and reviewer for Mathematical Reviews. In addition, he serves as a consultant to several corporations and government agencies.

STEVEN A. Y. LIN is a Professor of Economics at Southern Illinois University. He received his Ph.D. in economics and statistics from Iowa State University in 1967. He has also taught at the Universities of Colorado and Wisconsin. His main fields of interest are: Econometrics, Microeconomic Theory and Welfare Economics, Economic Development and Trade and Urban Economics. His publications include: Theory and Measurement of Economic Externality (ed), The Academic Press, 1976; Comparative Costs and Consequences (co-author), Iowa State University Press, 1972; "Transportation Sensitivity and Regional Growth," Regional Science and Urban Economics, 6(1976); "Modified Internal Rate of Return," Engineering Economist, 21:4; "Externality Tax and Subsidy," Theory and Measurement of Economic Externalities, 1976; "External Effects of Growth: Japan in Pacific Trading Area," Journal of Economics, Vol. 1, 1975; "Optimal Growth in a Surplus Labor Economy," Indian Journal of Economics, 1973; "Effects of Monetary Policy and Credit Conditions on the Housing Sector," Journal of American Real Estate and Urban Economics, I:1.

WILLIAM LOEHR is the Assistant Dean and is an Assistant Professor of Economics at the University of Denver. He has published extensively on comparative public policy issues. His publications include: Comparative Public Policy Issues, Theory and Method, 1974; "Fiscal Federalism, Spillovers and the Export of Taxes: An Extension," KYKLOS, 1974; Collective Goods and International Cooperation: Comments, 1973.

RACHEL McCULLOCH was born in Brooklyn, New York. She received her Ph.D. from the University of Chicago in 1973. Previously, Professor McCulloch has held positions with the Federal Reserve Board and the University of Chicago. She is currently an Associate Professor of Economics at Harvard University. Selected research and publications include: "Import Quotas and Resource Allocation," 1973; "When are a Tariff and a Quota Equivalent?" Canadian Journal of Economics, 1973; "A Note on Proportionally Distributed Quotas," American Economic Review, 1973.

JOHN CHARLES PATTISON was born in Ottawa, Canada in 1945, raised in Sarnia, Ontario and educated at the University of Western Ontario and The London School of Economics. He has lectured in Europe and North America at economics conferences, learned societies and university campuses. He has been an administrator at the OECD in Paris, France, a senior research officer at the Ontario Economic Council, and is currently a faculty member of the School of Business Administration at the University of Western Ontario. His economics writings have been published in books, journals and magazines in a number of countries and have been translated into other languages.

JOSEPH E. PLUTA is an Associate Professor of Economics at the Naval Postgraduate School in Monterey, California. He received his B.A. and M.A. degrees from the University of Notre Dame and his Ph.D. in 1972 from the University of Texas, where he was the recipient of the Ayres-Montgomery Award for Teaching Excellence. He served on the faculty at Texas as Assistant Director of Undergraduate Studies in the Department of Economics and taught at the University of North Florida before accepting his present position in 1974. In the fall of 1974, he worked as a consultant to the government of Vietnam and served in a similar capacity with the government of Taiwan in 1975. In both cases, his work involved teaching courses to high level government officials in the areas of public budgeting, macro and microeconomics, and the application of cost-benefit analysis to public policy issues in both countries with special emphasis on the planning-programming-budgeting system. For the past year, he has been Assistant Program Manager for International Courses at the Defense Resources Management Education Center, a position which has involved the administration of interdisciplinary, team-taught courses for government officials representing foreign governments from all over the world, especially the developing countries. Dr. Pluta's major research has centered on public expenditure patterns at Federal, state, and local levels in the U.S. as well as in European, Latin American, Asian, and African countries. He has also written on intergovernmental grants and in the field of the history of economic thought. His articles and book reviews have appeared in the National Tax Journal, American Economist, Journal of American History, Journal of Economic Issues, International Journal of Social Economics, World Affairs, Hispanic American Historical Review, Journal of Developing Areas, and other professional journals. He is currently involved in research on evaluating public programs in selected developing countries.

JOHN D. SHILLING received his Ph.D. in Economics from the Massachusetts Institute of Technology in 1971. Prior to completing his degree, he worked in Ghana on a research project in trade and development sponsored by Williams College and taught Development Economics at Boston College. He then spent two years as an economic adviser to the Government of Morocco Planning Secretariat helping to prepare the 1973-1977 Economic Plan. In 1973, he joined the Comparative Analysis and Projections Division of the International Bank for Reconstruction and Development.

ELIAS H. TUMA is a Professor of Economics at the University of California at Davis. He was born in Palestine in 1928 and left Israel for the United States in 1955. He received his B.A. from the University of

Redlands in 1958 and his Ph.D. from the University of
California at Berkeley in 1962. He spent one year as a
Post-Doctoral Fellow at the Near Eastern Center at the
University of California at Los Angeles, followed by two
years of teaching and research at the University of Saskatchewan, Saskatoon, Saskatchewan, Canada. Since 1965,
he has been on the faculty of the University of California
at Davis. He has held short-term consultant jobs with
the United Nations and the FAO. His publications include
several books and many articles: Twenty-Six Centuries of
Agrarian Reform, 1965; Economic History and the Social
Sciences, 1971; Peace Making and the Immoral War, 1972;
"Land Reform and Tenure," Encyclopedia Britannica, 1974
edition. He is a member of several professional societies
and is on the Editorial Council of the Institute for Middle Eastern and North African Affairs, and New Outlook.

The New Economics of the
Less Developed Countries

I
THE NORTH-SOUTH DIALOGUE

Nake M. Kamrany and John E. Elliott
University of Southern California

WORLD POVERTY AND NORTH-SOUTH ECONOMIC RELATIONS

In recent years, the traditional perception of a world separated into East and West, focusing essentially on military, political, and diplomatic matters, has been supplemented by an alternative view of the world in terms of a North-South division, focused on the political economy of development. In the longer run, indeed, the strategic importance, for world stability, prosperity, and progress, of dialogue and decision between the relatively prosperous North and the relatively and absolutely poorer South concerning world poverty and North-South economic relations should equal and may well surpass that of East-West rivalries.

This volume elucidates various policy dimensions of contemporary international issues of political economy especially pertinent to North-South relations. It aims at a scholarly and objective, though frankly normative, exposition of the major dimensions of the critical economic issues with a view to contributing in at least a preliminary way, to an analysis of the "new economic order" which some believe is now beginning to emerge in world society, an "order" characterized more by cooperative, collective ventures, relative to market processes, than in the past century, and less by the dominance of a very few large and powerful countries.

After a quarter century of experimentation with economic development in the poorer countries, the disarray and in some cases the calamitous results are so obvious that a fresh look and reexamination of traditional assumptions, methodologies, theories, and policies is needed. We do not believe that it is necessary to argue this point at length, since both supporters and critics of the record of economic development of the poor countries agree that reappraisal is necessary. More importantly, at the risk of overstating the case, it is noteworthy that the dramatic and significant in-

1

ternational economic changes which have taken place during the last half decade, as exemplified by the emergence of OPEC, resource shortages, the multinational corporations, and the new world monetary system, have rivaled those of the last century. These changes in themselves warrant a serious reappraisal and have introduced additional skepticism concerning the viability of the traditional framework of development economics. Moreover, the continuing impasse of the North-South dialogue pointedly illustrates the complexity and difficulty of determining what must be done to substantially reduce, if not "solve" the problem of world poverty. In relative terms, poverty in the non oil-rich Third World countries is more severe now than in the past despite decades of optimistic programs for economic development. The disparity between the rich and the poor countries is increasing and the resentment of the poor over the unshared affluence has become more serious. The mode of interaction between the poor and rich countries has changed from that of cooperation and partnership for progress in the 1950's to that of adversary bargaining in the 1970's, as exemplified in the recent deliberations at GATT (Kenya), the North-South dialogue (Paris), Conferences on Population and Food (Rome), and a number of conferences held by the poor countries (Manila).

Thus, transfer of wealth to the less developed countries, or LDCs -- its magnitude, rate, and composition -- has been a major international issue and one which may well be contributing to the emergence of a new world order. Five years ago, the United States and the rest of the technology-advanced countries were the main source of this transfer in the form of aid. Now, the OPEC members and multinational development agencies provide alternative sources of funding to compensate for the decline in the relative share of aid from the Western world. Part of the problem, for instance, in the United States, has been growing doubts by the American public concerning the goals and results of foreign aid programs. There is no doubt that the events of the last five years call for alternative approaches to aid from both the donors' and recipients' perspectives. The one percent of GNP aid target from the Western countries to LDCs set by the Pearson Commission of 1969 has not been achieved; indeed, by 1977, the actual aid transfer was only around one-third of the target.

The terms of trade of the LDCs are deteriorating. The OPEC price hike has accentuated this deterioration.

2

Debt service ratios of 25 to 40 are reaching anti-growth proportions; fragmented markets continue to constrain demand; inefficient and stagnant import substitution is failing to improve the balance of payments and is not alleviating the high unemployment rates of 20% to 35%. Supplier's credit, if available, remains exploitative and is insufficient or ineffective to uplift these economies. The multinational corporations have largely ignored the internal economic development of these countries. The linking of the International Monetary Fund's Drawing Rights to development finance and its effectiveness remain uncertain. Even if implemented fully, uncertainty remains as to its adequacy, especially in view of a worldwide shortage of capital and the reluctance of private financial institutions in the West, especially those of the United States, to advance further credit to what are perceived as high-risk ventures, especially since the magnitude of these credits have already reached $180 billion by mid-1977.

Debt refinancing has added enormous interest burdens, jeopardizing the credit-worthiness of many LDCs. Tied aid has made the cost of development prohibitive, while project aid carries with it undue rigidities and has forced LDCs to define their development plans in terms of the availability of credit and their restrictive uses specified by the donors rather than their own national interest.

Despite these factors, recent international efforts have involved little more than reaffirming the status quo and promising more dialogues and conferences. Needless to say, there is a case for a candid and forceful restatement of the central economic problems of LDCs and their prospective solutions, with a view to keeping in perspective realistic limitations imposed by institutions and resources. If existing economic prescriptions are extended to their logical conclusions, we will be faced with a picture rooted in the extension of the present order. For instance, if the Pearson Commission's GNP growth target of 5% per annum were to be realized in the 1980's (which is unlikely), a large number of LDCs would still remain very poor in the 1990's. The relative share of world income by LDCs would be diminishing, while the gap between the "rich" and the "poor" would be increasing. Needless to say, the international present uncertainty casts doubt upon the availability of funds and the urgency of attention needed for changing the lot of millions, indeed, billions, of people in the least developed nations.

3

These various issues are indeed complex, and the
task of addressing them adequately is a major one. This
volume is a modest beginning. It comprises nine invited papers by a group of young and upcoming economists
who have had an opportunity to sit around a table and
discuss with each other the issues and their respective
findings.[1] In contrast to a topical approach, such as
analysis of trade, investment, aid, growth, and so on,
authors contributing to this volume have addressed themselves to integrated policy issues that are fundamentally people-oriented, taking an interdisciplinary and
functional approach. In view of increasing world economic interdependence and its profound and continuing
global effects, there is a growing necessity to address
international issues in an integrated and normative
analytical context. This objective has been kept in
mind in preparing this volume. Moreover, in conducting
the research, various methodologies have been employed,
ranging from "common sense" observations to sophisticated tools. Since definitive generalizations cannot
be drawn from case studies in the field of world economic development, several papers have used comparative
studies to explicate and illustrate the various dimensions of the issues. Moreover, critical observations
have been made concerning the inadequacy of traditional
theories or tools of analysis. This volume aims at a
scholarly exposition of the various policy dimensions
of critical international economic issues. It does not
lobby for any policy nor is it the aim of the volume to
support or oppose any stance taken by any of the group
of nations such as the North, the South, OPEC, OECD, or
the LDCs. Whenever appropriate, policy prescriptions
have been drawn explicitly.

It should be noted that we are concerned here with
theoretical and policy issues rather than problems.
Issues evolve over time, but essentially remain with us,
while problems lend themselves to more specific solutions. Issues are dissonances that require management
and weighing of alternatives for better choices on a
continuous basis. This point is well illustrated in
an opening statement of the Economic Committee of the
League of Nations in 1937 which was then concerned with
a number of international economic issues.

> It is not without some hesitation that
> the Economic Committee has undertaken to
> prepare the present report. An effort
> for the normalization of economic rela-
> tions might well seem futile at a time

4

when the existence of grave disputes
fill all minds with uneasiness.

Nevertheless, the Committee has
thought its duty to continue its
earlier studies, because, in existing
circumstances, it seemed to it more
than ever necessary to make an effort
which might help to bring about economic improvement and thus contribute
to safeguard peace.

It does not fall to the Committee
to judge the possibilities of action
in this direction. That is the function of Governments. The Committee's
task is limited to lay before them the
material upon which they have to base
their decisions.[2]

Thirty years later we find that many of the recommendations of the report are valid today, including aboli-
tion of quotas, improving standard of living, need for
dynamic policies, limitation of armanents, provision of
better nutrition, need for new initiatives, and others.[3]

COMPETING POSITIONS CONCERNING INTERNATIONAL ECONOMIC
ISSUES

Clearly, new issues have also emerged onto the international economic scene. These issues have become
the basis of positions taken by various groups. The
complementary and competing elements of the various
positions will yield solutions with varying degrees of
stability or instability. Consequently, the future of
the world economic condition will range from a world of
harmony, prosperity, peace, and hope to one of conflicts,
stagflation, wars, and despair. While debate, bargaining, and dialogue center around equitable distribution,
no theoretical framework now exists that would produce
an "optimal" result. Moreover, these issues include multidimensional (socio-political and economic) considerations. Objectives sought for any one of them (e.g.,
buffer commodities, indexation, etc.) are invariably inconsistent to some degree with other goals. Therefore,
a holistic analysis is needed, i.e., an examination of
these issues which is not restricted to the traditional
framework of economic analysis. Because doubts have
been raised about the adequacy of the traditional approach to explain and elucidate these issues and their

5

related problems, it follows that before solutions are applied, we ought to engage in serious thinking in problem definition and examine the adequacy of existing theories and tools of analysis as well as the generation of required information for policymakers for their decision process.

Economic behavior emanating from competing North-South positions may be characterized as a system of multilateral bargaining or oligopoly for which existing economic theory cannot provide optimal solutions with precision. Many would argue that in the present economy, each major bargaining group assumes "a zero sum game" situation and attempts to either hold on to an advantageous relative position and/or improve its relative position. This situation lends itself to analysis through a form of dynamic game theory whose results depend upon politics, behavior of the OPEC countries, trends in Detente, role of the multinationals, the state of the economies of the OECD countries, the LDCs' ability to form selective cartels and a host of ethical, psychological, and intangible factors. It would appear that it will take both altruism and self-interest to bring these competing positions into closer convergence if not consensus.

The OPEC Position

As an oligopoly, the OPEC countries will raise the price of oil insofar as it appears profitable to do so. It will attempt to get OECD to agree on some indexation scheme. Its upper bound for price at any time will be influenced by considerations of aggregate demand for oil, slowing down of the rate of economic recovery of the West, fear of stagflation, possibility of rapid development of substitutes, alienation of the West, and the possibility of provoking a military response. They will try to counter the impact of the price hike upon the poor countries by providing aid and negotiating for more concessions from the OECD. The long run concern of the OPEC (assuming that the cartel will last) is to devise a strategy of self-sustaining economies prior to the exhaustion of revenue from oil -- an exhaustible resource.

6

The OECD Position

The basic strategy of the OECD countries is to try to organize the oil importing countries (e.g., The Washington Energy Conference of February 1974 and the formation of the International Energy Agency), break the OPEC cartel, preserve the pre-OPEC market system and its institutions, gain time through conferences (Conference on International Economic Cooperation -- the North-South Dialogue), reduce dependency upon oil and other imports, retain certain monopolies, and minimize the influence of the Soviet bloc upon both the LDCs and the newly rich oil exporting countries.

The LDC Position

The LDCs aim for higher commodity prices (inflation for OECD) and indexation, debt relief (budgetary problems for OECD), greater access to markets in the developed nations, more transfer of technologies (unemployment for OECD), worldwide dialogue on international economic matters, a common fund for commodities, fuller access to capital markets, and easier import terms for manufactured goods and oil imports. In the absence of any substantive power, the LDCs' strategy has been to work through the United Nations, making use of their majority vote to create specialized agencies that are sympathetic to its cause, such as UNCTAD (1964), UNIDO (1966), International Development Strategy (1970), and resolutions by the United Nations General Assembly.[4] In September 1975, the U.N. Resolution 3362 endorsed the linking of special drawing rights (SDRs) to aid and a 0.7 percent aid target, and price indexation.

RECENT STUDIES

Many issues of North-South relations and the need for a new world economic order have been addressed in a number of recent conferences and volumes. In the aptly titled In Search of a New World Economic Order, for example, H. Molmgren argues that:

> 1. There is a need to restore order and a high degree of collective discipline in world economic relations.
>
> 2. There is a need to provide suf-

7

ficient flexibility in the international mechanisms of adjustment so
that domestic economies may be managed effectively, and yet be allowed
to adapt on a continuing basis to
the evolution of the global economy.[5]

In a joint Japanese-American statement published
by the Committee for Economic Development, it is asser-
ted that the world is groping for a new order in international economic relations, including currency, trade,
investment, and foreign aid.[6] It further states that
"developing countries" are demanding recognition of
their special position in both the new political structure and the new international economic order.[7]

In 1974, the United Nations General Assembly's
"Charter of Economic Rights, and Duties of States"
heightened the following positions of the South and endorsed the following proposals:

1. Price support and indexation of LDC
commodities.

2. Transfer of .7% of GNP of the developed countries to LDCs in the form
of official aid.

3. Linking IMF-SDR to development aid.

4. The "right" of the primary producers
to form cartels.

The issue of the New Economic Order has also received considerable attention by the Club of Rome,
which has sponsored several analytical modeling efforts
as exemplified by the following:[8]

1. the Meadows/Forrester Models -- using
difference equations and drawing aggregation to overall world averages under
the assumption of differential growth
rates in production and consumption;

2. the Bariloche Model -- assuming complete independence of regions;

3. the Pestel/Mesarovic Model -- giving
free options to the users using basically
the Forrester framework;

4. the Linneman Group Model -- assuming
a static price elasticity of demand for
goods and demand elasticity of food production under existing market conditions.

Although often provocative, these models have been interpreted as having anti-growth biases. Their publication has often generated more heat than light since
they adhere to a "feast and famine" forecast and have
aroused emotional predilections of the "haves" and the
"have nots". Major objections to these models in the
Western countries have been directed at the implications for a new order involving alteration of the market system and its institutions. The central theme in
these approaches has been criticized because of their
speculative concern about the well-being for the present generation.

The Committee on Economic Stability of the Social
Science Research Council (USA) has contributed to several economic modeling efforts. These have produced
very useful models, including those of M.I.T.-Pennsyl-
vania-SSRC, and project LINK.

Eventually, through LINK -- an inter-country input-
out model -- it should be possible to quantify the impact of trade and investment on a global basis.[9]

The subject of international trade and investment
policies has been addressed by many scholars. Professor C. Fred Bergsten's contributions and pulling together the proceedings of many conferences provide a
wealth of materials on these major policy issues.[10]
Moreover, the seminal contributions of Emile Despres
have been the precursors of many of these recent efforts, whose aims are to transform the conventional and
narrow, self-centered policies that are being pursued
into a system of world prosperity and respect for human
dignity in the poor and rich lands.[11] Moreover, the
seven reports of the Tripartite association (European
community, Japan, and North America) have made major
contributions toward policy formulations concerning the
New Economic Order.[12] The uncertainty surrounding the
direction of the New World Economic Order is clearly
expressed in one of these reports:

As reflected in debates in the United
Nations, relations between the industrial and the developing countries seem

9

to have deteriorated sharply. It is
too soon to know whether these and related developments will halt or reverse the earlier trend toward closer
international economic cooperation or
whether the response rather will be to
expand to multilateral understandings
and institutions that have been created
to support world economic integration.
In this sense the world economy is at
a transitional point.[13]

In view of a continuing shift in the distribution
of power and a "multipolar" competition, the management
of these issues can be no longer the responsibility of
a single nation or bloc of nations; it must be the
shared responsibility of the world community at large.
It follows that the problems as well as the incentives
of the various participants need to be taken into account. Moreover, one could argue in favor of a major
movement towards a "willed future" that is consistent
with the quality of life under managed growth.[14] In
response to these issues, the Europeans have advocated
models of autarky for themselves.[15] Suddenly, world
economic relations has become perceived as a zero-sum
game. This is really a very unfortunate trend. Just
as the world is beginning to find new ways for at least
a portion of the LDCs to pay their own way in economic
development, an aura of pessimism has set in, especially in Europe. Self-sufficiency and autarky are being
advocated as a means of economic "survival."

In the LDCs, the apparent trend toward autarky has
been interpreted roughly as follows:

When the prices of commodities, materials, and energy were kept low, a
system of free trade was advocated by
rich countries. Now that energy prices
have been increased due to the emergence
of OPEC (the champions of the Third
World) and the probabilities of other
oligopolies have been created for
other commodities and materials with
the possibility of better prices (indexation), a system of autarky is being
proposed. Such a system, if adopted,
may slow down the rate of growth of
selected LDCs and the living standards
of the advanced countries, especially

those of Western Europe. It can also
create major political and military
upheavals, the costs of which would be
enormous.

In one sense, world economic relations do constitute a zero-sum game. Clearly, it is not feasible to
increase the relative share of world income for all
countries or blocs of countries simultaneously. It is
possible to increase the absolute size of each although
the rate of increase for some may be faster than for
others and the relative gaps may diminish and/or shift.
But, even this modest aim will require a good dose of
enlightened self-interest.

ORGANIZATION OF THIS VOLUME

In the remaining chapters, an attempt is made to
explicate the position and prospects of the non-oil
producing less developed countries. The objective is
to elucidate the various alternatives which are open to
these countries to achieve specific growth targets or
basic consumption needs and the likely consequences of
these options upon the internal and external policies
of these countries and the external policies of donor
countries. A heuristic macroeconomic analysis is made
to estimate the foreign aid requirements of these countries (1975 - 2000) to achieve specific growth targets
per annum and to identify the underlying economic performance and political will in order to meet the requirements of these conditional scenarios (Chapters II
and III). A modified version of the Chenery-Strout
model is employed to generate these forecasts for 29
countries specifying performance criteria and assigning
the parametric values for the marginal propensity to
save, import rate, rate of growth of exports and target
growth rate of the GDP.

John D. Shilling and Nicholas Carter in Chapter II,
and Nake Kamrany in Chapter II, explicate the conditions under which the LDCs may stand on their own and
participate in the world economy as equal partners. The
most revealing points in these chapters are the implicit positions taken that foreign aid by itself is unlikely to break the vicious circles of poverty, that
the task of breaking them is the responsibility of the
LDCs themselves, and that the international role of
assistance now belongs to several groups of nations,
i.e., OPEC, OECD, Eastern Bloc countries, China, and

11

other blocs that may develop.

Shilling and Carter have examined the position and prospects of 29 non-oil producing countries to the year 2000. They have elucidated the various alternatives that are open to these countries to achieve self-sufficiency and the likely consequences of these options over the next quarter of a century. Their scenarios are conditional upon the internal and external policies of these countries and the policies of the donors with regard to them. These include resource endowments, the development policies the countries were following prior to the crisis, the amount of aid that OECD, the Soviet bloc, and OPEC will make available, the conditions attached to the aid, the internal policies that these countries will adopt, and the countries' reaction to various crises, as well as of the direct effects of the crises themselves. Equally important is the role or roles which these countries will play individually and in various groups with each other and with the donor groups.

Kamrany provides an interdisciplinary evaluation of the options open to the six countries in the Sahel-Sudan region of West Africa which suffered major drought, 1972-74. These include Chad, Mauritania, Mali, Niger, Senegal, and Upper Volta. Four of these countries were classified as the least developed of the LDCs by the United Nations. The top and bottom limits of development options are explicated under various assumptions that are made explicit as conditions for internal and external performance. Kamrany concludes that under the most optimistic set of assumptions, four of the countries' per capita income will remain below $150 by the year 2000, implying major structural and policy changes (internal and external) and/or discoveries of new marketable resources as necessary ways to break through the vicious circles of poverty. The range of foreign aid required to achieve a 5% annual target growth is estimated at $5 billion, under the assumption of high export performance, and about $9 billion, under the assumption of relatively modest export performance. Kamrany has further pointed out that the burden of solutions and implementations of development programs should rest with the Sahel-Sudan countries and that programs of development should not be determined and imposed by the donors, as has been the case so far. With respect to internal performance, substantial upgrading of macroeconomic parameters are needed.

12

The methodological innovation of both the Shilling/
Carter and Kamrany approaches may be sought in their attempt to heuristically estimate the parametric values
for savings, investment, exports, imports, capital-output ratio, and related rates of change rather than rely
solely on values derived from historical trends. Regression trends generated disconcerting results.

In Chapter IV, Professor Steven A. Y. Lin challenges the adequacy of the traditional measures of per
capita gross national product for classifying countries
into "developed" and "underdeveloped" categories. The
need for this is well articulated by the Brookings Institution, as it observed:

> the existence of growing affluence and
> growing ills has led many to the con-
> clusion that the vision of general pros-
> perity as a solvent of social ills has
> been a chimera...that GNP turned out to
> be a small god....[16]

Lin has proposed a framework that breaks away from the
conventional GNP accounting. It attempts to (1) develop a unitary index of "measurable welfare" in natural units of goods and services for approximately 88
countries using the 1960-70 period, (2) analyze the
possible interrelationships between the "welfare" or
"level of living index" and the development strategies
and structure of these countries, and (3) draw policy
implications and suggestions concerning development issues. The taxonomic distance and the ordinary (or relative) composite index (SM) for the level-of-living are
used. It provides for a unique approach in systematically measuring and analyzing the level-of-living gap
between the rich and poor countries for the decade of
1960-70, using a multidimensional composite index. It
is a useful tool to assist in working out strategy for
assisting the poor nations. It is also an internally
verified measurement of the level-of-living gap and its
relation to the resource allocation indices of each
country.

While the economic growth performance of the LDCs
has been unsatisfactory over the last two decades,
changes in structural, institutional, social, environmental, and distributional developments have become of
growing concern, especially as they relate to justice,
equity, and the overall well-being of the masses of
population. One may observe that the aid programs of

the last quarter century represent transfers from the
poor in the rich countries to the rich in the poor countries. Although a number of recent studies have pointed
to the increasingly unequal income distributions that
have accompanied economic growth, there is no inherent
incompatibility between growth and social objectives.
Nor should the poor record of the past mislead us to
such a belief, although some trade-off, by necessity,
would have to be made. Given this increasing concern,
international development institutions such as the
World Bank have begun to shift their attention from activities which are purely growth-oriented to those which
attempt to strike a balance between economic growth and
equity.

In Chapter V, Professor William Loehr has addressed
the issue of growth and income distribution policies.
He has observed that researchers have tried to single
out certain macro variables, such as socioeconomic dualism, as leading to declining shares of income for the
poor. Others have examined specific policies in such
areas as the fiscal system, agriculture, or technology.
Despite this intense effort by economists to discover
the causes of increasingly unequal income distributions,
and to devise policies to offset present trends, there
is little consensus as to causes. Policy has, therefore, been ad hoc aiming for "solutions" which may not
be solutions at all, but merely attempts to eliminate
glaring problems in the short run. The relationship
between growth and distribution factors such as uneven
distribution of human resources, varying economic growth
rates, barriers to economic mobility, the structure of
ownership and property, the social and political organization, and dualism -- are cogently reviewed and related to cross-sectional studies. Loehr concludes that
no generalization can be made between growth and distribution. He illustrates his point by examining income
distribution and growth in eight countries using the
Gini index with the following results:

> 1. Rapid growth (Korea, Taiwan),
> increasing equality in distribution;
>
> 2. Rapid growth (Brazil, Mexico),
> decreasing equality in distribution;
>
> 3. Slow growth (Sri Lanka, Costa
> Rica), increasing equality in dis-
> tribution;

        4. Slow growth (India, Columbia),
        decreasing equality in distribution.

Loehr's findings suggest the need for further research
concerning growth and distribution, including consideration of such policy prescriptions as the role of small
enterprise, issues related to the protection of the
poor and "near poor", reduction in the growth rates of
population, intersectoral shifts with balance between
rural and urban equity and growth, and social welfare
policies.

        The issue of the effectiveness of public expendi-
tures to enhance social welfare is addressed by Professor Joseph E. Pluta (Chapter VI) using data on public
education and health expenditures in Brazil, Columbia,
and Ecuador. Surprisingly, the role of public expenditure in the development process is an area that few
economists and other social scientists have explored
carefully. Especially lacking has been a systematic
format for analyzing the effectiveness of public investment in human resources in the LDCs. Pluta's findings
provide a convincing case supporting the view that expenditure increases were accompanied by favorable results in terms of selected output measures of effectiveness while expenditure stagnation cutbacks were accompanied by adverse behavior of such measures. Pluta
further observes that aid programs have emphasized technical development to accelerate trade, a priority which,
despite its obvious importance, is likely to have little effect upon the development of human resources.
Moreover, he points out that decisions to increase education and/or health expenditures will be accompanied
by difficult political decisions, since it would involve either cutbacks in other areas or increases in
taxes to finance additional outlays.

        On methodological grounds, Pluta notes that, in
measuring social effectiveness, a shift in emphasis
toward output measures would enable more accurate evaluation procedures based on cost, effectiveness, and
efficiency criteria. He adds further that the procedure of relating multiple output measures of effectiveness to expenditure patterns over time adds perspective
to the question of what such expenditures have attempted
to accomplish, a question often answered incorrectly
(or at least vaguely) by exclusive reliance on input
measures.

For nearly a quarter of a century, economic development of the LDCs has been treated with the traditional economist's "positive" view, with the assumptions that the behavior of the decision makers, both leaders and nonleaders, are based on economic rationality, are consistent with complete and fixed preferences, and tend toward equilibrium, so that supply and demand are balanced, and the economy is efficient, so that no agent can improve his lot without diminishing that of another. In reality, economic actors process their decisions with partial information, adapt to internal and external conditions using suboptimal strategies, and development paths are not smooth or optimal. As Professor Richard Day has stated, "They often involve situations in which unforeseen crises emerge out of formerly advantageous changes and patterns in which some segments of a population -- or some whole countries -- become worse-off while others become better-off....People, as well as nations, however, are often inconsistent, the economy appears frequently, if not always, to be more or less in disequilibrium, and improving conditions for some at the expense of worsening conditions for others is a commonplace occurrence, with economic competition producing losers as well as winners."[17]

There is, indeed, a need to understand and explain how development problems and crises emerge from the dynamic structure of the developing system. Sufficient study of development from this point of view may help identify policies which can anticipate potential crises and moderate or eliminate them by preventive action. Moreover, it is in this context that the LDCs could arrive at realistic policy options concerning their internal policies and external bargaining positions.

Professor Elias H. Tuma (Chapter VII) identifies a number of misconceptions concerning the position of the LDCs vis-a-vis the rest of the world in their role as producers of raw materials and under the mistaken assumption that the market system would produce optimally both with respect to efficiency and a welfare-inducing system for all participants. Tuma suggests a distinction between strategic and nonstrategic primary products. Exchange of the strategic products, whose price elasticity of supply may be zero, depends primarily on nonmarket arrangements such as agreements, barter, and international political power. Reliance upon the traditional system has found the LDCs to remain poor, highly dependent, vulnerable, and underdeveloped. An appreciation of the interdependence between economics

16

and politics may produce a system that is equitable,
viable, stable and fairly predictable. Thus, Tuma recommends the incorporation of power and vulnerability
as a significant characteristic of control over strategic resources, since they affect both the producers
and the consumers. His prescriptions include lessening
of dependence upon raw material exports, increasing the
relative share of finished and semi-finished exports,
improving technical, economic, and political positions,
synchronizing export earnings to absorptive capacity,
and encouraging structural changes toward industrialization to produce the machinery, not just to operate it.
Tuma illustrates his innovative theoretical construct
by critically examining Iran's strategy of development.

In Chapter VIII, Professor Rachel McCulloch ex-
pounds upon the major bargaining issues of the North-
South dialogue and various proposals that have been
made. She argues that multilateral agreements could
be favored on "second best" grounds. However, if commodity prices are set artificially high, the largest
absolute share of the transfer of wealth would go to
certain developed nations rather than to LDCs since
the developed nations produce the largest absolute share
of these products. Consumer dependence on raw materials could be eroded by development of subtitutes, although possibilities of substitution in supply has
proven costlier than anticipated. Moreover, she points
out that it is difficult to generalize about the probability of successful cartelization by producer nations.
Moreover, McCulloch argues that price and revenues could
be stabilized by adhering to export controls, buffer
stocks, and import-export agreements between producer
and consumer nations. In the context of the new economic order, she favors more emphasis upon investment
rather than commodity policies, except for stabilization
of export earnings with compensatory financing preferably through the IMF. Moreover, the World Bank may have
to substitute for private investment flows which are
likely to dwindle in coming years as a result of mili-
tancy over resources and if the LDCs implement the provisions of the U.N. Charter of Economic Rights and Duties
of States. McCulloch's exposition is a fine summary
of points of conflict in the North-South debate and possible positions of workable compromise at some cost of
efficiency; although the concept of efficiency in international exchange is indeed illusive and never existed
anyway.

17

In Chapter IX, Professors Michael D. Intriligator
and Dagbert L. Brito present an overview of a theory of
power and the international distribution of rights and
resources. Such a theoretical development is indeed
needed since events of the recent past have made it increasingly clear that the distribution of wealth among
nations and the distribution of the gains from trade
is a function not only of markets and initial resources,
as in the classical theory of international trade, but
also of the power of the nations involved. The OPEC
cartel was able to use an embargo and the threat of
future embargoes to shift the distribution of economic
rents from the oil consuming countries to the oil producing countries, i.e., from production and consumption
of petroleum. This display of economic power has served
as an example to other producers of primary products
and has caused them to consider the possibility of similar actions to shift the distribution of the gains from
trade. The North-South dialogue, detente, increase in
world population and its concentration in poor countries,
and the proliferation of nuclear power are among other
major developments which underscore the importance of
the role of power in changing or maintaining the distribution of wealth among nations. Intriligator and Brito
suggest that the relationship of a nation's power in its
various forms to its share of the world's wealth is becoming a question of increasing practical as well as of
theoretical interest. They summarize a general equilibrium model which addresses the allocative process of
the role of power in an explicit theoretical framework,
including bargaining and learning behavior, and its practical implications to address such issues as cartel
behavior, trade agreements, and the structure of the
international monetary system.

One of the important requirements of international
conflict solution and international progress is the existence of an institutional framework and institutions
that could effectively serve that purpose. The majority
of the development agencies,including the World Bank,
were established to manage the development process under
the old world economic structure. And a majority of the
secretarial staff of these agencies were the former colonial administrators whose views of that world were
embedded in the acceptance of the exchange between the
privileged and the nonprivileged and a system whereby
the bargaining positions were totally lopsided in favor
of the rich and the powerful. In the absence of any
other power base, the LDCs capitalized on whatever limited advantage their number could gain from them. (In
1955, the United National had 59 members; as of mid-1977,

18

the number increased to 150 members, two-thirds from the LDCs). The establishment of the United National Conference on Trade and Development (UNCTAD) in 1964 provided a forum for the LDCs to articulate their position for trade instead of aid, especially under the leadership of its first director, Raul Prebisch. The establishment of the United Nations Industrial Development Organization (UNIDO) in 1966 and the United Nations International Development Strategy for the Second Development Decade in 1970 extended the scope of discussion to industrial development, and issues of food and population, environmental pollution, and related subjects. However, since the formation of OPEC, the strategy of the LDCs has shifted to a call for reform of the existing order and a demand for an integrated and comprehensive approach to cope with the essence of poverty, as spelled out in the United Nations Charter of Economic Rights and Duties of States (December 1974, Resolution 3362; passed in September 1975 to negotiate compromises). Since then, several proposals and conferences have been advanced without any resolution in sight. One of the crucial questions concerning the North-South dialogue is the suitability and effectiveness of the existing international institutions and their administration, bureaucracies, and the overall framework.

Dr. John Pattison and Professor Fratianni (in Chapter X) have addressed this crucial question. They have examined international institutions through the analytical framework of the theory of clubs, uncertainty, and information. They conclude that these international institutions do not represent a proper correspondence between the systematic needs of the world economy and institutional capability, either in terms of the allocation of tasks to organizations, or of nations as members of these bodies. The inadequacy of these institutions make the formulation and implementation of reform difficult. They recommend that consideration of equity and efficiency should determine the optimal number of members in an organization and an understanding of how an international institution could effectively function as it relates to voting, budgets, staffing, and incentive system.

FOOTNOTES

[1]Conference on Major International Economic Issues,
held at the University of Southern California,
Los Angeles, California, December 15-16, 1976.

[2]League of Nations. "Remarks on the Present Phase
of International Economic Relations," September, 1937.

[3]Ibid.

[4]Several U.N. resolutions have been passed in support
of the International Development Strategy. See
United Nations publication A/AC, 176/2-3, September, 1975.

[5]Molmgren, H. "Need for a New System for World Trade
and Payments," in Corbet, H., and Jackson, R.
(eds.) In Search of a New World Economic Order,
1974.

[6]Toward a New International Economic System. Committee
for Economic Development, 1974.

[7]Ibid.

[8]See Mesarovic, M., and Pestel, E. Mankind at the
Turning Point, 1974; Meadows, D., et al., Limits
to Growth; and Proceedings of the Third Symposium
on Global Modeling (Food and Agriculture), International Institute for Applied System Analysis,
Schloss Laxenberg, Austria, September 22-25, 1975.

[9]Ball, R.J. (ed.) The International Linkage of National
Economic Models, North-Holland, 1973.

[10]See Bergsten, C. Fred. Toward a New World Trade Policy:
The Maidenhead Papers, Lexington Books, 1975, and
many additional publications by Bergsten. Also,
for a broader treatment see Helen Hughes (ed.),
Prospects for Partnership, The Johns Hopkins Press,
1973.

[11]Meier, G. M. (ed.) International Economic Reform:
Collected Papers of Emil Despres, Oxford University
Press, 1973. Also, for a significant contribution
to the reform of the international commercial
system to be pursued in the context of the liberali-

zation of world trade, see In Search of a New World Economic Order, Corbert, H., and Jackson, R. (eds.), John Wiley, 1974.

[12]The seven reports published by The Brookings Institution are as follows:
Reshaping the International Economic Order, 1972;
Reassessing North-South Economic Relations, 1972;
World Trade and Domestic Adjustment, 1973;
Toward the Integration of World Agriculture, 1973;
Cooperative Approaches to World Energy Problems, 1974;
Trade in Primary Commodities: Conflict or Cooperation?, 1974;
The World Economy in Transition, 1975.

[13]The World Economy in Transition, The Brookings Institution, 1975.

[14]This concept was advanced by Professor Hasan Ozbehhan of the University of Pennsylvania in the preliminary defunct prospectus of the Club of Rome project, 1969-70.

[15]We are referring to several Monday luncheon seminars at the Harvard Institute for International Development where these views were expressed, 1973-76.

[16]Agenda for the Nation, The Brookings Institution, 1968.

[17]Day, Richard H. "Cooperative Dynamics and Development Policy Analysis." Paper presented at the International Development Conference, 1975.

II
THE OUTLOOK FOR DEVELOPING COUNTRIES

John Shilling and Nicholas Carter
*International Bank for Reconstruction and
Development*

Not since the hopeful period of the late 1950s and early 1960s, when the first U.N. Decade of Development program was announced, has so much attention and concern been focused on developing countries. The tone, however, has changed from the spirit of cooperation and progress that characterized that earlier period to one of recrimination and conflict. This reversal of attititude and rhetoric follows a world economic crisis precipitated by the combination of sharp world-wide price increases and then a sharp fall in demand for least developed countries' exports in the wake of the deep recession in the developed countries. Although reflecting disillusionment at the very partial achievement of earlier goals for aid and development, the current pessimistic mood is much more a result of world-wide changes in perceptions than it is of fundamental changes in the situation of the developing countries. This is not to diminish the severity of the shock absorbed by the developing countries as a whole, but for most it has been only one of several short-run set-backs, and for a few it has even been a net benefit.

In strict economic terms, the developing countries suffered less immediate loss in income and consumption growth than did the developed countries; however, the onset of the crisis and the reaction to it served to emphasize the huge disparities of wealth and income that have increased over the past decade, and the relative powerlessness of most developing countries to control many factors directly affecting their economic well-being. Many developing countries have taken the necessary domestic policy actions to adjust to the new external conditions; at the same time, they have also begun a more strident political dialogue with the developed countries aimed at achieving a greater role in international economic decision making and a more favorable distribution of resources - encouraged in large part by the example of OPEC.

New relative prices, new sources of demand for the
least developed countries' exports, and new sources of
supply for aid have sharply increased the pressure on
the least developed countries to modify existing programs for development and to restructure their modern
sectors to meet the new world economic conditions. The
trebling of foreign borrowing (in nominal terms) by
least developed countries has played an important role
in the adaptation and restructuring process. The readjustment is by now well underway, although it is unlikely that the transition will be completed before 1980
even if there are no further major shocks to the system.

The outlook for the developing countries following
a period of adjustment, is a function of their resource
endowments, the development policies the countries were
following prior to the crisis, and more importantly, the
countries own policies in reaction to the crisis, as
well as of the direct effects of the crisis itself. Although generalizations are of limited validity given the
heterogenous nature of developing countries, we wish to
emphasize the importance of the domestic policy adjustments to the largely uncontrollable external shocks.
The policies and mechanisms that guide the transition
from the pre-1973 "equilibrium" (Old Economic Order, if
you will) to the post-1980 "equilibrium" (New Economic
Order, whatever it turns out to be) will be crucial in
determining just what that new "equilibrium" will be
like, i.e., whether the developing countries will be
able to return to the high growth rates of the late
1960s and early 1970s, or whether they will enter a prolonged period of relative stagnation. In short, the
fundamental characteristic of the new relative equilibrium depend in large part on the developments during
the transition. It is not a simple case of comparative
statistics.

THE GROWTH OUTLOOK FOR DEVELOPING COUNTRIES

The fundamental development problems of the least
developed countries have not changed as a result of the
events of the past three years, although the relative
magnitude and importance of some major factors have.
The boom and inflation in the OECD, the increase in the
price of oil and other commodities, and the subsequent
stagnation in many developed countries was a unique
conjuncture that has directly affected the environment
in which the developing countries must operate. Although
other developing countries suffered sharp declines in

their immediate barter terms of trade, increased current account deficits, and corresponding increases in foreign borrowing, these countries also suffered internal disruptions including sharply increased inflation, budgetary deficits, unemployment and declining economic activity. These internal problems resulted from the external crisis itself and from the effects of each country's adjustment policies.

In the following sections we will examine the key developments prior to the crisis, the impact of the crisis itself, the recovery and readjustment process, and the longer-term outlook. In a final section we will discuss the major internal and external factors which affect this outlook.

Developments Leading Up To The Crisis

Prior to 1974, a number of low income developing countries were already experiencing economic difficulties due to the effects of bad weather (a drought in the Sahel and flooding in South Asia), poor domestic policy conception or execution (maintaining overvalued currencies, high domestic subsidies, inefficient pricing policies, or inefficient investment allocation), and external economic set-back (declining terms of trade, loss of markets).[1] For these countries, the total growth of GDP had averaged little more than 3% per year over the preceding decade, or less than 1% per capita. The international community was not insensitive to the needs of these countries; major aid and relief programs were mobilized, particularly for those affected by natural disasters. Although such aid programs alleviated much short-run suffering, they had little impact on long-run problems of development. Aggravated by the current economic crisis, the fundamental problems will remain the over-riding obstacles for these countries.

For the middle income countries[2], the period leading up to 1974 had been one of increasing growth and prosperity. For many of them, booming exports had greatly eased the foreign exchange constraints, and they appeared to be entering a period of self-sustaining rapid growth.

In 1972-73, the prices of primary product exports and the levels of primary product and manufactured exports of the developing countries were rising rapidly. The export price index (1967-69=100) stood at 148 in

25

1973; and manufactured exports of the middle and higher income non-oil-exporting countries (NoLDCs) were growing at 20% in real terms from 1965 to 1973 (32% for 1971-73). Except for some low income countries whose primary exports were not enjoying the generally favorable price increases (e.g. Sri Lanka with tea, Bangladesh with jute and Tanzania with sisal), even the moderate inflation in the prices of manufactured imports was not troublesome.

Table I shows the terms of trade indices and the export price indices for ten groups of developing countries, for OPEC and for all non-oil developing countries. For many parts of the world, export prices rose steadily during the early 1970s, particularly in the non-OPEC Middle East and in parts of Latin America. The accelerating inflation in imports was mild compared to the boom in exports until late in 1973.

This inflation also produced some benefits for the non-oil developing countries by reducing the real value of their outstanding debt, whose nominal value was $68 billion in 1973[3], and by easing the burden of the debt service relative to their current value exports. Their aggregate debt service ratio declined 30% from 1971 to 1973. The total current account deficit of these countries was $9.6 billion in 1973 and foreign exchange availability was diminishing as a major constraint on development for a number of countries. This increasing prosperity was partly based on the boom in exports to the OECD countries and the inflationary rate of international reserve creation, but it nevertheless meant real gains in income and growth potential even among the poorer countries as Table II shows.

TABLE I

EXPORT PRICE (XPI) AND TERMS OF TRADE (TTI) INDICES FOR
DEVELOPING REGIONS 1967-76
(1967-69=100)

Year	South Asia		India		Low Income Africa		Latin America I[1]	
	XPI	TTI	XPI	TTI	XPI	TTI	XPI	TTI
1967	98	106	102	96	96	101	98	101
1968	104	98	96	104	98	99	99	100
1969	99	95	102	100	105	100	103	100
1970	99	81	94	84	110	102	113	103
1971	101	75	102	92	107	93	116	101
1972	105	79	113	91	111	86	128	104
1973	149	72	143	88	138	95	172	114
1974	225	72	168	74	166	86	224	109
1975*	186	69	190	74	159	74	208	92
1976*	184	67	200	76	181	79	219	91

TABLE I
(continued)

Year	Latin America II²		Korea & Malaysia		Philippines & Thailand	
	XPI	TTI	XPI	TTI	XPI	TTI
1967	97	97	100	101	99	98
1968	97	97	96	95	99	100
1969	108	105	103	103	101	102
1970	114	109	103	101	105	100
1971	105	97	94	94	102	90
1972	108	93	98	90	99	84
1973	143	103	125	92	143	101
1974	197	108	165	81	240	97
1975*	197	94	167	81	224	81
1976*	206	92	181	81	230	77

TABLE I
(continued)

Year	Middle Income Africa		Middle East (non-OPEC)		South Europe		OPEC		Total (no LDCs)	
	XPI	TTI	XPI	TTI	XPI	TTI	XPI	TTI	XPI	TTI
1967	91	93	97	99	98	112	99	98	98	100
1968	95	94	100	101	99	96	99	100	98	99
1969	113	111	103	98	102	94	102	101	104	101
1970	105	101	103	96	110	94	107	102	107	99
1971	96	90	103	91	117	95	117	108	107	94
1972	99	86	124	97	125	93	134	119	113	93
1973	136	95	156	108	158	93	196	145	148	99
1974	165	94	263	128	213	86	472	284	201	95
1975*	164	82	274	126	215	79	582	298	197	86
1976*	180	84	272	118	234	81	614	292	209	85

*Estimated/Projected

1 Brazil and Mexico

2 Selected other Latin American countries

TABLE II

GROWTH RATES OF SELECTED NON-OIL DEVELOPING COUNTRIES
GROUPS PERCENT PER YEAR
1961-73

	1961-65[1]	1966-70[1]	1967-73[2]
Africa	4.8	5.0	7.8
East Asia	5.5	7.2	7.8
Middle East[3]	8.2	7.6	6.0
South Asia	3.8	4.4	3.2
Western Hemisphere	5.3	5.8	7.1
			5.9
Low Income No LDC			3.3
Middle Income No LDC			7.0
Southern Europe	7.2	6.3	6.3

[1]from IBRD Annual Report 1976
[2]Selected Countries
[3]Includes Oil Producers

Most countries were being expansionary in this
period, stimulated to some extent by increasing world
liquidity and the rapid expansion of world capital markets. With easing external constraints, many developing
countries were less careful with their own internal policies - allowing inefficient protection levels, rising
domestic subsidies, and inappropriate investment projects that would not have been possible under earlier
circumstances. By themselves, these policy "lapses"
were not serious, but when the price of oil shot up in
1973, followed by most other prices in 1974, many economies were left in exposed and vulnerable situations.
Projects conceived and launched prior to 1974 became
much more expensive to complete after 1974. Minor indirect subsidy programs became large subsidies, drain-
ing government budgets as a result of price increases
of food and petroleum products. In all, the developing
countries were no better prepared than the developed
countries to cope with the events of 1973-74.

The Crisis And Its Effects

The period of growth and optimism ended for most developing countries in 1974-75 as prices of their imports rose sharply in relation to export prices (OPEC excepted, of course), as the OECD entered a severe recession, and as the international economic structure abruptly shifted. Despite heavy borrowing to prevent falls in aggregate consumption and international ad hoc measures designed to ease balance of payments squeezes (e.g., Oil Facility, U.N. Emergency Operation), a majority of the people in these countries suffered declines in real income. An arresting, but by no means comprehensive measure of this impact is the terms of trade decline from 1973 to 1975. Table I shows that only in the Middle East has the terms of trade index remained anywhere near the 1973 levels. For other non-oil developing countries the index has fallen by 15% or more. The adverse movement in the non-oil developing countries terms of trade resulted in a net loss to them of about $4.5 billion in 1974 and a further $2 billion in 1975, which however followed net gains in 1972-73.

The current account deficits of the non-oil developing countries increased sharply from $9.6 billion on the current account in 1973 to $30.4 and $39.2 billion in 1974 and 1975 respectively. Although these deficits have been balanced by sharply increased capital flows to the non-oil developing countries, as shown in Table III, this additional financing does not eliminate the real burden of the deficit. It postpones the burden into the future, and reduces it only by the grant element in the concessionary financing, which has been low for much of the additional financing in 1974-75. The non-oil developing countries will have to adopt serious internal policy changes if they are to reduce their deficits, or the OPEC-OECD countries will have to agree to maintain a higher level of net transfer in the future, or both.

31

TABLE III

FINANCING NON-OIL DEVELOPING COUNTRIES' DEFICITS

US $ Billions

	1972	1973	1974	1975
Current Balance	-8.8	-9.0	-30.5	-39.2
Direct Investment	2.3	4.0	4.8	5.0
Official Grants	2.8	3.0	4.2	4.0
Net M&LT Public Loans	6.6	9.3	17.5	20.4
(Banks)	(1.3)	(3.7)	(6.7)	(7.2)
(OPEC)	-	-	(2.4)	(4.4)
(Other)	(5.3)	(5.6)	(8.4)	(8.8)
Net IMF	0.4	-0.1	1.6	1.6
(Oil Facility)			(0.9)	(1.5)
Capital NEI	2.2	0.9	4.7	5.2
Changes in Reserves	-5.5	-8.1	-2.3	3.0

Source: J. Holsen & J. Waelbroeck "Less Developed Countries and the International Monetary Mechanism".

The increase in the price of oil and of other imports has affected the developing countries in several
ways beyond the direct addition to their import bill.
The oil price rise aggravated the inflation in the OECD
countries, and it turned slowing OECD growth into a
major recession. Both of these developments in the industrialized countries worked to the detriment of the
non-oil developing countries by increasing their import
prices while reducing demand for their exports.

The developed countries have been able to absorb
resources in the form of manpower and exports from the
non-oil developing countries to cushion their inflationary tendencies in the early 1970s; they were also able
to use the non-oil developing countries to cushion the
recession of 1974-75, both by cutting back imports of
goods and labor and by passing on some of their higher
oil import bill to the non-oil developing countries in
the form of higher export prices. OPEC however took up
some of this slack by absorbing increased levels of
goods and manpower from the non-oil developing countries.

The Short-Term Responses To The Crisis

The short-run reactions of the non-oil developing
countries were quite varied. Most non-oil developing
countries however tried to ride out 1974 with minimal
policy changes. In this group, a number of the more

32

diversified and stronger economies postponed making fundamental adjustments because of political elections, the prospect of oil bonanzas in the near future and/or continued high export earnings in 1974.

A few countries, realizing that their circumstances were fundamentally changed, reduced imports, reduced growth and investment targets, and sought to make more efficient use of investments. These countries, like the majority of the non-oil developing countries, relied on short-run measures, financing their growing deficits out of reserves, increased commerical borrowing, and the ad hoc international financial measures.

The less fortunate among these countries have now exhausted their reserves and credit and their recovery will be protracted under the best of circumstances, but some countries have been forced by the crisis to undertake policy measures long overdue and have increased economic efficiency.

The net result has been that real income and consumption slowed but did not decline for the non-oil developing countries as a group during the crisis. In a few exceptional cases, countries were able to borrow enough abroad to maintain both consumption and investment at the expense of domestic saving and indebtedness. Their overall rate of growth, although cut about in half for 1974-75 remained positive. These countries were able to borrow enough because the absolute level of their increased needs, as expressed through the current account deficit, was small in relation to the wealth of the developed world and the newly-acquired liquidity of OPEC. In addition to substantial increases in nominal official capital flows (which allowed a small real increase), private sources vastly increased their lending to developing countries. The amount rose from about $3 billion in 1973 to nearly $15 billion in 1975. The slack demand for capital in the recession-stricken OECD, as well as the increased liquidity from OPEC facilitated this diversion of resources. In fact, since the OECD had balanced its current account by 1975, the non-oil developing country deficit roughly offset the OPEC surplus and the financial flows were the necessary counterparts to the real transfers implied by the OPEC surplus non-oil developing country deficit relation.

These short-run effects, which have so far been the object of most activity because of the enormity of the immediate problem, have generally been accomodated.

33

Now that recovery seems to be underway in most countries, it is important to highlight the long-run effects and requirements to see what long-run adjustments need to be made and how the long-run outlook is affected by these elements.

Many of the short-run phenomena are indicators of long-run changes in relative prices or other aspects of the world economic structure. In the short-run, the problem has been adapting to the fact of the change itself, while the long-run problem will be adapting to the changed situation. In this regard, many of the countries that benefited from gains in the terms of trade and rapidly increasing foreign exchange earnings in the short-run, will still face long-run problems as the terms of trade stabilize and foreign exchange earnings level off again. Imports will no longer be able to grow at the rates permitted when the terms of trade were improving and adjustments will have to be made. Put another way, the key to the short-run has been the ability to adapt to a changing world economic situation. The key to the long-run will be the success a country has in adapting to a new relatively stable long-run situation. In the latter, appropriate domestic policy will once more emerge as the most important factor.

Recovery To 1980

The adjustment to the changed circumstances is following a variety of courses, but recovery is taking place.

Although the developing countries have experienced a severe shock, there is a sense in which their adjustments are less unsettling than those of the developed countries, which suffered real income declines. Having less well developed modern sectors, they have had to face less fundamental restructuring. They still face the same basic problems of structuring an efficient modern sector, and these problems are now different as a result of the real price shifts that have occured.

Our projections indicate that most developing countries should recover from the crisis by 1978-80 if there are no further major shocks (see Tables IV and V).[4] By that time, their growth rates will have returned to long-run trend patterns, losses in import capacity will have been offset, and investment and domestic saving will have returned to sustainable levels. The real level of foreign borrowing should decline during this period as nominal current deficits stabilize or decline slightly and inflation continues at about 7%. Although the nominal levels of debt still appear large, real net foreign borrowing should return to more normal pre-crisis levels of under 2% of aggregate GDP. As in the past, there will continue to be wide inter-country variation. It will take some time, however, to work off the bulge of foreign debt built up during the crisis.

TABLE IV
THE CRISES AND RECOVERY TO 1980
NoLDCs[1] SELECTED INDICATORS

	1971	1972	1973	1974	1975	1976	1978	1980
Growth of GDP%	5.7	4.8	6.8	5.6	3.8	4.3	5.4	5.7
Real growth of exports%	4.9	10.8	7.1	-1.1	3.4	7.8	7.9	7.8
Real growth of imports%	6.1	2.6	8.0	13.7	1.3	-0.7	5.2	5.6
Export Price Index (1967-69=100)	7.0	113.0	148.0	201.0	197.0	209.0	251.0	291.0
Import Price Index (1967-69=100)	4.0	122.0	150.0	211.0	230.0	245.0	284.0	326.0
Terms of Trade Index (1967-69=100)	4.0	93.0	99.0	95.0	86.0	85.0	89.0	89.0
Real Growth of Consumption	6.1	3.5	6.8	5.1	5.4	3.3	4.6	5.2
Balance of Payments (current $US Billions)								
Resource Balance	-7.4	-6.0	-5.3	-22.5	-29.9	-25.7	-22.7	-21.7
Factor Payments	-1.8	-1.5	-1.4	-1.5	-2.5	-3.4	-6.1	-8.5
Current Account Balance	-7.8	-5.6	-4.2	-21.0	-29.6	-26.4	-26.4	-27.5
Gross M & LT Borrowing	9.8	13.3	15.5	21.5	31.9	33.6	39.9	47.7
Less Amortization	-4.5	-5.3	-6.9	-7.2	-7.3	-10.0	-17.2	-24.0
Other Capital Account-Net 4	2.5	-2.4	-4.4	-6.7	5.0	2.8	3.7	3.8
Debt Service								
-as ratio to exports (%)	13.4	12.9	12.3	10.4	11.5	13.2	15.7	16.5
Real Net Borrowing ($ Billion 67-69)	4.8	6.0	5.8	6.8	11.9	10.7	8.8	7.9
-as Percent of Real GDP	1.8	2.2	1.9	2.2	3.6	3.1	2.3	1.9

[1]IBRD Sample of 41 Major Countries
[2]Two Year Average for Growth Rates and ICORS
[3]These were estimated before the full effect of the coffee boom was known. Higher coffee prices would raise the export price indices and term of trade indices on the order of 5-10%.
[4]Including Direct Foreign Investment, IMF, and Reserve Change

TABLE V

GDP GROWTH RATE OF NoLDC GROUPS (% p.a.)

	1970-73	1973-76	1976-78	1978-80	1980-85
Low Income	1.9	2.7	4.1	4.2	4.4
South Asia	1.6	2.7	4.3	4.1	4.3
Low Income Africa	3.5	2.8	3.7	4.5	4.7
Middle Income	7.4	5.2	5.7	6.3	6.7
Latin America I[1]	9.3	5.3	5.4	6.4	7.1
Latin America II[1]	5.1	2.6	5.4	5.8	6.0
East Asia	8.4	6.5	7.5	7.4	7.5
Middle Income Africa	3.8	3.9	4.9	4.9	4.7
Middle East (non-OPEC)	4.3	7.2	6.6	6.6	6.6
South Europe	6.4	6.2	5.2	5.8	5.9

[1]See Table I for groupings

The Long-Run Outlook

Our longer projections show that is is feasible for the developing countries to achieve after 1980 near-ly the same growth rates they enjoyed in the 67-73 peri-od - about 7% for the middle income countries and slight-ly more than 4% for the low income countries. This out-come is by no means assured and depends a great deal on the internal policy adjustments the developing countries can make to the new external factors as well as on the external factors themselves. The developing countries must formulate their long-run adjustment policies, as before, within the limitations of their own resources, the levels of net official aid that will be made avail-able to them, their access to foreign private capital markets, and the progress they can make to improve their export earnings from the OECD and OPEC countries. Among these factors, it is clear that with respect to their balance of payments the non-oil developing countries have comparatively few fully independent policy options and these limitations also shape the constraints on do-mestic policy options. The developing countries are dependent on the policy decisions and future developments concerning trade, aid, and industrial development taken in the OECD and OPEC countries.

The growth rates presented in Table V for 1980-85 assume that OECD growth rates will return to historical levels averaging 4.9%, that trade opportunities will continue to develop, albeit at a somewhat slower rate than during the late 1960s, and that real capital flow will remain constant. For the period 1980-85, alterna-tive tests were made to determine the effects of varia-tions in these assumptions. Variations in OECD growth rates produced about .5 percentage point change in non-oil developing countries growth rates for each 1.0 percentage point change in OECD rates.

More dramatic changes would occur if the developing countries could expand their manufactured exports more rapidly, both by diversifying and penetrating new product markets in the OECD, and by expanding their exports to OPEC and to other developing countries. If the rate of growth of manufactured exports were to return to the rates achieved before the crisis, the growth rates for GDP could rise to as much as 5% for the low income countries (if they can adapt their policies quickly enough) and to cover 8% for the middle income countries, which have already demonstrated their ability to sustain high rates of growth. Additional capital flows of about $3-4 billion a year in 1980-85 could achieve a similar result in the low income countries, again assuming the necessary policy adjustments. For the middle income countries, however, $3-4 billion difference in capital flows would have little direct effect as that represents less than 1% of total foreign exchange flows: trade is far more important for these countries.

In order to achieve these projected growth rates, most non-oil developing countries (and all of the low income ones) need continued availability of real external resources at least as great as what is currently available, either through aid or trade. In fact, a fundamental point of dispute in all these "North-South" conferences, trade conferences and producer-consumer conferences is "How much additional resources can the OECD-OPEC countries be induced to make available to the Non-oil Developing Countries."

The precise mechanism of effecting any additional transfer - whether by increased concessional aid, by commodity price supports, or by increased preferences for NoLDC exports - is important in determining the specific policy measures to be undertaken by the non-oil developing countries, but it is secondary to determining the level of additional transfer to be granted to the non-oil developing countries. The OECD countries have suffered real income losses and are undergoing painful structural change; and the OPEC countries have begun ambitious industrialization plans that will soon more than absorb the current account surpluses of most members; so that neither the OECD countries nor the OPEC countries are currently inclined to increase their real resource transfer to non-oil developing countries a

38

great deal, whatever the mechanism suggested, except on
a highly selective basis. It is within this framework
that the non-oil developing countries must conceive
their internal adjustment policies, and that the international community must formulate its long-run response.

MAJOR FACTORS AFFECTING THE OUTLOOK FOR DEVELOPING
COUNTRIES

In a world as interdependent as ours, the economic
destinies of all countries are affected by the interplay
of both internal and external factors as the recent crisis has so amply demonstrated. The internal factors,
reflecting resource endowment (including human resources),
development strategy and its implementation, and the
current stage of development constitute the physical
and structural framework from which each country can
shape its future. The external factors, reflecting
trading prices and volumes, external aid and capital
flows, and integration into world markets and price
structures, determine the external constraints and
rules of the game within which each country must shape
its policy. These factors are not entirely independent;
various domestic policies and endowments encourage certain external reactions, and various external factors
condition domestic policies. More favorable external
factors can ease the constraints faced by a country,
but unless the country can efficiently take advantage
of these improvements in the context of appropriate
domestic policy, little is gained from the external benefit. In the following section, the external factors
will be discussed in more detail; in the subsequent section, the internal factors will be discussed.

The External Factors:

Exports provide the largest source of foreign exchange earnings, usually well over 90%, and are the
principal means of converting the country's more abundant resources and factors into scarce goods through
imports. To the extent that the economy is open to
trade, this exchange of goods also exposes the economy
to world price and efficiency criteria. For most countries, the prices received for their primary product
exports are determined by overall supply and demand

39

interactions on the world commodity markets. The developing countries as a whole have little control over the volumes or prices of their commodity exports in the short to medium term. Individual countries can, of course, undertake specific policies to expand (or contract) their share in the total market, and change their relative position in the medium term. In the long run, the aggregate investment decisions of the producers of any given commodity can affect the long-run supply function, thereby affecting both prices and volume.

Expansion of the volume of traditional exports is limited primarily by the growth of demand in the OECD markets and the extent to which markets in the OPEC and centrally planned economies can be opened. Even as OECD growth recovers and demand increases, traditional exports cannot be expected to expand very rapidly because of low income elasticities of demand for primary products.[5] Until recently, concerted efforts by the producers to control either price or volume have not been very successful. The OPEC oil embargo and price increase is, of course, and important exception, and it has had profound effects, both on the structure of world prices and economic relations and on the perceptions of other primary producers as to possibility of administering prices. OPEC countries have managed to increase their real incomes greatly at the expense of the rest of the world, generating a large current account surplus in the process. This does not, however, free them from the laws of economics. They have spent their new resources far faster than expected, and far beyond their capacity to absorb productive investment. Many will soon face problems as increasing imports begin to exceed stabilizing export earnings, requiring sharp readjustments in domestic policy and reductions in investment plans.

The promotion of manufactured exports, including additional processing of primary products, offers the greatest hope for export growth. Greater participation in these world markets can also have very beneficial side effects in encouraging efficiency and proper resource allocation by exposing the developing countries to international prices and competition. The recent high growth rates of a number of non-oil developing countries have been based on very rapid growth of industrial exports. They have been able to expand their small share of manufactures in OECD imports because it

is a highly elastic market for them. The future of
manufactured exports from an increasing number of developing countries depends a great deal on the continued willingness of OECD, and to a lesser extent to OPEC
countries, to restructure their own industrial plant
in order to allow for the transfer of more labor-intensive industries to the non-oil developing countries.
Continued trade liberalization, or at least the pre-
vention of any backsliding toward more protectionism,
is among the most important conditions for this development. It should be noted here that the developing countries as well as the developed countries are guilty of
imposing import restrictions against other developing
countries, thus inhibiting potentially beneficial trade
among themselves. Policies to increase exports of non-
oil developing countries and to maintain and expand
access into markets should have very high priority in
any "new economic order".

The value of a country's exports plus whatever net
foreign saving it can attract, determines the value of
the imports a country can afford. And the relative
prices of the imports determine the real level of transfer a country can achieve. These relative prices, generally expressed in the terms of trade, are another important external factor for developing countries. Increasing terms of trade means a higher level of real
resources available to the economy for a given level of
exports, while declining terms of trade mean the opposite. There have been clear increases and decreases in
the relative prices of a number of commodities, and
some countries have benefited or have been harmed by
systematic movements in their own terms of trade. However, long-term movements in the terms of trade in
either direction are not in and of themselves indicators
of the well-being of a country. An improvement in terms
of trade due to export shortfalls and resulting price
rises may not benefit a country.[6] On the other hand,
if a country is rapidly expanding its exports by lower-
ing prices to penetrate new markets, then the falling
terms of trade are in fact an indications of the success
of its policy.

In response to the structural decline in the terms
of trade in 1974, some middle and higher income non-oil
developing countries have been able to reduce their imports by stringent measures, such as reducing so-called
non-essential imports and buying down - purchasing lower
price and lower quality versions of goods in order to
save foreign exchange. For the poorer countries, there

41

is much less leeway to reduce imports because their poverty has already forced their imports to near minimum levels. Further import substitution also offers some hope of mitigating the external resource constraint; but as has already been demonstrated in the 1960s, this policy is usually dependent on continued high levels of imports, particularly in smaller countries where markets are restricted. Alone it is not sufficient to sustain high real growth rates. Most non-oil developing countries have already exploited the easiest and most profitable opportunities for import substitution, so except for the larger and more diversified of the developing countries, accelerated import substitution probably will neither reduce the demand for imports nor, if past experience is any guide, necessarily be an efficient use of scarce foreign resources.

A final major external factor in the outlook of the developing countries is the availability of foreign savings in the form of official grants and loans, private loans and direct investment. The availability of official capital is largely determined by the donor countries, both directly and through the international institutions, and by private lenders on the basis of their own political and economic criteria. While direct investment is also a function of the receptivity of the recipient country, the developing country can only assure that certain domestic conditions to attract investment are met. The final decision to invest rests with the investor.

The official aid from traditional DAC donors will probably continue to decline as a share in the GNP of DAC countries through 1980 and then remain constant as a share of GNP thereafter. The sharp increase in the share of OPEC will probably reverse itself and slowly decline as the OPEC countries absorb their own surpluses. (Table VI)

TABLE VI

THE OFFICIAL AID PACKAGE

	1960	1965	1970	1975	1980	1985
ODA as % GNP-DAC	.52	.44	.34	.32	.30	.30

	1973	1974	1975	1977	1980
Total Offical Aid	15.0	21.2	26.2	30.5	32.4
($ Billion)					
Share of:					
DAC (%)	81.3	66.0	56.5	59.0	76.2
OPEC(%)	8.0	26.4	37.4	35.1	17.5
Other(%)	10.7	7.6	6.1	5.9	6.3

The real level of aid increases over the next decade, but still falls well below the target of .7% of
GNP established for the second Development Decade.
The emergence of OPEC as a major aid donor has primarily
benefited Arab and Islamic states.

The international institutions act primarily as
intermediaries in channeling resources from the OECD
and OPEC countries to the non-oil developing countries
and these institutions are limited by the political
decisions of donor countries. The IMF may be able to
transfer about 0.5 billion a year for the next five years
by means of the Trust Fund and other expanded facilities.
The World Bank's capital has been increased by $8.6 bil-
lion, which will allow it to maintain a constant level
of commitment at the 1978 levels, and it now appears
likely there will be a further increase. IDA V sub-
scriptions and thus commitments will amount to $7.6
billion for 1977-79. Possible expansion of resource
transfer through the existing international institutions
is limited by the willingness of the OECD institutions.
A number of new international institutions have been
created or proposed in the past two years to transfer
resources to the non-oil developing countries for either
specialized (IFAD) or general purposes. To the extent
that these institutions can generate additional resources
to transfer to the developing countries they will add to
the official flow.

Projection of the availability of private source
capital for the least developed countries is more difficult. It is much more dependent on specific market conditions and judgments about credit worthiness. Our
country projections assume private flows consistent
with expected availability of private capital and the

conventional criteria of individual country's credit worthiness. This implies there will be little expansion over the high levels reached in 1974-75 in nominal terms, and a decline in real terms for the net flows.

The level of foreign capital available to any developing country is generally small in comparison with domestic savings and investment or to total foreign exchange resources[7], but it is often desired because of its special attributes. Strictly speaking, foreign capital, in the form of foreign exchange, is no different from foreign exchange earned by exports. But, officials loans and grants, particularly from the multi-national institutions, bring valuable technical assistance in project identification, preparation and execution, and they often aid in improving the overall efficiency of the economy beyond the range of specific projects. Private lending can provide similar assistance, although its record is mixed in this area. Direct foreign investment often brings a whole package of technology, technical assistance, marketing, and indirect investment which can be very beneficial to a developing economy, although it presents the problem of perceived or actual foreign interference.

These external factors contain elements that are beyond the control of the developing countries. They form the constraints within which the country must shape its policies. However, one of the attributes of the "new economic order" has been to try more vigorously to use international negotiation and political pressure to change some of these external factors, e.g. proposals for a common commodity fund or for debt rescheduling. Whether or not these actions are successful, they will not reduce to necessity of good domestic policy. And good domestic policy can influence the effects of the external factors on the economy. For example, the ability of a country to export enough to pay for its desired imports is as much a function of policies that encourage efficient production as it is of high external demand or generous resource endowment. The demand for imports is a function of domestic income and demand regulation policy as much as it is of the industrial and investment plan of a country. Similarly, the overall absorptive capacity of a country in terms of project preparation and management and its receptiveness to foreign capital helps determine the amount of foreign capital that will be available to it.

The Internal Factors:

The most important internal factors affecting a
country's prospects are its resource endowment (human
and natural), size of population and income, and level
of industrialization or modern development. While at
any moment of time these factors are fixed, new resources can be discovered, manpower can be trained, industrialization expanded and incomes raised -- what we
call economic development. Or conversely, resources
can be wasted, skilled manpower idled or turned to non-
productive tasks, inefficient investment pursued with
no real income increases realized -- what we call stagnation. Although it takes little analysis to see that
a rich initial endowment makes rapid development easier,
it is neither a necessary nor a sufficient condition.
By appropriate policy, the necessary resources can be
created or purchased, just as inappropriate policies
can waste rich resources.

The role of resources is overshadowed and dominated
by the internal factors that control their use: the development strategy of the country and the policies
used to implement it. With good domestic policy, rapid
development is feasible without large net external resources, but access to external resources can facilitate
and speed up development in conjunction with good domestic policy. On the other hand, without appropriate domestic policy, no level of external resources can do
much to aid development. Inevitably, this analysis
places domestic policy and related internal factors
squarely in the middle of the development problem, while
external factors play a supplementary role that may be
important at certain stages, but rarely is crucial.

There are some relatively costless policy options
that can increase a country's economic and bureaucratic
efficiency by removing bottlenecks, by improving the
quality of administration, and by reducing or eliminat-
ing wasteful and non-productive expenditures. The possibility and desirability or implementing such measures
has always existed, but the present crisis has made
implementation all the more imperative. Some countries
have already structured their economies to be highly
efficient (Korea, Malaysia) so they have less scope
for further improvements among these lines. For some of
the other countries, the impetus of the crisis may have
been sufficient to force needed improvements in efficiency - as was the case with the accelerated rate of exploitation of the Bombay High oil reserves in India, and
with the economic stabilization program in Zaire.

45

Most domestic policy alternatives are difficult
and involve serious trade-offs among different goals.
The most important constraint faced by the NoLDCs after
the crisis has been low foreign exchange availability
due to terms of trade deterioration and to weak export
markets. Since policies that reduce import demand
generally reduce investment and growth rates as well,
countries have faced difficult trade-offs. The detri-
mental effect on growth, however, can be diminished
by structural shifts in the composition of investment
away from low productivity sectors into more immediately productive projects, (such as is being done in Kenya) and by shifts into sectors with lower import requirements such as agriculture instead of industry.

A re-examination of investment strategies is probably the most important policy action to be taken in
order to achieve the projected post recovery growth
rates. Large-scale industrial projects - whether for
import substitution or export promotion - have often
proved to be relatively inefficient and costly in terms
of domestic resources and foreign exchange. This sort
of investment needs to be reduced in favor of more investment and research/development in agriculture, labor
intensive industry, and small-scale production with
higher returns and lower costs in terms of both domestic resources and foreign exchange. The poorer NoLDCs
could also save considerable amounts of foreign exchange
by reducing their net food imports, if proper agriculture policy is followed; this necessitates adequate
producer prices and input supplies at reasonable times
and prices, i.e. improving their terms of trade between
rural and urban sectors.

As imports of capital and intermediate goods have
become relatively more costly, there is greater reason
to develop and use new or modified technology more appropriate to the factor proportions and resource availability of the non-oil developing countries. As such
technology is implanted, the non-oil developing countries
can benefit from improved efficiency, including higher
capacity utilization, will have greater capacity for
increasing the skill levels of a larger segment of their
work force, and should become more self-sufficient in
satisfying their needs for capital and intermediate
goods.

The range of choice among policies varies widely
among the non-oil developing countries. With few exceptions the richer, more industrialized and flexible

economies have the resources and control to be able to change policies more easily.

They have diversified economies and access to large amounts of capital from private sources. For these countries, the major tasks involve insuring that policies to restore growth do not sacrifice other targets of equity, improved income distribution, and creation of employment. They must also guard against middle term liquidity crises as their private debt and debt service burden escalates. While their growth rates may be slightly below the high levels of recent years, they will still be comfortably above rates of population growth.

There is a middle group of countries whose long-run prospects have been somewhat diminished by the recent events but who have developed to a point where they can undertake efficient investment and utilize increased external resources to achieve satisfactory growth rates. It is important that these countries receive continued official aid in order to facilitate internal policies to improve efficiency and maintain growth.

Finally, there is a group of generally low income countries whose dim and uncertain prospects have been further shadowed by the recent events. These countries need improved domestic policy and large inflows of external resources and merely to keep economic growth even of slightly ahead of population growth. Some lack the ability to mobilize sufficient domestic resources and suffer from shortages of manpower and administrative capacity. Their need predates the crisis, but has been aggravated by it. With a major effort by them and by the international community, they still can move to the threshold of sustained economic development in the coming decade.

Increasing the net foreign resources available to the poorer non-oil developing countries and to a lesser extent to the middle income countries is of primary importance. If the real level of total official flows does in fact only remain constant over the next decade, then there must be a shift in its distribution toward the poorest and least developed of the non-oil developing countries. This will not only increase the possible growth rates of these countries, but also improve the distribution of resources on a world-wide basis as these countries do not have access to resources on any other terms (i.e. commercial credit).

47

We think the outlook we have presented is reasonably optimistic. The developing countries have not suffered a cataclysmic defeat as a result of the recent economic crisis. They have suffered a major setback, from which they are recovering. Most of them are facing more a difficult external situation, but with the aid and cooperation of the developed countries, there is no reason why they cannot adjust their internal policies to the new circumstances and continue to achieve satisfactory rates of growth.

FOOTNOTES

[1]Low income being defined for this paper as below
$200 per capita annual income as reported in
the 1975 World Bank Atlas.

[2]Those with an annual per capita income of over $200
per capita, ibid.

[3]IBRD Annual Report, 1975, excluding Southern Europe
and Middle East.

[4]The projections are based on two-gap consistency
models which essentially trade off growth rates
and exogenous export projections against import
demand and foreign capital availability in terms
of each country's estimated parameters.

[5]Producers of individual products will continue to
experience fluctuating earnings as prices fluctuate (e.g. copper or coffee) unless stabilization agreements are reached.

[6]A good example is Peru, where fishmeal has been a
large percentage of exports, but in recent years
price has risen as production dropped. With a
1963 base the index currently stands at about
125, if this is adjusted to current export weights,
the index is perhaps less than 100.

[7]There may be exceptions to this for small countries
for short periods of time, e.g. the Sahel in the
early 1970s when almost all investment was foreign saving, but such a relation is not sustainable.

III
THE CASE OF THE LEAST DEVELOPED OF THE UNDERDEVELOPED COUNTRIES: THE SAHEL-SUDAN REGION OF WEST AFRICA

Nake M. Kamrany
University of Southern California

INTRODUCTION

The United Nations has identified 25 countries as the least developed of the Less Developed Countries in the world.* Per capita income (around $100) was the main criterion used for this classification. The purpose of this subcategorization by the U.N. was to induce and encourage grants and concessional "soft" loans for these countries. Aid -- its quantity and conditions -- is indeed one of the main points of contention in the present North-South dialogue and bargaining. The major problems faced by these countries are articulated in various speeches and articles. Following is a synopsis.

The terms of trade of these countries are deteriorating and the OPEC price hike has accentuated this deterioration. Debt service ratios of 25 to 40 are reaching antigrowth proportions, fragmented markets continue to constrain demand, inefficient and stagnant import substitution is failing to improve the balance of payments and not alleviating the high unemployment rates of 20% to 30%. Supplier's credit if available remains exploitive. The multinational corporations have largely ignored these countries. The possibility of linking the International Monetary Fund's Drawing Rights to development finance and its effectiveness remain uncertain.

---

*Included are: Afghanistan, Bangladesh, Bhuton, Burundi, Chad, Central Africa Republic, Dahomey (Benin), Ethiopia, Guinea, Haiti, Laos, Mali, Madagascar, Malawi, Niger, Rwanda, Sri Lanka (Ceylon), Sierra Leone, Somalia, Togo, Uganda, Upper Volta, Vietnam, and Yemen.

Debt refinancing has added enormous interest burdens jeopardizing the credit-worthiness of many LDCs and tied aid has made the cost of development prohibitive, while project aid carries with it undue rigidities and has forced LDCs to define their development plans in terms of the pleasures and objectives of the donors rather than their own national interest.

In spite of the above situation, recent international efforts have suggested little more than reaffirming the status quo and promises of more dialogues and conferences. Needless to say, there is a case for a candid and forceful restatement of the central economic problems of LDCs and their solutions, with a view to keeping in perspective realistic limitations imposed by institutions and resources. If the existing economic prescriptions are extended to their logical conclusions, we will be faced with a picture rooted in extension of the present order. For instance, if the Pearson Commission's GNP growth target of 5% per annum is realized in the '70s (which is unlikely), a large number of LDCs would still remain very poor in the '80s. The relative importance of LDCs would be diminishing, while the gap between the "rich" and the "poor" would be increasing. Needless to say, the present uncertain international economic issues cast doubt upon the availability of funds and the urgency of attention needed for changing the lot of billions of peoples in the least developed nations.

This paper summarizes the findings of a case study and an attempt is made to (1) examine the foreign aid requirements for the Sahel-Sudan countries of West Africa to achieve an annual growth of 5% and (2) to identify the underlying conditions to be met -- both internal and external -- for these countries to effectively utilize the aid program and reach a status of self-support in the long run. Included in the case study were Chad, Mauritania, Mali, Niger, Senegal, and Upper Volta. All except Senegal were classified among the Least Developed of the Underdeveloped Countries by the United Nations. These economies were examined with respect to their (1) capacity to respond to major droughts, (2) capacity to break the vicious circles of poverty, and (3) capacity to create self-supporting economies in the long run.

SUMMARY OF FINDINGS

The countries of the Sahel-Sudan region are sus-
ceptible to major and frequent droughts. The most recent drought of 1972-74 caused substantial losses of
lives and property. It also demonstrated that the capacity to respond to major drought is extremely limited
on the part of these countries.

For the period 1975-2000, the range of foreign aid
required to achieve 5% annual target growth was $5 bil-
lion under the assumption of high export performance
and about $9 billion under the assumption of relatively
modest export performance. Under both assumptions the
occurrence of another major drought was not considered.
The wide range in the amount of foreign aid was due to
the varying assumption concerning the internal and external performances of these countries as summarized
below:

> a) The donor countries shift the burden
> of solutions and implementations of de-
> velopment programs to the Sahel-Sudan
> countries, rather than have programs
> determined and imposed by the donors.
>
> b) Specific assumptions are made con-
> cerning the performance of these coun-
> tries with respect to the savings rate,
> the investment rate, the capital-output
> ratios, import rate, and rate of growth
> of exports. These assumptions point to
> substantial upgrading of the internal
> performance and are spelled out later
> in this paper and in Appendix A.

An interdisciplinary approach in forecasting the
macroeconomic options of the sub-Sahara countries was
followed.

The Chenery-Strout model was found most appropriate
as a forecasting tool, since it explicitly recognizes the
three important constraints relevant to these economies:
(1) the absorptive capacity, (2) the savings gap, and
(3) the balance of payments gap. The parametric values
have been estimated heuristically rather than by the
least squares method. This was possible since sufficient information was generated from an interdisciplinary research team studying the region's long-term options both from the engineering and social technological

perspectives. A strictly statistical approach produced disconcerting results.

The initial values for 1970 and the values of the parameters were made to estimate the foreign aid requirements of these countries to achieve annual 5% growth rate of the GDP over the next 25 years. A departure from the Chenery-Strout approach was embedded in our assigning time path values to the parameters rather than values derived from historical data. Our assumptions regarding parameter values were made explicit, which also pointed to required trends (a policy variable) if these economies were to achieve certain macroeconomic targets. Three sets of projections were made for each country under alternative assumptions regarding the parameters, in order to capture the top and the bottom limits of development options and provide a useful frame of reference for policy analysis. Our procedure for estimating capital-output ratios was designed to "average-out" the influence of minor droughts. Five-year averages have been computed. Our results show that under the most optimistic set of assumptions, four of the countries' per capita income will remain below $150 (in 1971 prices) by the year 2000, implying major structural changes and/or discoveries of new marketable resources as a way to break the vicious circle of poverty.

The importance of the limited absorptive capacity is brought to focus when the value of the rate of growth of investment (β) is shown to be zero for Chad and Upper Volta when the Chenery-Strout model was strictly followed. The model indicates that it will take 15 years for these economies to reach a sustained growth rate of 5%, even if donors' assistance closes the "two gaps" and the capital-output ratio is improved from 6+ to 4. It follows that investment in human capital should receive high priority.

The sensitivity of foreign aid upon growth was examined under these sets of alternative assumptions concerning capital-output ratios, the saving rate, and the rate of growth of exports. It pointed to the concerted effort required for export promotion and import substitution requiring regional cooperation to achieve growth targets. This point becomes more significant when it is shown that even if the capital-output ratio (K) is made more efficient from 6 to 4, reliance upon foreign aid will not be reduced significantly unless it is accompanied by an improvement in the trade sector. The trade gap dominates in each country studied; nevertheless, dependence upon foreign aid will remain under the best of assumptions. The annual net inflow of foreign aid required (1975-1990) to achieve a sustained growth rate of 5% will be doubled over the annual average amount received during 1965-1971 (except for Mali and Senegal and the special case of Mauritania). Weather fluctuations and investment in infrastructure kept the capital-output ratios quite high, 6+. If this factor is not lowered to 4 or better, either GDP will not achieve its target by the year 2000, or foreign aid requirements will become prohibitive.

PROBLEM IDENTIFICATION

Although the total area of the Sahel-Sudan region is approximately two-thirds that of the United States, its 23 million inhabitants represent a population only approximately 11 percent of the U.S. The majority of the people live at a subsistence level, depending primarily on agriculture and animal husbandry for their existence. The drought of the past few years has exacerbated the chronic problem of moderate malnutrition and has drastically reduced herds. Only extensive assistance from the international community prevented widespread loss of human life.

Disaster relief has helped to minimize the effects of the drought and very significant amounts of foreign assistance have financed a variety of projects and programs in the area for many years. However, these funds were either inadequate or not always directed to the most effective ends. New approaches are clearly necessary if the region is to become self-sustaining and begin an era of positive economic development and widespread improvement in the quality of life of its people.

Critical Questions

Employing a functional approach to examining the whole development problems of the Sahel-Sudan region, several critical questions were raised.

First, Climate Changes: In view of the region's five consecutive years of drought, a fundamental question raised was: is the climate changing? Although others disagree (Bryson 1973, Bryson 1974, Bryson and Giordano 1974), we maintain that the present drought should not be considered indicative of a climatic change. Analysis indicates that long droughts are not statistically unlikely; six or more consecutive years of drought could take place in the region once in a century. Furthermore, the region must expect to cope with recurrent droughts of random frequencies and varying intensities, at different locations.

Second, Long-Term Self-Sufficiency: The second critical question that emerged was related to the region's long-term self-sufficiency. Given its climatological characteristics, would the area be capable in the long run of supporting its population on a sustained basis? This question was addressed first from a technological viewpoint. Our deliberations ranged from assumptions of utopian conditions to computations of the region's carrying capacity, given the known resource potentials and conditions (including both average rainfall and drought).

The answer to the second critical question was, yes: with the known resources and under varying rainfall conditions, it is possible, technologically speaking, for the region to support the population projected from the year 2000 on a sustained basis. If the answer to this question had been negative, the factor of migration would have to have been given greater weight in terms of the options realistically open to the people in the area.

Third, Plausible Diagnosis: These conclusions, then, led us to a third question: what are the underlying reasons for the region's present inability to provide sustained support for its population? What are the plausible diagnoses and remedies?

We maintain that the loss of human lives and livestock and the region's increasing desertification result primarily from an overstressed, frail ecology; the drought simply accelerated the occurrence and intensity of these conditions. Even without the drought, had the pressures from livestock and population continued the region would have encountered the same problems within a decade or slightly longer. Thus the essence of the problem is ecological imbalance, emanating from sociocultural and institutional variables and intensified by natural and climatic conditions. To remedy this situation, new social technologies are as necessary as new engineering technologies.

Since we are examining the entire region and at-

56

tempting to conceptualize its problems in a unified, comprehensive framework, we are necessarily abstracting from the many differences that exist among the individual countries. However, these countries do share a number of structural problems. These common characteristics are examined in order to discern their implications.

The bottlenecks to development of the region can be conceptualized as a set of interacting problems or vicious circles incorporating resources, socio-cultural variables, and institutional factors.

The Interacting Problems, or the Vicious Circles

1. The Agricultural-Ecological Vicious Circle, or Interaction Between Agriculture and the Ecology

Climate in the Sahel-Sudan region is the predominant factor in determining agricultural production. Yet the development economists, by and large, have neglected to treat this variable rigorously and adequately. Progressive deterioration of the region's ecology is due both to recurrent droughts (22 recorded over the last 400 years, at varying degrees of frequency and intensity) and to human factors -- the socio-cultural behavior of 24 ethnic groups whose instincts for survival, sustenance, and improvement have paved the way to a "tragedy of the commons," or what economists call the "fallacy of composition."

The northern cattle-raising and southern sedentary farming areas are both caught in a vicious circle. The region's climate has been and will remain subject to extreme variation in annual precipitation, which have in turn caused variations in the agricultural output achieved by the farmers and led to a system of cattle-raising that leads to seasonal weight fluctuations in the animals. A relatively long period of cattle-grazing (8-10 years as compared to 3-4 years under European or American conditions) is therefore required before animals reach maturity. Significant increases in cattle population (50 percent increase in 1970 over 1960) have caused range depletion, which, in turn, has lowered the carrying capacity of the grazing land; repetition of the process has reduced the land's grazing capacity even further. According to preliminary calculations, the region's 1970 cattle population exceeded the carrying capacity under the most favorable set of conditions and policies we tested.

57

In the area of sedentary agriculture, a similar phenomenon is observable. Frequent periods of adverse climatic conditions and pressures of increasing population have, over time, reduced soil fertility. In the absence of modern agricultural technologies and fertilizers, the traditional farming system depends on fallow periods to restore soil fertility. Since little new arable land is available, the rate of soil fertility decline (with use time) has been higher than the rate of soil recovery with fallow time. For example, from 1961 to 1970, the fallow time in Niger declined by 50 percent, while farming technology and application of fertilizers did not change substantially.

The foregoing problems are exacerbated by the patterns of energy consumption, in which nearly 90 percent of the energy is drawn from wood resources. The rate of wood consumption in Upper Volta, for example, is now estimated to equal the rate of net reproduction of trees. If this trend continues and alternative sources of energy are not developed, the problems of deforestation and desertification will be magnified.

Finally, overgrazing of the fragile range had led to an increase in the amount of the sun's energy reflected by the ground. This increase could in turn have an adverse effect on cloud formation and on the frequency and quality of precipitation.

2. The Human Opportunity Vicious Circle, or Interaction Between the Productive Capacity of the Area and its Institutions

Failure to develop adequate social institutions has influenced both the modern and traditional sector's production functions since colonial times. The interaction between agriculture and the ecology has led to low population, low output, and subsistence living conditions in the traditional sector. This low productive capacity in the rural areas has led to a failure to develop institutions which would in turn foster development of the rural sector. A lack of institutions for saving, credit, and investment means that the rural sector relies on traditional forms of savings (e.g., more cattle), which are counterproductive to maintenance of the ecological balance and thus the productive capacity of the area. Lack of availability of credit, together with low investment in agricultural technology exacerbates the problem of low productivity. Failure to de-

58

velop productive capacity has led to a lack of employment opportunities which has in turn resulted in outmigration and loss to these areas of many of the most able people.

The rural areas also suffer from inadequacies in health care facilities and infrastructure, an education system unresponsive to social needs, and lack of other social amenities. As a result of these restricted opportunities, the well-being of the region's inhabitants -- especially when measured in terms of the potential that might be realized if adequate services were available -- has deteriorated over time.

3. The Traditional-Modern Vicious Circle, or Relations Between the Traditional and Modern Sectors

Pricing policies for agricultural production, taxes, and other fiscal policies have favored the modern sector at the expense of the traditional sector. These policies have siphoned resources from the traditional sector and increased the migration of rural labor to the cities.

However, the rapid rate of migration from the traditional sector into the modern sector has created problems within the modern sector. The rate of migration into the modern sector has been much higher than the rate of increase of employment opportunities, thus creating a very high unemployment in the cities. Moreover, minimum wage laws, overvalued currencies, and a very low level of worker skills have created conditions adverse for competition in the international markets. The rapid migration to the cities has also led to inadequate housing, sanitation, water systems, health care, and nutrition, and thus to a generally poor quality of life among the urban masses.

These policies and conditions have fostered certain internal inconsistencies. Since the prices of both imports and the modern sector's products have been held quite high, the growth of a market for industrial goods has been inhibited in the traditional sector. That sector's elasticity of income demand has been disregarded in pricing, income, and tax policies. Industrial policies have been geared to foreign markets, neglecting rural demands and the need for a synergistic system linking industry and agriculture.

59

Additional Problems

A number of additional problems over which these countries now have little control have limited their development. These include:

1) Restrictive economic policies -- The monetary union to which these countries belong results in restrictive monetary and fiscal policies in which there is limited flexibility.

2) Poor foreign trade situation -- The region's exports are subject to short-term fluctuation on both the demand side (world market) and the supply side (because of climatic conditions), while prices of imports have been steadily rising.

3) Dependence on other countries -- The growth of the Sahel-Sudan countries is heavily dependent on foreign aid, on European markets, and on outlets for the region's products on the countries to the south.

4) High population growth rate -- The population growth rate has been and will probably remain high for some time. The resultant high dependency ratio is a detriment to economic development.

5) Underdevelopment of human resources -- Lack of trained indigenous personnel will continue to impose a major constraint upon the region's absorptive capacity and keep the region dependent upon foreign technical assistance.

For the economies of the Sahel-Sudan region to support their populations at a self-sustaining level, these interacting problems would have to be addressed and their effects minimized.

The determination of the answers to the basic question of the ecology and long-term self-sufficiency, together with the identification of persisting and interacting problems, provides the basis for the framework within which development alternatives can be identified and evaluated.

MAJOR DEVELOPMENT ISSUES AND POLICY IMPLICATIONS

From the foregoing observations, it is quite clear that foreign aid could not by itself break the three vicious circles of underdevelopment. Many of the problems enumerated for the Sahel-Sudan region are shared by the rest of the LDCs. It will require substantial reorientation of the internal policies of these countries as well as new criteria for aid on the part of the donors. With respect to the goals of economic development, the record of foreign aid (by all donors) is widely regarded as having failed. For example, financial viability criteria for IBRD project aid may preclude the redistributional aspects so badly needed. Otherwise, the rich in the poor countries will be richer if the income redistribution impact of aid is not taken into consideration.

Issue 1: The Primacy of Political & Social Factors

In the six countries of the study area, political and social factors outweigh economic considerations. The six countries are inhabited by approximately 23 million people who share many affinities as well as divergences. Their affinities stem from the fact that after centuries of colonial rule they have been engaged since 1960 in the process of nation-building, painstakingly trying to develop the institutions, organizations, and cohesiveness necessary for politically and economically viable nation state. The primacy of their political and social ideals is clearly pronounced in each nation's plans for social and economic development.

Associated with the primacy of the political/state considerations is the countries' common and firm objective of improving the quality of life of their citizenry. While some of the basic indicators of the quality of life (Q/L), such as adequate amounts of food, shelter, clothing, and social amenities, can apply to any individual in any part of the world, those components of the Q/L that go beyond the basic necessities are cultural and value-bound. And it is the Africans themselves who are best qualified to define their own criteria for the optimal quality of life within their own geographic, cultural, ethnic, and social context. For both historical and environmental reasons, however, it has not yet been possible for a majority of the inhabitants of this area to free themselves from the struggle for the basic necessities of life. In this

61

struggle, all of the six countries have a common cause.

Conclusion 1

The allocation of resources in these countries is influenced more by political and social considerations and by the African definition of the optimal quality of life than by economic profitability. Thus, any successful development strategy, whether for a single country or for the area as a whole, will have to pass the quality-of-life, political and social tests of the African decision makers, i.e., the civil servants, who will be asked to implement the strategy, and the affected population whose acceptance or rejection of it will have a major bearing upon its success or failure.

Issue 2: Variability of Climate

The Sahel-Sudan area is subject to multiannual variations in climate, especially in precipitation. While it is true that topography and soil, as well as social and governmental structure, differ in important ways from one part of the Sahel-Sudan region to another, one climatic feature is common to the entire area. This is the variability in precipitation from year to year. The periods when precipitation is below some threshold value of economic importance may not always be coincident over the entire region, but the fact that there will be periods without enough rain is the one aspect of the climate that is dependable.

Whether the current prolonged drought is just the sort of event to be expected from time to time through random chance or whether it is a manifestation of a shift to some different climate, the implications for modeling climatic impact on economic, ecological, and societal events are almost the same. Even though the 1972-73 drought ended, the pattern will almost certainly repeat itself in the future.

The concept of a high degree of variability in the timing and the amount of monsoon-line precipitation must be included in any development strategy. An attempt to portray the climate of the area in terms of long-term "normal" precipitation will lead to unrealistic conclusions.

Conclusion 2

Possible strategies for countering climate variability and warding off famine in the area as a whole need to be realistically developed.

Policy measures to help reduce the risk and uncertainty associated with climatic variability should include both regional cooperative programs and national supply policies.

These programs and policies should include the stabilization of the food supply by establishing reserves of animal and human foodstuffs, together with a system of storage silos, monitoring, and distribution. Such a program is technically feasible.

Another essential program is the establishment of a water-distribution system that would draw upon reserves of the major surface-water sources and would also develop schemes for groundwater utilization and desalination.

Issue 3: Geographic Significance of Development Planning

The subdivision of the area into the climatic zones of desert, subdesert, Sahel, Sudan, woodland, and riparian (river valleys with a potential for irrigation) is illustrated in Figure 2. This infraregional variation strongly suggests the significance of geography for development planning.

Conclusion 3

Obviously, the climatic conditions in this region have a great bearing on determining the type of development project that can have some hope of success. In general terms, the following geographical distinctions appear to merit further consideration:

> Desert (37% of area) -- Little or no
> agricultural development; limited
> animal production with controlled
> grazing (similar to grazing activities
> in northwestern Sonora and parts of
> southwestern Arizona).

Subdesert (27% of area) -- Very limited
agricultural development; some animal
production with controlled grazing
(similar to grazing activities in parts
of west-central Arizona).

Sahel (16% of area) -- Animal-grazing
projects (based upon range improvement).
Crop production limited to a few small,
scattered areas where local terrain conditions offer acceptable crop-production
risk probabilities.

Sudan (9% of area) -- Dry-land crop
projects, utilizing improved technology
and plant varieties.

Woodland (8% of area) -- Dry-land crop
projects, as in the Sudan.

Riparian (2% of area) -- In the river-
valley areas (such as the Niger delta)
irrigated crop (and forage) production
is possible. Before large-scale ir-
rigated-agriculture projects are undertaken, the hydrological constraints must
be determined.

Issue 4: Ecological Fragility of the Area

From the viewpoint of agricultural productivity
(both field crops and animals), and stated in oversim-
plified terms, most of the area suffers from an ecological imbalance and has a basic problem of insufficient
rainfall even in "normal" times.

Conclusion 4

Any long-term strategy for the region requires
identification of zones offering ecological opportunities and of corrective measures concerning the ecological balance. Some of the implications include, but
are not restricted to the following:

1) The necessity of limiting grazing to
match the carrying capacity of the land.

64

2) The necessity of developing (as has been done in the southwestern United States and in Australia) an animal-supply policy suitable not only for maintaining grazing lands but also for improving economic practices. The existing cattle-raising practice of cyclical fattening over a long period of time is four times as expensive as are more efficient management practices.

3) The necessity of fertilizer.

4) The necessity of developing new sources of fuel, such as, perhaps, solar ovens or, for urban areas, bottled gas.

Issue 5: The Impact on Development of Population Growth Trends

The urgent need for both urban and regional planning becomes manifest if we examine several basic population changes occurring in these societies.

Population Growth. In the 1960s, the estimated rate of population increase in Africa as a whole was the third highest in the world (2.5 percent per year), surpassed only by Latin America (2.6 percent per year) and South Asia (2.9 percent per year). Estimates made by the United Nations indicate that, within the next decade, Africa will surpass the two leading regions, attaining the highest rate of population growth in the world, and that this trend will continue until at least the end of the century. The specific part of Africa with which this report is concerned, the countries of the Sahel-Sudan, has a current growth rate ranging from 1.7 percent per year in Chad to 3.5 percent per year in Niger and averaging 2.0 percent per year for the region as a whole.

This high rate of growth, in spite of the still very high infant mortality rate, indicates that the population will, for some time, become increasingly biased toward youth. This bias will be intensified as better health practices reduce infant mortality. The population of African countries is already young, with children under 15 years of age usually forming about 43 percent of the total. The distribution of the population by age groups is extremely important for de-

velopment considerations because it gives some indica-
tion of the manpower potential of the population. It
also provides a measure of its dependency load, consumption needs, and social requirements for both the present
and the future.

This high rate of growth must also be analyzed with
reference to the carrying capacity of the region. Obviously, it is not possible to adduce population pressure from a knowledge of population growth alone. Pop-
ulation-growth figures can take on meaning only when
related to the resource base of the region and the opportunity structure of the social and natural environment.

Urbanization. A significant proportion, although
by no means all, of the demographic growth is being
transferred from the country to the cities of the region. The actual levels of urbanization in the African
countries are of less significance than the rate at
which these levels are rising. At present, Africa is
the least urbanized region of the world. However, it
has the highest urban growth rate. In most countries
of the region the urban population is increasing at
twice, and sometimes at as much as four or five times,
the rate of the total population, and in general the
population in the cities is increasing faster than that
in the towns.

From 1965 to 1985, urban growth, continuing at an
average rate of 7 percent per year, will lead to a
quadrupling of the urban population. Urban growth of
this magnitude surpasses all other urban growth ever
witnessed in the most dynamic of the developed countries
and suggests a number of problems of balance and development:

> 1) The cost of the infrastructure neces-
> sary to support urban development and the
> impact of urban growth on the general
> balance of the country;
>
> 2) Industrialization and unemployment;
>
> 3) The provision of food supplies for
> the centers (economic problems of re-
> sources and of urban incomes; also,
> problems of external financial equili-
> briums).

Migration. The relatively early development of the coasts of West Africa, leading to their rapid integration into the modern economic system, was accompanied by migratory movements. To a greater extent, the population of the large cities of West Africa --Lagos, Accra, Abidjan, Dakar -- is of Sahel-Sudan origin. This general migratory movement covers the complex convergence of separate and distinct movements related to professional specialization of certain ethnic groups and nations (Edioulla and Maur traders and jewelers and, more generally, Senegalese artisans, administrative and cultural workers from Togo and Dahomey, Sudanese soldiers recruited by colonial authorities, and so on).

In the recent past and continuing in the present, several large migrations have taken place. These migrations are closely related to the situation of originally agragarian economies and may be understood as instances of collective adaptation by societies not in a position to take their place in the modern productive system. This adaptation is effected by the production of goods that can be exchanged in modern markets. Among these trends, two are dominant: (1) Sarakole migration, whose origin in the Sarakole country lying in the valley of the Senegal River and split between present Senegal, Mali, and Mauritania; and (2) a Voltaic migration, principally Mossi.

The first movement is very old and has its origins, perhaps mythical, in the role of traders and traveling merchants which was assumed in the past by the Sarakole peoples. At present, it is dispersed between several destinations (aside from Dakar, of course, which serves as a stop off point): Coastal West Africa, Central Africa (Congo, Zaire), and Europe, specifically France, where the yearly immigration figure is 85,000.

The second migration, from Upper Volta, began with the development of the south part of the Gold Coast (presently Ghana) between 1920 and 1950. It continued in the Ivory Coast, which has now become its nearly exclusive destination. Better known statistically than the first, this migratory trend is significant and of consequence for the social balance of the countries of origin as well as of the countries of destination.

Not only does the migratory trend from Upper Volta attain an unusual amplitude (more than one-third of the active population), but it is tending toward a more rapid growth rate than that of the population at large.

Thus Voltaic manpower is in the majority in several modern activities in the Ivory Coast (industrial plantations, industrial workers, dock workers, and so on) and has a considerable role in the village-plantation economy, of whose work force it furnishes a large part.

Other smaller migratory trends effect a transfer of population, following a relatively complex network, from the Sahel-Sudan region toward the lower coast.

Spatial disparities in population growth. The consequences of the unprecedented rate of urbanization and forward migration have a significant impact on the variations in population growth rates from area to area and promise to have an even greater impact in the future. We have noted that urban populations are expanding at an overall rate of 7 percent per year. The important corollary here is that the rural areas are also severely affected. We have already suggested the consequences of emigration for the manpower sector of Upper Volta. The same principle holds for migration from rural to urban areas within a country. The great majority of migrants are men under thirty, whose emigration strongly affects the age-distribution, skill, manpower, and growth patterns of the rural areas. The general pattern of population growth rate is thus (1) high growth rates in fast-developing cities, or core areas with the overall population increase exceeding the rate of natural increase, (2) an overall population increase somewhere nearer the rate of natural increase in the peripheral zones adjacent to the fast-developing cities or core areas, and (3) a net exodus of people from more distant areas, resulting in population growth rates below the rate of natural increase.

Disparities and problems of economic development. The striking contrasts in population growth from area to area have had important economic causes and consequences. European colonization and postindependence economic modernization began, in general, on the coast, expanding subsequently toward the interior. Thus, the coastal regions have long offered the greatest opportunity for participation in economic activities. The differential opportunities afforded by the development of a modern economic system in the coastal areas, particularly the coastal areas to the southwest of the Sahel-Sudan region, have resulted in a migratory trend toward this region, especially to the coastal cities of Dakar, Lagos, Abidjan, and Accra.

This population movement must be taken into account in any development strategies proposed for the region. In all probability, an account of migration gains and losses, country by country, will show a net loss of labor and skills, including scarce and essential entrepreneurial talents, for sections experiencing out-migration. If these present urbanization and migration trends continue, we might expect (1) a regular increase in the gap between the urban and rural sectors of the national economies and (2) a regular increase in the gap between the needs of the Sahel-Sudan region and the production capacity of its systems.

Conclusion 5

Urbanization and migration are key elements in the development process. Population movements tend to be responses to economic incentives and thereby reflect economic differentials from area to area. The large amount of spatial disparity, as demonstrated by these indices of growth from area to area, is indicative of the urgent need for urban and regional planning.

The aims of urban and regional planning may be summarized as follows:

1) To establish the nature, location, and dimensions of the changes taking place in the rural, urban, and regional sections of the Sahel-Sudan area, with emphasis on the spatial aspects of such changes;

2) To identify the problems of development arising from these changes, particularly the location of the problems, their repercussions on the countries' expanding physical framework of cities, towns, villages, roads, and railroads, and their implications for the rapidly growing movement of people and goods from place to place; and

3) To formulate possible public policies in regard to the location of future investment in economic activities, urban and rural infrastructure, communication networks, and the like, which are designed to attack urban and regional problems where and as they arise, before they become serious threats to national, regional, and local interests.

69

Issue 6: Regional Cooperation in the Development of the Industrial Sector

The pattern of industrialization observed from the preindependence period to the present point to the fact that the six countries of the Sahel-Sudan region have developed industries very slowly. With the exception of those in Senegal and perhaps some in Chad, the majority of industries in existence now (not including electrical-generating and water facilities) did not exist before 1960.

With the exception of those in Senegal and Mauritania, the industries established have been based on processing organic products, particularly food products.

In all of the countries except Senegal the majority of their industrial production are based on two or three commodities. In most cases, production is far below capacity. In Chad, however, prior to the drought, the slaughterhouses and ginning mills were operating close to capacity.

Problems plaguing industrial growth in the Sahel-Sudan countries can be summarized as follows:

Markets. The domestic market is small, and there is limited access to external markets because of tariff barriers created by the coastal countries, e.g., Ivory Coast maintains a tariff on slaughtered meat.

Production. There is little value added to imported or exported commodities.

Labor, management, and unemployment. There exists a fundamental structural problem with African government policymaking schemes to bias investment decisions against labor-intensive methods. There is a problem of "noncommitted" or migrant labor, while at the same time there is a virtually unlimited supply of labor. There are a few managerial skills being developed.

Non-African entrepreneurs. Except in Senegal, there is no encouragement of African entrepreneurship.

Land tenure. Communal land tenure has made it difficult to attain land for industrial use and has created a barrier for small businesses wishing to acquire loan capital through land-collateral borrowing.

Capital. There is a lack of domestic capital available for development of small industries by African entrepreneurs.

Infrastructure. High transport costs are an important obstacle to overcome.

Regional integration. Regional political federations, customs unions, free-trade areas, common markets, or industry-preference agreements are needed to protect developing industries. Fragmentation of the market and duplication of productive units are already problems.

In areas where foodstuffs are produced, smaller industries located in the agricultural areas are more successful. They have fewer transport requirements, need less skilled labor, and are capable of adjusting to fluctuating market demands more readily. Also, the introduction of small-scale processing, such as the proper drying and smoking of freshwater fish in Chad, will increase productivity and reduce waste.

Conclusion 6

Although some growth of small farm-related processing industries is possible now, any large-scale industrial development will require a high degree of regional cooperation and agreements on allocation of capital, prices, production, distribution, marketing, and related matters.

Issue 7: The Influence of Economic Rigidities

Resource development will have to be accompanied by optimal monetary, fiscal, international, and market policies in order to be effective in terms of maximum per capita contribution. The existing system in the area suffers from a number of rigidities:

> 1) Producer or supplier pricing policies are usually fixed for long periods of time. For example, the price of cotton in Chad was fixed for 14 years. If these prices are subsidized, then the export sector is subsidized at the cost of food crops and farm diversification. If the price is fixed below the relative market price, market forces will lead to sub-

stitute products at the cost of inadequate foreign exchange earnings, or, if substitution is not possible, the farmers will not render husbandry adequate for optimal per-acre production.

2) Similarly, wage rigidities exist whereby government employees (mostly in the urban centers) are paid wages that are 30 to 40 times the per capita income of the rural population. Government employment constitutes from 30 to 50 percent of the total wage-and-salary employment in the area, and its lure has contributed to labor surpluses in the urban areas. Wage flexibility will be a prerequisite if the industrial sector is expected to grow competitively.

3) Banking institutions do not reach the rural employment market where low productivity and low income prevail. Only 3 percent of the total employment in the area is in the money sector. Rural employment represents 90 percent of the total in Chad, Mali, Niger, and Upper Volta, 85 percent in Mauritania, and 75 percent in Senegal. Savings in the rural area find no other outlet than more livestock and other traditional forms of investment, which have been found to be counter-productive. The traditional sector subsidizes the modern sector by providing it with foreign-exchange earnings and other surpluses, but receives no feedback that would contribute to rural productivity.

The role of the banking system in the modern sector is also precarious. Except for those of Niger and Mauritania, the monetary systems are tied to France, where reserves ($350 million) are kept. This practice amounts to a short-term loan from the area to France.

France is the major donor of aid and long-term loans to the area. The contents and effectiveness of France's aid and long-term loans (most of them tied loans)

would have to be evaluated against the
monetary arrangement with France where
the reserves are kept without interest
in order to arrive at net benefits. Moreover, the banks in the area are geared
to provide loans to large foreign-owned
companies to the exclusion of small indigenous enterprises. The fixed interest
rate (4 percent) and minimum-deposit requirements ($240) for savings accounts
are other illustrations of the inadequacy
of the banking system. It is unlikely
to respond to, much less lead the way in,
development opportunities.

Conclusion 7

Unlocking economic rigidities will be a prerequisite of an effective development strategy.

Issue 8: The Gap Between Targets and Achievements

A cursory survey of the development plans of the
six countries of the Sahel-Sudan reveals that by and
large the realization rates of the plans have been low.
As a result, successive targets have been set lower,
as evidenced by the case of Senegal, where annual GNP
growth-rate targets for the first, second, and third
plans were set at 8 percent, 6 percent, and 5.5 percent,
respectively. A major cause of this gap may be the orientation of the plans and the donors' aid. It is important that projects be designed and selected in terms of
the demands they make on scarce decision-making skills
both among the decision makers in the countries and the
donor-agency personnel. For example, a very large project might well absorb all of the scarce decision-making
capabilities at the top both in a country and at an
agency desk and might also incur substantial lags in
funding. A gap of about 50 percent has been observed
between aid committed and actual disbursement in some
cases, e.g., IDA loans to Niger for 1967-71. Small alternative projects, on the other hand, could possibly
be dealt with by decision makers at lower levels and
might be subject to fewer funding delays. (Of course,
large projects might also be decision-skill efficient
relative to small projects.)

Conclusion 8

The development effort in the area requires an effective implementation strategy to close the gaps between targets and achievements. This conclusion suggests more program aid and sectorial· aid, together with consideration of small-scale projects. Project scale (both large and small) should be related to constraints not only on financial resources but on decision-making resources, both in the countries of the region and in donor agencies.

APPENDIX: MACROECONOMIC PROJECTION

Our choice of the projection model of the Sahel-Sudan countries was influenced by the presence of three most important constraints, namely: (1) the savings constraint, (2) the balance of payments constraints, and (3) the absorptive capacity constraint. Also, it should be noted that in this projection, foreign aid requirements do not include emergency food requirements as a result of any major future droughts. We believe that for this region a clear distinction would have to be drawn between emergency aid requirements to ward off famine or compensate for drought devastation and aid requirements for economic growth. Since emergency assistance will be a function of climatic condition and no reasonable means are available to predict the behavior of the climate of the region, emergency aid would have to be considered on an ad hoc basis until a world wide or a regional system of aid for such purpose is instituted. In this exercise we identified seven macroeconomic variables, seven parameters, and seven equations with an assumption of a target growth rate of 5 percent per year (a target set by the U.N. development decade of the '70s), under alternative sets of assumptions which we considered plausible.

The projections for the GNP and foreign aid requirements of each of the countries and for the region as a whole (from 1995 though 1999) are summarized on a five-year basis in Tables 1 through 4.

Our model includes the following:

Variables:

V_t	Gross National Product
I_t	Gross Investment
S_t	Gross Domestic Savings
C_t	Consumption
M_t	Imports of Goods and Services
E_t	Exports of Goods and Services
F_t	Net inflow of Foreign Capital

Parameters:

$\bar{r}$	Target Growth Rate of GNP
α	Marginal Propensity to Save
β	Maximum Rate of Growth of Investment
κ	Incremental Gross Capital-Output Ratio
μ	Marginal Import Rate
ϵ	Rate of Growth of Exports

Relations:

$$V_t = V_o + \frac{1}{k} \sum_{T=1}^{t-1} I_T$$

$$S_t = S_o + \alpha (V_t - V_o)$$

$$I_t \leq (1 + \beta) I_{t-1}$$

$$V_t \leq (1 + \bar{r}) V_{t-1}$$

$$M_t = M_o + \mu (V_t - V_o)$$

$$E_t = E_o (1 + \epsilon)^t$$

$$V_t = S_t + C_t$$

$$F_t = \max \{I_t - S_t, M_t - E_t\}$$

Our base year is 1975 for which 1971 data is used with the assumption that due to the severe drought from 1971-1974, the 1975 level of the economic variables are about the same as those of 1971. This assumption could be wrong either upward or downward since no detailed surveys of the impact of the drought or its delayed effects have been undertaken. We also believe that our projections are optimistic because of the values of the parameters which we have assumed. For instance, our calculations have shown that the marginal capital-output ratio for Senegal was 6; we have trended this value to reach 4, which means a substantial improvement over the projected period. For the remaining five countries a figure of 4 is assumed which may be quite less although it falls within reasonable range of the performance of the developing countries. Such improvement in the

76

value of capital output ratio assumes substantial improvement in administration, economic management, and the incentive structures. Likewise, in our alternative sets of projects, the rate of growth of investment has been trended from 8 percent to 10 percent, and the marginal propensity to save has been trended from 10 percent to 25 percent -- such trends will require substantial improvement in rural credit and in the banking system. Also improved trends have been indicated in the rate of growth of exports which assumes more realistic producer prices and countermeasures to minimize the cyclical effects of the climate. Likewise, the values of the marginal input rate for our second set of assumptions have been raised substantially -- a factor which depends upon the performance of exports as well as donors' aid. We have further assumed that foreign aid would effectively contribute to development.

The principal advantages of the Chenery-Strout model are: (1) it is not very stringent for data requirements, and (2) it explicitly incorporates the three most important development constraints that seem to be relevant for the Sahel-Sudan countries -- the domestic savings constraint, the balance of payments constraint, and the absorptive capacity constraint. By varying the values of various parameters within plausible limits, the model can be used to generate alternative feasible growth paths for the economy.

Instead of using constant values of the various parameters we assumed that some of them, e.g., the marginal propensity to save, the rate of growth of exports, the maximum feasible growth rate of investment, etc., will change in a favorable direction over time. Thus, instead of using a single value for each of the parameters derived from historical data, we have used time paths. Historical data influence these time paths through the choice of initial values and growth rates. This is a reasonable thing to do because the values of parameters based on historical data are very low. Deriving estimates of foreign aid requirements on the assumption that the low historical parameter values will continue to operate for the entire projection period, can therefore, be seriously misleading. We do not claim, however, that our particular choices of time paths are in any sense optimal. They are feasible in the sense that several underdeveloped countries have been able to achieve through determined efforts. The important conclusions were:

77

(1) The absorptive capacity constraint will prove
to be a very significant bottleneck, particularly in
Chad and Upper Volta. In both of these countries annual gross capital formation has actually declined over
the period 1964-71, the only period for which data is
available. Taken literally, this would imply a negative value of the rate of growth of investment. The
value of investment as a proportion of GDP in each of
these countries is quite low initially, and if assumed
the historical trend, it will take more than 15 years
merely to achieve the target growth rate. Clearly, a
larger amount of technical assistance and a comprehensive manpower training program are key elements if better growth performance is to be achieved.

(2) For Mauritania, the values of parameters based
on historical data are such that the model indicates
that enough savings and foreign exchange will be available to sustain a 5 percent growth rate of GDP. In
fact, even for an 8 percent growth target, the model
predicted no bottlenecks. These results must be treated
with caution, however, since most of the investment in
the past decade was carried out by foreign investors
who brought with them not only the financial resources
but also the required skilled personnel. Even though
the earnings from existing mines will be sufficient to
finance investment and import requirements implied by
an 8 percent growth rate, the absorptive capacity constraint may prevent the economy from achieving such a
growth rate, if foreign investment and the concomitant
inflow of skilled personnel slows down or stops altogether. Thus, even though Mauritania may have ample
financial resources, continuation of technical assistance, and assistance in manpower development programs
seems necessary for the target growth rates.

(3) The estimates of foreign aid requirements are
quite sensitive to the assumed values of the parameters,
particularly the marginal savings rate, the capital output ratio and the rate of growth of exports. Detailed
sensitivity tests were performed only for Senegal. It
is hoped that the results of these sensitivity tests
will also shed some light on the impact of these parametric variations on the total foreign aid requirements
for the six countries.

(4) Two estimates of total foreign aid requirements
were derived, one on the assumption of a sustained growth
of exports at an annual rate of 6 percent, the other on
the assumption that they will grow at 3 percent during

1975-79, at 4 percent during 1980-84, and at 5 percent thereafter. Other assumptions remained the same for the two sets of projections. In the former case, about $5 billion worth of foreign aid will be required during 1975-2000, and in the latter case about $9 billion. Clearly, these estimates also depend upon whether or not our expectations regarding saving effort, etc., as implied by our assumed parameter values, are fulfilled.

(5) The Sahel-Sudan region has experienced two kinds of droughts -- (a) minor droughts, when there is below normal rainfall only for one or two years, and (b) major droughts such as the one recently experienced, when rainfall stays at subnormal levels for three years or more. Our procedure for estimating the capital-output ratio does try to take account of minor droughts. But we cannot "average out" the influence of major droughts, which can cause severe dislocation throughout the economy besides a decline in output. Thus, if a major drought occurs within our projection period, the variance between the actual and projected figures will be much greater than normal.

79

TABLE 1: FOREIGN AID REQUIREMENTS OF THE SAHEL-SUDAN COUNTRIES, 1975-2000

PERIOD	AID REQUIREMENTS UNDER HIGH EXPORT PERFORMANCE		AID REQUIREMENTS UNDER RELATIVELY MODEST EXPORT PERFORMANCE	
	BILLIONS 1971 CFAF	MILLIONS 1971 DOLLARS	BILLIONS 1971 CFAF	MILLIONS 1971 DOLLARS
1975 - 79	230.69	902	273.82	1,070
1980 - 84	261.62	1,023	382.89	1,497
1985 - 89	271.85	1,063	424.91	1,661
1990 - 94	265.15	1,037	530.99	2,076
1995 - 99	251.69	984	675.02	2,639
TOTAL	1,281.00	5,009	2,287.63	8,943

TABLE 2

FOREIGN AID REQUIREMENTS TO ENABLE THE SAHEL-SUDAN
COUNTRIES TO ATTAIN 5 PERCENT GROWTH OF GDP,
IF RELATIVELY MODEST EXPORT PERFORMANCE IS ASSUMED.
(ALL FIGURES IN BILLIONS 1971 CFAF
EXCEPT THOSE FOR MALI WHICH ARE IN BILLIONS 1971 MF)

PERIOD	CHAD	MALI (in MF)	COUNTRY MAURITANIA	NIGER	SENEGAL	UPPER VOLTA
1975 - 79	49.46	30.69	-	41.97	124.31	42.73
1980 - 84	57.06	56.51	-	76.12	166.62	54.83
1985 - 89	69.77	96.92	-	120.70	112.33	73.65
1990 - 94	92.28	145.74	-	176.23	84.89	104.72
1995 - 99	104.78	208.07	-	247.10	69.81	149.29
TOTAL	395.34	537.93	-	662.12	557.96	425.22

TABLE 3

PROJECTIONS OF THE GROSS DOMESTIC PRODUCT OF THE
SAHEL-SUDAN REGION (BILLIONS OF CFAF, 1971 PRICES)

YEAR	CHAD	MALI (in billions MF)	COUNTRY NIGER	SENEGAL	UPPER VOLTA	MAURITANIA
1975	80	167	95	208	85	–
1980	87	204	118	205	96	–
1985	102	259	151	339	112	–
1990	124	330	193	432	137	–
1995	157	422	246	552	175	–
2000	200	538	314	704	224	–

REFERENCES

Kamrany, Nake M. "The Three Vicious Circles of Under-development: The Sahel-Sudan Case of West Africa," Socio-Economic Planning Science, Vol. 9, 1975.

Picardi, A. C., and Seipert, W. S. "A Tragedy of the Commons in the Sahel," Technology Review, June/July, 1976.

Billings, Martin, and Nelson, Garry. "Approaches to Agricultural Development in the Sahelo-Sudanian Zone." United States Agency for International Development, 18 January 1974.

Brochier, Jacques. "Quelques Observations sur les Blocages de la Croissance dans l'Agriculture Senegalaise: Blocages et Freinages de la Croissance et du Development en Europe, Asie, Afrique et Amerique Latine." Reprinted from Revue Tiers-Monde, Vol. vii, no. 30 (April-June 1967). Dakar: ISEA.

Charlick, Robert B. (Cleveland State University). "Rural Development in Francophone Africa -- Administrative Demonstration or Induced Participation?" Paper presented for panel on "Trends in African Rural Development" of the African Studies Association in Denver, Colorado, November 3-6, 1971.

Davis, Jackson; Campbell, Thomas; and Wrong, Margaret. Africa Advancing: A Study of Rural Education and Agriculture in West Africa and the Belgian Congo. New York: Negro University Press, 1969.

de Wilde, John C. "The Case Studies: Experiences with Agricultural Development in Tropical Africa," Vol. II. International Bank for Reconstruction and Development. Baltimore: Johns Hopkins Press, 1967.

Food and Agriculture Organization of the United Nations. "Notes on the Ecology of Rice and Soil Suitability for Rice Cultivation in West Africa." United Nations Development Program. Rome, 1971.

Manetsch, Thomas, et. al. "A Generalized Simulation Approach to Agricultural Sector Reference to Nigeria." United States Agency for International Development, 30 June 1971.

Mifsud, Frank M. "Customary Land Law in Africa." FAO Legislative Series #7. Rome: Food and Agriculture Organization of the United Nations, 1967.

Sheets, Hal, and Morris, Roger (Project Director, Carnegie Endowment for International Peace). "Disaster in the Desert (failures of international relief in the West African Drought)." Washington, D.C.: 1974.

Bryson, Reid A. "Climatic Modification by Air Pollution, II The Sahelian Effect." The Institute for Environmental Studies, University of Wisconsin at Madison. Report 9, 1974.

Dresch, Jean. "Drought over Africa." UNESCO Courier, Vol. 26 (August-September 1973), pp. 44-47.

Grant, James. "Some Notes on Drought in Africa and on Control of Weather." Symposium on Drought in Africa, School of Oriental and African Studies, University of London, July 19-20, 1973.

Lamb, H. H. "Statement to Symposium on Drought in Africa." Symposium on Drought in Africa, School of Oriental and African Studies, University of London, July 19-20, 1973.

Landsberg, H. E. (Institute for Fluid Dynamics and Applied Mathematics). "Statistical Characteristics of the Annual Rainfall Totals at Bambey and Zinguinchor, Senegal." College Park: University of Maryland.

Sherbrooke, Wade C., and Paylore, Patricia (Assistant Director of Office). "World Desertification: Cause and Effect." Arid Lands Resource Information Paper No. 3. University of Arizona, Office of Arid Lands Studies, 1973.

Skinner, Elliot P. (Department of Anthropology, Columbia University.) "The Breakdown of Sahelian Ecosystem: Ecological, Demographic and Socio-Cultural Factors in the West African Drought Areas."

Hance, William A. "Population, Migration, and Urbanization in Africa." Department of Geography, Columbia University, 1970.

Morely, G. E. "Food Storage in Developing Countries and

the Role of the Tropical Stored Products Center."
Symposium on Drought in Africa, School of Oriental
and African Studies, University of London, July
19-20, 1973.

Organization for Economic Cooperation and Development,
Development Center Population Unit. "Population
Assistance to Africa 1969-70."

"The World Food Supply," Vol. III of "Report of the Panel on the World Food Supply." (Report of the President's Science Advisory Committee, Donald F.
Hornig, Chairman.) September 1967.

DeGregori, Thomas R. (Case Western Reserve University).
"Technology and the Economic Development of the
Tropical African Frontier," Chapter IV, 1969.

de Wilde, John C. "The Development of African Private
Enterprise," in two volumes, Vol. II: "Country
Annexes." Report #AW-31, December 10, 1971.

Meinel, Aden, V., and Meinel, Margorie P. (Optical Sciences Center, University of Arizona: Helio Associates, Inc.) "The Village Energy Center: A New
Option for Solar Energy Utilization by Sahel Communities?" July 1973.

Organization for Economic Cooperation and Development.
"OECD at Work for Industry and Energy." Paris,
July 1973.

Skinner, Elliot P. "African Urban Life: The Transformation of Ouagadougou." Princeton, New Jersey:
Princeton University Press (Department of Anthropology, Columbia University), 1974. 3 copies.

Fischer, John L. "Development of the Beef Industry in
Africa: A Paper on Improving Technical and Capital
Assistance." A Study for the Agency for Interna-
tional Development, Bureau for Africa, Agriculture
Division, Washington, D.C., 1969. Mimeographed,
University of Arizona.

Nestel, Barry; Pratt, D. J.; Thome, M.; and Tribe, Derek.
"Animal Production and Research in Tropical Africa."
Report of the Task Force commissioned by the Afri-
can Livestock Subcommittee of the Consultative
Group on International Agricultural Research.
Washington, D.C., 1973.

Pino, John A. "Livestock Production in Tropical Africa." Discussion paper prepared for "Bellagio IV" Conference, November 1970.

Kamrany, Nake M. "The Sahel Drought: Major Development Issues," Ekistics, 1977.

Kamrany, Nake M., and Kazimi, A. "An Interdisciplinary Approach to the Chenery-Strout Growth Estimation: The Case of the Sahel-Sudan Region of West Africa," Center for Policy Alternatives, Massachusetts Institute of Technology, June 1976. (Submitted to the Annual Meeting of the Western Economic Association Meeting, San Francisco, California, June, 1976.)

IV
COMPARATIVE QUALITY OF LIFE

Steven A. Y. Lin
Southern Illinois University

Historically, well-being of mankind has been close-ly related to trends in the production of goods and ser-vices. But as the size of population grows and the fi-nite capacities of the earth are hard pressed, shrinking natural amenities per capita and the indirect effects of economic growth have begun to markedly affect our daily lives. In some situations, social disintegration and political repression are greatly diminishing the quality of life.

Generally speaking, there are three important fac-tors affecting the quality of life--per capita goods and services, per capita natural amenities, and social and political improvements. While our system of economic accounting measures rather well the goods and services produced by man, we have no comparable techniques for collectively measuring the amenities provided by nature or the indirect effects of growth.[1] Nor can we success-fully combine these three factors into a single indicator.

The purpose of this paper is rather modest. We focus on analyzing the well defined and quantifiable as-pects of the total life situation--the levels of living.

The main objectives of this paper are threefold: 1) to develop a unitary index of "measurable welfare" in natural units of goods and services for approximately 88 countries during the decade 1960-70, 2) to analyze the possible interrelationships between the "welfare" or "levels of living index" and the development strate-gies and structures of these countries, and 3) to draw the policy implications and suggestions with respect to the international issues concerning trade and develop-ment, and the levels of living.

WELFARE INDICATORS

Is the "welfare" or the "levels-of-living" gap between rich and poor countries increasing? The answer is frequently affirmative, although no precise measurement of the gap has been effected. This paper attempts to measure the gap between industrialized (rich) and less developed countries using the composite indices.

As defined internationally, levels of living refers to the satisfaction of needs or wants in certain well defined and quantifiable aspects of the total life situation (UN, 1961; UNRISD, 1970). This conception is much wider than the one-dimensional notion of Gross National Product (GNP) which is based on productivity. Such variables as GNP or consumption per head do not measure the satisfaction of needs but the market values of the means that could be (but not necessarily are) used for satisfaction of these needs.[2] However, constructing an aggregate welfare index is not without problems. The main problems arise in defining the notion of welfare; in determining, on theoretical and/or prgamatic grounds, the structure of the index (and, in particular, selecting and assigning weights to its components); in selecting and operationalizing the component indicators; and in the actual process of measurement itself. In the following, we will focus our discussion in these important problems.

Generally, there are three aspects of social conditions which may be measurable by separate sets of indicators: demographic indicators, social relations indicators and welfare indicators (Drewnowski). The last one is what interested us here.

The distinction between demographic and welfare indicators is relatively clear. It might be noted that demographic indicators can sometimes become substitutes for welfare indicators proper. Mortality, for example, which is obviously a demographic variable, may be a good proxy indicator of health. While this is permissible, it is still desirable to distinguish the different categories conceptually.

Welfare indicators are observable and measurable phenomena which contain information about the degree of satisfaction of human needs. As an indirect method for measuring welfare of an individual or a population, the welfare indicators selected could never comprehensively cover all the components of welfare. However, even such an imperfect way of measuring welfare is superior to not measuring it at all or using indicators such as G.N.P. and consumption per head (Beckerman; Beckerman and Bacon). G.N.P. or consumption per head do not measure the satisfaction of needs but the market values of the means that could be used for satisfaction of these needs.

There are two distict ways of looking at welfare:
the flow of and the state of welfare. The degree to
which housing, education, and health and nutritional
needs are satisfied would constitute the flow of welfare. Indicators for this dimension of welfare are
expressed in their specific units per unit of time,
such as consumption of animal protein per capita per
day, average number of persons per room, and electricity consumption per capita. The state of welfare
refers to the state in which the population finds itself at one particular time, such as literacy rate and
consumption of calories. It constitutes yet another
dimension of the welfare aspect of special conditions.
The flow of welfare corresponds <u>roughly</u> to what is
generally termed the level of living.

There are several features an indicator must possess to be fit for measuring welfare. First of all
the welfare indicators should indicate the direction
of welfare. In other words, an upward movement of an
indicator's numerical values must correspond to the
improvement in the satisfaction of needs. For example,
an increase in the daily intake of animal protein improves the satisfaction of the need for food and consequently increases the flow of welfare. Animal protein intake is therefore an appropriate indicator for
measuring welfare. Similarly, the rate of urbanization
can be a proxy for 'industrialization' which reflects
welfare in certain ways. Consequently, the urbanization
rate may be accepted as an indicator for measuring welfare.[3]

The values of the indicator has to be normalized
or scaled, especially for international comparison. We
will discuss more about this shortly.

The welfare positions of individuals within a population are obviously unequal. The simple way of obtaining an indicator value valid for the whole population is to find an average value of that indicator per
head of the population, which is how it is usually done,
but this procedure ignores an important feature of the
welfare problem, namely the distribution of that satisfaction among the population. Unless it is assumed that
some people are entitled to more welfare than others, a
position of greater equality brings more welfare to the
population (within given possibilities) than a position
of inequality. It is therefore necessary to take account
of distribution in the procedures for measuring welfare.
It has to be noted that this is a value judgment rooted
in a very widespread egalitarian ideology. In addition,
the data for income distribution is hard to come by.

The concept of human welfare cannot be free from value judgments. This is a problem which must be recognized. Value judgments would have to enter the measurement of welfare at various stages. The very selection of component indicators is not value-neutral. The system of needs which we have in mind when selecting indicators is of course culture-determined. It is more of the European-culture-derived system of values.[4]

The most controversial value judgment involved is with the assignment of the weights in aggregation procedure for measuring welfare, such as for example to construct a composite level-of-living index. To arrive at a composite index particular components of the level-of-living (such as housing, education, health and nutrition) have to be weighted one against another. Certainly, the weights depend on time and space. Decisions involving political judgments on the relative importance of various level-of-living components are a matter of course when policies are determined and development plans formulated. Those decisions constitute objective facts which may be significant in establishing procedures for constructing aggregate level-of-living and state-of-welfare indicators.

An aggregate index is as good as the system of weights on which it is based. The proper procedure for establishing a system of weights is to derive it from some system of preferences, such as policy statement. As the index which we are looking for is supposed to measure the welfare of a nation, conceptually the preferences which express the aspiration and govern the policies of that nation should be used. This means that the level-of-living index should be computed with weights reflecting the same system of preferences by which planning was guided.

More complications arise in the international comparison of the level-of-living. If weights for the index were based on a national plan, they would be valid for that particular nation but not for cross-country comparisons.[5] To overcome this difficulty we have to construct a synthetic system of weights reflecting common features of a number of plans. The validity of such weights will also be limited in time and space but will transcend one nation. So long as we do not have a system of weights based on sound theoretical principles, a system of equal weights seems to be the simplest. More discussion on the weights will be taken up shortly.

90

METHODOLOGY AND DATA

There are, say, m countries belonging to the world community. Each country, q_i (i = 1,----,m), is characterized by n variables X_1, X_2, ----, X_n. In other words, each country may be looked upon as a row vector X_i= (X_{i1}, X_{i2},----, X_{in}).

There is also a discrete, non-negative function $W_i = W(X_i)$ which plays a role of a measure of relative level of living of particular country q_i. A country q_i is considered to have a "higher" level of living than a country q_j (i ≠ j) if and only if $W(X_i) > W(X_j)$.

In this connection, the following question arose. Are all variables (X_1, ----, X_n) equally important in judging the level of living or are some of them more and some less important? Before answering this question we should be discussing what criterion do we use to distinguish between "more" and "less" important variables. There are two possible ways of selecting such a criterion. The first consists in accepting as a criterion one of the variables X_1, X_2, ----, X_n (say the variable X_n). In this case, we are using a so called endogenous criterion. Another case is the exogenous criterion which is equivalent to selecting some additional variable, say X_{n+1}.

Following is an example using endogenous criterion. Suppose that the variable X_n represents the consumption per capita. This variable has been accepted as a measure of the level-of-living and therefore it can play the role of a criterion: the more important is a particular variable X_j the larger is the $r^2(X_n, X_j)$, where r refers to the correlation coefficient. Naturally, the weight assigned to X_j will be larger when r^2 is larger.

An example of using an exogenous criterion is to use the distance d_{oi} which measures the achieved level of, say economic growth of a given country X_i to the "ideal country" X_o. The more important is a variable X_j the larger is the value $r^2(d_{oi}, X_j)$. In a sense, using the "ideal country" for comparison is an example of employing exogenous criterion.

In our study of the international comparison of the levels-of-living over time, there are no fixed final goals for each component of the level-of-living for each country. The achievement in each particular year is surpassed by the next year's achievement so that the competing countries are confronted all the time with ever-

91

receding goals. These goals are being achieved by the most advanced countries which form a sort of a spearhead of all the competing countries. Distances between the spearhead countries and the rest depend on the relative speeds with which the two groups are moving. Thus the measurement of the level-of-living gaps when the goals are continuously moving requires different methodological concepts and tools than those relevant to situations of fixed goals.

A variation of the exogenous criterion may prove to be useful under this circumstance. Our reservations on comparing to the most industrialized country notwithstanding, the most advanced country can be used as a criterion country, and all of the selected variables for measurement of the levels-of-living from ith country can be measured against that of the most advanced country. This multi-dimensional distance can be used then as the ordinal measurement of the international comparison of the levels-of-living. Taxonomic method (Hellwig) can be used in measuring this distance. Suppose I_1 and I_2 are the values for ith country, on the variables 1 and 2, and C_1 and C_2 the corresponding values for the 'criterion country,' the formulating for this taxonomic distance is $d(I,C) = \sqrt{(I_1 - C_1)^2 + (I_2 - C_2)^2}$. This same formula holds true for the situations involving more than two variables.

Explicitly, the weight for each component variable is treated equally. It seems to be the simplest when there is no theoretically sound alternative. However, the taxonomic distance is not value-neutral from the most advanced country's perception of the importance of different component variables. The resulting weights of each variable implicitly reflect the value-judgment of the most advanced country. It is biased toward that of the European-culture-derived system of values.

Furthermore, there is one more serious drawback in using the taxonomic distance for measuring the welfare gap. It is its inability in identifying the direction of the gap (i.e., better than or worse than the ideal country) without supplementary information, for it is an absolute value. However, it still provides an excellent measurement of similarity or dis-similarity among the countries in terms of the multi-dimensional welfare indicators. The smaller the taxonomic distance (d-value) the closer (or similar) the ith country is to the 'criterion country.'

92

Contrasting to taxonomic distance, the following composite index does provide the directional sign in addition to being an ordinary measurement of welfare. Suppose I_1 and I_2 are the values for ith country, on the welfare components (or variables) 1 and 2, and C_1 and C_2 the corresponding values for the 'criterion country,' the formula for this ordinal (or relative) composite index is $R(I,C) = \sum_{i=1}^{2} \pm \frac{I_i}{C_i}$ for i=1,2. The same formula holds true for the situations where there are more than two variables.[6] The sign $(\pm)$ of the specific ratio (I_i/C_i) depends on whether the specific component is an addition to or subtraction from the total welfare. $R(I,C)$ provides the ordinary (or relative) value of ith country's welfare in comparison to the 'criterion country.' This composite R-value, of course, can be converted into an index (SM) assigning the value of 100 to the criterion country, for easier comparison.

In this study, both the taxonomic distance and the ordinary (or relative) composite index (SM) for the level-of-living are computed. Due to data availability, eighty-eight countries have been selected for the analysis. The years covered are 1960, 1965 and 1970. Twenty-one component indicators (or variables) have been chosen for this international comparison. It covers six fields: health, nutrition, education, housing and communications. These twenty-one component indicators include:

(1) Expectation of life at birth
(2) Crude birth rate (-)
(3) Crude death rate (-)
(4) Newspaper circulation (per 1,000)
(5) Radios (per 1,000)
(6) Steel consumption (K_g per capita)
(7) Energy consumption (metric ton of coal equivalent) per capita
(8) Number of physicians (per 1,000)
(9) Telephones (per 100)
(10) % wage earners and salaried employees in total economically active population
(11) % economically active population employed in electricity, gas, water, sanitary, transportation, storage, and communications
(12) % GDP derived from manufacturing
(13) Sum of value of imports and exports (per capita) in U.S. dollars
(14) Combined primary and secondary enrollment as % of 5 - 19 age group
(15) Vocational enrollment as % of 15 - 19 age group
(16) Consumption of protein (per capita, per day) in grams

93

(17) Adult males in agriculture as % of total
      male labor force (-)
(18) Electricity production, KWH per capita
(19) Infant mortality rates (-)
(20) Number of persons per room (-)
(21) Expenditure on food as % of total pri-
      vate consumption.
Components 2, 3, 17, 19 and 20 are thought to
correlate negatively to the aggregated welfare
of each country.

The data are taken from available statistical sources,
mainly United Nations' Publications (UN; FAO). The choice
of the period 1960-1970, like the choice of country, is
determined by data availability.

Among those 88 countries, countries at the lowest
development level are under-represented (many newly
independent African countries, and certain large but
less developed Asian countries) because the availability
of statistical data is correlated with development levels.
Also the socialist countries with centrally planned economies are excluded because of a basic incomparability
of some indicators. (A 'Global Material Product' cannot
be reasonably compared with GNP at factor cost in United
States dollars, if for no other reason than the multiple
exchange rates for a dollar in those countries.)

As the component indicators are expressed in very
different and incomparable measure units it is necessary,
before proceeding to any aggregation procedure, to stand-
ardize them. Various methods of standardization are
possible and the choice of a certain one involves some
degree of arbitrariness. This is an unavoidable short-
coming of any research involved with aggregation procedure (such as our taxonomic distance and relative index).
It has to be noted also that the absolute value of our
indices (d- and R- values) are not neutral to the origin
of measurement (i.e. selection of 'ideal country').

The standardization formula used in this study is as
follows:
$$X_j = \frac{X_j - \bar{X}_j}{s_j}$$

where $\bar{X}_j$ and s_j are, respectively, the arithmetic mean
and the standard deviation of the variable X_j. This procedure of transformation is also called the normalization
of the data. The same procedure is applied to every
component variable before computing the taxonomic distance and relative index.

94

Taxonomic Distance and the Relative Levels-of-
Living Index

The United States is chosen as the 'ideal country'
and the taxonomic distance of the other 87 countries
are computed with respect to U.S., using the formula
discussed in the last section. The results for 1960,
1965, and 1970 respectively are presented in Table 1.

As expected, the less developed countries general-
ly have larger d-value (i.e. lower level-of-living) than
the industrialized countries. All countries except
Luxemburg have lower levels-of-living than the United
States. According to these 21 component indicators,
Luxemburg has substantially higher level-of-living than
U.S. mostly due to her small size of population yet
highly industrialized economy. Countries like India,
Ethiopia, Vietnam, Haiti, Zambia, Pakistan, Honduras,
Thailand, Sudan, Gambia, Kenya, Indonesia, Ghana, Burma,
Uganda, Morocco, Madagascar, and Liberia are substantially dissimilar to and lower than U.S. in terms of the
welfare indicators chosen. However, readers are remind-
ed to interpret these results with caution. As indicated
earlier, the index computed here has the built-in bias
toward European-culture-derived system of values. Furthermore, the other important factors affecting the
quality of life, such as environmental amenity or dis-
amenity is not included as a component in our computation
of the index, due to the lack of data.[7] Canada, Germany,
Japan, England and Belgium are by far the closest to U.S.
in terms of the level-of-living.

Taxonomic distance is not particularly sensitive in
detecting the widening gaps of the level-of-living between other countries and the U.S. The process of squar-
ing the differences between the specific country and the
'ideal country' for each component indicator in computing
the composite index buries a lot of information.[8] Over
the selected years of 1960, 1965 and 1970, the observed
level-of-living gaps between rich and poor countries have
been relatively stable. This observation is contrary to
the findings derived from the relative levels-of-living
index which will be discussed momentarily.

The relative level-of-living values (R) are computed
for 87 countries again using the United States as the
'ideal country.' The results are presented in the left-
hand side of Table II. For easier comparison, the level-
of-living values are converted into an index using the U.S.
values of the respective years as 100. This level-of-
living index (SM) is presented in the right-hand side of

95

Table II. This index not only provides the magnitude
but also the signs (+). India, Ecuador, Ethiopia,
Vietnam, Haiti, Zambia, Pakistan, Sudan, Kenya, Indonesia, Burma, Uganda, and Liberia again show up to be
pretty low in the levels-of-living in comparison to
U.S. This finding is consistent with the earlier finding using the taxonomic distance. Germany, Canada,
England, Sweden, Switzerland, Netherland, Belgium and
Austria are by far the closest to U.S. This finding
again is consistent with that of the taxonomic distance,
except Japan. Luxemburg is again by far having a higher level-of-living than U.S. From Table II, one can
clearly observe that the level-of-living gaps between
rich and poor countries have been widening over the
decade of 1960-1970. This finding coincides with a similar assertion and analysis made by others (Gostkowski,
Elliot), using a different component indicator and approach.
Note that the level-of-living gap between rich and poor
countries may be even larger than presented here, for
many countires at the lowest development level are under-
represented in our study. Many newly independent African
countries and certain large but less developed Asian
countries are not included in our study for lack of data.

As we alluded to earlier, there are no fixed final
goals for each component of the level-of-living for each
country in their international competition for better
living over time. The achievement of a country, in a
particular year, is surpassed by her following year's
goal. Each country is confronted also with ever-receding
goals all the time with the most advanced countries
acting as a sort of spearhead for all of the competing
countries. Gaps in the level-of-living between spearhead
countries and the rest depend on the relative speeds with
which the industrialized (rich) countries and LDCs are
moving.

Table III is presented in order to compare the relative speeds with which the rich countries and LDC are
moving. In order to compute this speed, 1960s values
of the R-values for each country for the three selected
years are computed. Then, the R-values for each country are
compared over time. The speed of movement in the levels-of-
living is represented by the difference of R-values between
selected years (1960, 1965, and 1970) for the respective
country.

Table III indicates that either computing the speeds
for the two periods 1960 to 1965 and 1965 to 1970 separately or computing for the whole period 1960 to 1970, the
LDCs' speeds of improvement are generally much slower than

that of industrialized countries. Thus, the widening
gaps between the two groups in terms of the level-of-
living can be attributed to the compounding effects of
both LDCs' original low level-of-living and their slow
speeds of improvement.

Relationships Between the Levels-of-Living Index and the Development Strategies

In practice there is a good deal of confusion about
the place of level of living indicators within development models. In the broadest interpretation improvement
in level of living becomes synonymous with development,
a challenge to national income as an indicator of welfare. In the international development strategy the
improvement in levels of living is seen as both "determining factors and end results in development."

Comparing the recent experience of less developed
countries with the earlier development and present structure of the developed countries, it is observed that
continuous structural change is related to the growth
of income rather than that different structural relations
characterize developed and less developed countries,
however defined (Chenery and Syrquin). Applying these
findings to the formulation of policy, 50 sample countries are classified according to the structural similarities of their development strategies. Four principal
patterns of resource allocation are identified: primary
specialization, balanced allocation, import substitution,
and industrial specialization. The countries in each
classification followed somewhat different sequences of
development, stemming partly from initial differences
in size, resource endowments, and access to external
capital and partly from differences in social philosophy
and organization. This typology provides a basis for
comparing the policies of countries having similar structural characteristics. It also provides a basis for comparing the policies of these countries with respect to
their "levels-of-living." Thus some light can be shed
on the place of the level-of-living indicators within
the development model in its end-and-mean continuum.

With special interest in the transitional developing
countries, the data for fifty countries which are not the
least developed, the fully developed, and not the transitional countries in which growth has been seriously disrupted during the decade of the sixties (1960-1970) are
compiled in Table IV (Chenery and Syrquin, pp. 102-103).[9]

In last two columns of Table IV, the level-of-living index (SM) for 1965 and 1970 are listed for comparison. There is a completed set of data for a total of 44 countries instead of 88 countries in Table IV, due to the availability of data. Countries in the categories of primary specialization and import substitution are generally having lower levels-of-living.

To analyze the relationships between each index of resource allocation and the level-of-living, the pairwise simple correlation coefficient between each of the allocation index and the level-of-living index (SM) is computed. The results are presented in Table V. A_1 through A_{10} are the 10 indices of resource allocation:

A_1 -- 1965 population in millions
A_2 -- 1965 per capita GNP
A_3 -- 1960-1970 growth of per capita GNP in %
A_4 -- Relative export level
A_5 -- Trade orientation
A_6 -- Production orientation
A_7 -- Capital inflow
A_8 -- Income shares of upper 20%
A_9 -- Income shares of lower 40%
A_{10}-- Gini coefficient

The value inside the parenthesis below each correlation coefficient is the number of observations available in computing each specific correlation coefficient. Each S-value indicates the type 1 (one-tail) error for the significance of the respective correlation coefficient.

Generally, the correlations between the 10 (re-source) allocation indices and the taxonomic distance (d) are lower than that of the level-of-living index (SM), except the correlation coefficient between 1965 per capita GNP and the taxonomic distance. The latter relation is negatively correlated and has the largest correlation coefficient of 0.81. It implies the higher the per capita income the lower the taxonomic distance or vice versa. The relation is as expected.

The level-of-living has positive correlation with per capita GNP, growth of per capita GNP, relative export level (export as % of GDP), and income shares in % of lower 40% population group. It has negative correlation with the size of population, trade orientation (above-normal primary product exportation), product orientation (above-normal primary product specialization), capital inflow (excess of import over export) and Gini coefficient (the higher the coefficient, the less equal the distribution). The signs fôr all of the correlation coefficients are as expected.

It is conceivable that the different patterns of resource allocation may have a delayed, instead of contemporaneous, relationship with the levels-of-living. For this reason, the correlation coefficient for the same relationships is also computed for 1970s d-and SM values and the results are presented in Table V. The results are consistent with that of 1965, except the magnitudes of the correlation coefficients are generally larger. This finding suggests a certain degree of time-lag relation between those resource allocations and the level-of-living.

An interesting observation is that the per capita income has a very strong relation with both the taxonomic distance and the levels-of-living index. Especially for the countries of similar allocation pattern, the rank order by per capita GNP is quite close to that by the level-of-living index. However, one cannot stretch this implication too far. Mexico has similar per capita GNP as that of Uruguay, but the Uruguay has a much higher level-of-living than that of Mexico. This difference between the two measurements may be due mainly to the different income distribution pattern of the two countries. Uruguay has more equal income distribution (Gini coefficient of 0.42) than that of Mexico (Gini coefficient of 0.58), as indicated in Table IV. It is also easily visualized from Table IV that Taiwan, for example, has a much lower per capita GNP than Mexico yet her level-of-living index is much higher than that of Mexico which has different allocation pattern. It demonstrates that there are still substantial differences between the one-dimensional GNP measurement and the multidimensional level-of-living index. A similar phenomenon is observed between Brazil and Mexico. Brazil's per capita GNP is about one-half that of Mexico. Yet, Brazil's level-of-living is much higher than that of Mexico.

There are numerous reasons for Taiwan's higher level-of-living than Mexico. In addition to having a different allocation pattern, Taiwan's income distribution is more equal than that of Mexico. The Gini coefficient for Taiwan is 0.32 and that for Mexico is 0.58. As we discussed earlier, income distribution could be an important factor affecting the level-of-living. Due to the paucity of income distribution data (we only have 44 countries' data for 1965), the income distribution is not incorporated

99

in our computation of the level-of-living index. For example, Mexico and Uruguay have a pretty compatible allocation pattern including per capita GNP yet the levels-of-living is quite different due to different income distribution pattern. On the other hand, Jamaica and Mexico have similar per capita GNP and Gini coefficient thus similar levels-of-living index, though the other allocation patterns are different between these two countries. The correlation coefficient between the level-of-living and the Gini coefficient is in the neighborhood of 0.2, as indicated in Table V.

International Development Issues and Suggestions

As we discussed earlier, the rich-poor gap in the levels-of-living had been widening during the last decade both absolutely and relatively. In addition to a quantitative economic difference, it is increasingly a gap in values, in social organization, in contrasting life styles and in perceptions of the world in which we live. Ominously, it is a gap over which the world community may find it increasingly difficult to communicate effectively.

Reasons for the gap are numerous. It is an economic gap, a technological and educational gap. It is a complex phenomenon. A high population growth rate in the poor countries also acts to widen the gap. The low levels of living tend to perpetuate these trends from one generation to the next. In the absence of external factors capable of breaking the cycle, these conditions will no doubt continue indefinitely into the future. It points to the fact that the levels-of-living serve not only as targets for development plans but also for assessing the results of development.

The direct or indirect interrelationships identified in the last section concerning the levels of living indicators and structural similarity of development strategies can be used to assess the national or international development policies designed to narrow the rich-poor gap. Considerations ought to be given to the effects of such policies as the trade and economic integration, multinational economic groupings, and the programs designed to reduce export instabilities of less developed countries.

Every country's welfare or quality of life depends to quite an extent on the resources and cooperation of other nations. As incomes rise, dependence on imported

100

goods and raw materials, and the share of global output
crossing national borders increases. Closely related
to this increase in international trade is the growth
in international production and the spread in multinational corporations. This institution, with its
efficiency in combining resources and disseminating
technology, plays an important role in raising material
affluency and in integrating the international economy.

Using this institution as catalyst, industrial
countries can assist less developed countries in transferring technology and pursuing research specifically
suited to the social needs of LDCs such as helping
LDCs in increasing food output by developing new techniques for cultivating land, reduce plant and animal
diseases, improve food-storage systems and methods.
Increased dialogue between rich and poor countries
should be encouraged to promote the attitudes, moti-
vation and mores congenial to economic and social developments.

As noted in the last section, the production and
trade orientations biased toward primary products have
substantial adverse impacts on the level-of-living.
The underlying reasons for this relationship are numerous. The instability in the production and export
earnings related to primary products could be one of
the main reasons.

Rich and industrialized countries can also help
LDCs in stabilizing the export earnings to enable them
to reduce wild price fluctuations of the commodity
markets and develop a realistic strategy for social and
economic developments. The common market's recently
proposed Stabex plan (Wall Street), for example, es-
tablishes a $450 million fund to be used to help 46
African, Caribbean, and Pacific states whose exports include such primary products as cocoa, coffee, copper and
cotton. UNCTAD (United Nations Conference on Trade and
Development) earlier (Wall Street) proposed to extend
the number of countries involved and the list of primary commodities to cover cocoa, coffee, copper, cotton,
hard fibers, jute, rubber, sugar, tea and tin.

Promoting vocational training is also important in
addition to investing more in social overhead capital.
The important bottleneck-breaking programs in raising
level-of-living are the transportation and communication
infrastructures that spur efficient industrial and agricultural output.

Most important of all, the poor countries must recognize that they are in an anxious race between demography and development. As noted in the previous sections, uncontrolled human fertility may pose a greater threat to future well-being of any country than any other single factor. Slowing population growth is a prerequisite to solving the widening gaps in the levels-of-living between rich and poor countries. Also following the findings of the last section, the importance of a more equal income distribution in improving the level-of-living for LDCs cannot be overemphasized.

CONCLUSIONS

The findings of this study indicate that the level-of-living gaps between rich and poor countries over the decades of 1960-1970 had been widening. The widening gaps between the two groups during the period were attributed to the compounding effects of both LDCs' original low level-of-living and their slow speeds of improvement.

The level-of-living of each country has positive correlation with the following allocation indices: per capita GNP, growth of per capita GNP, relative export level (export as % of GDP) and income-shares in % of lower 40% population group. It has the negative correlation with the following allocation indices: the size of population, trade orientation (above-normal primary product specialization), capital inflow (excess of import over export) and Gini coefficient. There is a certain degree of time-lag relation between those resource allocations and the level-of-living. Though a very strong positive relation exists between per capita GNP and the level-of-living index, it is a better measurement of the "welfare" or "quality of life" than the one-dimensional GNP measurement.

Reasons for the level-of-living gaps between rich and poor countries are numerous. It is a complex phenomenon. A high population growth rate in poor countries acts to widen the gap. The low levels of living tend to perpetuate these trends over years or generations. Slowing population growth and improved income distribution would help substantially in reducing the gap. However, in the absence of external factors capable of breaking this vicious cycle, the condition of gaps will no doubt continue indefinitely into the future.

Rich and industrialized countries can help LDCs in transferring technology and pursue research specifically

suited to the social needs of LDCs using the existing
institutions, such as multinational corporations. They
can also help LDCs stabilize the export earnings to
enable them to reduce the wild price fluctuations of
the commodity markets and develop a realistic strategy
for social and economic development.

[1]Nordhaus and Tobins (1972) attempt to adjust the GNP
number in order to get a more meaningful measure of
economic welfare. Their "Measure of Economic Welfare" attempts to reclassify GNP expenditure as consumption, investment, and intermediate; correction
for some of the disamenities of urbanization. Similarly, the work done by the Economic Council of Japan
supplements the usual production-oriented economic
accounting with consumption oriented welfare accounting, which explicitly recognizes the conservation
costs, environmental costs, and urbanization costs
(Economic Council of Japan, Zapf, pp. 480-482). However, the latter elements represent only a small
part of the natural amenities (or disamenities) and
indirect effects.

[2]They express the intermediate changes of economic activity which constitute the costs of generating the
ultimate outcome of that activity, that is, welfare.
Similarly, such variables as employment or income
cannot be considered social indicators. Employment
is only the means to earn income and income is only
the means to acquire goods. It is still very far
from actually satisfying the needs.

[3]This indicator is not explicitly integrated in our
composite index for we are short of 1965 data. Concerning this urbanization rate, one may argue it is
not a good indicator for measuring welfare for it
can also be a proxy for the "degree of disamenities".
Its influence on welfare thus may go either way depending on the circumstances. Consequently, it may
not be a good welfare indicator.

[4]For example, the "number of children in the family"
indicator, usually as an example of non-welfare indicator, might be a welfare indicator in another
culture where the number of children is considered
a blessing and desirable.

[5]This difficulty is not a unique problem for the international comparison of the level-of-living. Similar
difficulty arises in international comparisons of
the development levels (Baster).

[6]Additive welfare components are assumed here. Let
W(x) be the vector of welfare indicators (or components). We assume that there exists F, a positive monotonic transformation such that total welfare F W(x) is additive. It is analogous to the
assumption made by Strotz and Lancaster (1957;
1966) on the additive total utility function. Each
individual welfare indicator (or component) may be
a function by itself (not necessarily additive) of
the yet lower level welfare components.

[7]An attempt is currently underway to remedy this deficiency
by using appropriate proxy variables.

[8]We can subtract instead of adding the square difference
of a specific component indicator if the specific
indicator is a negative to the total welfare. However, this revision will not contribute much precision to the measurement, for the squared difference
makes the sign less meaningful.

[9]Following are explanations on each different indicator
on Table 4. Since the level and composition of exports are affected by different policies and have
different implications for other development processes, it is useful to treat them separately in
classifying countries. The level of exports is
readily measured by the ratio of the actual export
level in the country (E) to the value predicted for
the country's size and income level (E). The effect
of the capital inflow is indicated by its share in
GDP.

Chenery and Syrquin (Chapter 2) indicate that there
is a normal shift in the composition of exports as
the level of income rises, as shown below:

PER CAPITA INCOME LEVELS	NORMAL EXPORTS	NORMAL PRIMARY EXPORTS	NORMAL MANUFAC. EXPORTS	NORMAL TRADE BIAS
	E	E_p	E_m	T
($)	($)	($)	($)	
50	8.5	6.4	.5	.69
200	43.6	27.1	6.8	.47
500	121.9	59.8	32.5	.22
1000	260.3	96.2	96.9	.00
1500	403.1	117.1	178.4	-.15

(In this table, all values are per capita based on a population of 10 million.)

From this average pattern a normal trade bias can be defined as:

$$T = \frac{E_p - E_m}{E}$$

Deviations from this average composition can be measured by the difference between the actual trade bias and normal bias. This leads to the definition of the following trade orientation index (TO):

$$TO = \frac{E_p - E_m}{E} - \frac{E_p - E_m}{E} = T - T$$

where the predicted values of E_p, E_m, and E are determined from equation

$$X = \alpha + B_1 \ln Y + B_2 (\ln Y)^2 + \gamma_1 \ln N + \gamma_2 (\ln N)^2 + \Sigma \delta_j T_j$$

where

X = dependent variable (E_p, E_m, or E)

Y = GNP per capita in 1964 U.S. dollars

N = population in millions

T_j = time period (j=1, 2, 3, 4)

α, B_1, B_2, γ_1, γ_2 and δ_j are the constants.

T which corresponds to 1950-54, 1955-59, 1960-64, and 1965-69.

The production pattern is summarized by the following index of production orientation (PO), which is analogous to the trade orientation just described:

$$PO = P - P = \frac{(V_p - V_m)}{V} - \frac{(V_p - V_m)}{V}$$

where P is the normal production bias and P is the actual bias, where V_m is value added in production in manufacturing and construction, and V_p is that of agriculture and mining. As in the case of the trade orientation, positive values indicate a bias toward primary production or a lag in industrialization.

Capital inflow is defined as the total imports of goods and services less the total exports of goods and services. Factor payments and transfers to and from abroad are excluded from the calculation. Incidentally, capital inflow is also equal to gross domestic investment minus gross domestic saving.

Relative export level is export as percent of GDP. It is the exports of goods and nonfactor services valued at current market prices of merchandise (f.o.b.). It includes transportation, insurance, and other services sold to the rest of the world but not including factor payments from abroad (i.e., payment accruing to domestically owned factors of production operating abroad, which represent the claim of domestic residents on the GDPs of other countries). The value of gifts in kind and other exports financed by means of international transfers is included, but the value of military equipment transferred between governments is excluded.

Income shares: income distribution, highest 20 percent and lowest 40 percent (Jain and Tiemann). Gini coefficient is obtained from Chenery et al. (1974). Noted, lower value of Gini coefficient represents a more equal income distribution.

Since the classification of countries is based on their departure from the average patterns of production and trade, a normal range is defined for each of three measures and a country is classified accordingly as high, low, or normal for each dimension. The width of the normal range was chosen (Chenery and Syrquin, p. 104) to include roughly 40 percent of the observations for each measure. The level and orienta-

tion of production is taken as the basic criteria
for the typology; the level of the capital inflow
is used to subdivide the categories where it is important. For the capital inflow a distinction is
made between high (over 4 percent), normal (0 percent to 4 percent), and negative values.

Four main patterns of allocations are identified on
the basis described above according to the following
values of the indices. The resulting classification
is given in Table 4.

1) Primary Specialization
    a) Primary-oriented exports (TO greater than .10)
    b) Primary-oriented production (PO greater than .07)
    c) Export level usually above normal

This group corresponds to the established concept of
an export-led growth pattern based on favorable primary resources. In the 1960s, it included thirteen
transitional countries having a total population in
1965 of 116 million (plus Nigeria, which was temporarily disrupted by civil war).

2) Balanced Production and Trade
    a) Normal export orientation (TO - .10to + .10)
    b) Normal production orientation (PO - .07to + .07)

This group of fourteen countries can be subdivided
into nine having normal levels of capital inflow and
exports and five with high capital inflow (F equal to
or greater than .04). The total population for the
whole group was 174 million.

3) Import Substitution
    a) Primary export orientation (TO greater than .10)
    b) Low total exports (exports below .75 of normal
       levels)
    c) Production not primary oriented (PO less than
       + .07)

This group includes nine countries having a total population of 216 million plus India, which will be treated
as a special case because of its exceptional size.

4) Industrial Specialization
    a) Industrial export orientation (TO less than -.10)
    b) Industrial production orientation (PO less than
       -.07)

108

This category can also be usefully subdivided into seven countries with a high capital inflow (F more than .04) and six with more normal levels of F. The total population for the whole group was 240 million in 1965.

TABLE 1

TAXONOMIC DISTANCE (d) FOR SELECTED YEARS

COUNTRY I.D.		1960	1965	1970
1	IREL	13.166	13.046	13.069
2	GREC	14.395	14.109	13.985
3	GERM	9.290	9.704	10.024
4	FRAN	11.068	10.888	11.059
5	FINL	12.119	11.768	11.668
6	DFNK	10.795	10.933	11.233
7	BULG	12.910	12.722	12.591
8	AUST	11.222	11.593	11.776
9	MAUR	15.803	15.283	15.045
10	JAPN	11.664	10.598	10.434
11	ISRL	13.437	13.358	13.347
12	INDI	16.100	16.046	16.229
13	ECUD	15.890	15.706	15.543
14	CTIW	14.930	14.830	14.762
15	NZEA	11.702	11.553	11.805
16	ENGL	9.607	9.853	10.157
17	SWTZ	11.575	11.186	11.548
18	SWED	10.157	10.085	10.452
19	SPAN	13.793	13.162	13.055
20	POLE	12.102	12.284	12.431
21	NORW	11.596	11.029	11.026
22	NETH	11.853	11.185	11.402
23	LUXB	14.476	14.135	14.244
24	ITAL	12.217	11.738	11.870
25	ETHP	17.734	17.820	17.806
26	YUGO	14.003	13.658	13.656
27	LEBN	14.790	14.545	14.493
28	KONG	14.654	14.388	14.527
29	VIET	17.089	17.070	17.065
30	DOMC	16.159	16.079	16.034
31	HAIT	17.540	17.635	17.663
32	MALT	14.731	14.477	14.507
33	NICR	16.485	16.365	16.420
34	SURN	15.883	15.656	15.614
35	TURK	16.054	15.901	15.829
36	URGY	14.372	14.097	14.229
37	ZAMB	17.761	17.682	17.587
38	ALGE	16.793	16.782	16.609
39	IRAQ	16.006	15.899	15.925
40	PAKT	17.251	17.173	17.254
41	RICO	13.457	13.078	12.664
42	MALY	15.971	15.707	15.499
43	PORT	14.104	13.906	13.886

110

Table 1, Continued

COUNTRY I.D.		1960	1965	1970
44	HOND	16.159	16.133	16.073
45	THAI	16.478	16.295	16.136
46	CZEC	10.819	10.739	11.092
47	TRIN	14.417	13.632	13.190
48	LEIS	15.243	14.450	14.002
49	USOA	.000	.000	.000
50	FLSV	15.624	15.455	15.589
51	UOSA	13.785	13.563	13.578
52	MEXI	15.400	14.555	14.754
53	CYPR	14.392	13.917	13.769
54	CEYL	15.770	15.371	15.323
55	CHIL	14.572	14.212	14.159
56	BRAZ	15.083	14.864	14.694
57	GUAT	16.259	16.033	15.922
58	COST	15.350	15.212	15.103
59	CANA	10.007	8.722	8.656
60	EGYP	15.915	15.358	15.172
61	BELG	10.666	10.542	10.688
62	HUNG	13.339	12.516	12.431
63	AUSL	11.254	10.776	11.068
64	ARGT	13.140	12.467	12.202
65	SUDN	17.183	16.951	16.823
66	KENY	17.043	16.723	16.674
67	VENZ	14.809	14.357	14.157
68	GAMB	17.015	16.925	16.978
69	GUAD	15.467	15.003	14.822
70	BRUN	15.553	14.826	14.612
71	SKOR	15.594	15.086	14.733
72	PHIL	16.235	16.086	15.946
73	INDO	16.998	16.932	16.843
74	COLM	15.526	15.058	15.115
75	JAMC	15.551	14.758	14.433
76	CHAN	16.925	16.685	16.385
77	ROMN	13.254	12.965	12.850
78	ALBN	15.183	15.090	14.901
79	SAUD	16.437	16.311	16.303
80	JORD	15.774	15.805	15.958
81	IRAN	15.826	15.595	15.592
82	BURM	17.491	17.377	17.344
83	PERU	15.155	15.204	15.204
84	TUNS	16.156	15.899	15.824
85	UGAN	17.479	17.312	17.285
86	MORC	16.544	16.582	16.562
87	MADR	16.917	16.636	16.633
88	LIBR	16.913	16.909	16.906

TABLE 2

LEVELS-OF-LIVING INDEX FOR SELECTED YEARS

COUNTRY I.D.		R			SM		
		1960 (U.S.=100)	1965 (U.S.=100)	1970 (U.S.=100)	1960 (U.S.=100)	1965 (U.S.=100)	1970 (U.S.=100)
1	IREL	-10.286	-14.817	-16.211	-19.637	-28.287	-30.947
2	GREC	-33.215	-34.583	-33.589	-63.411	-66.022	-64.125
3	GERM	29.893	32.047	33.734	57.068	61.277	64.400
4	FRAN	4.022	1.840	1.996	7.679	3.512	3.810
5	FINL	1.465	-2.924	.558	2.796	-5.581	1.066
6	DENK	25.015	24.613	21.453	47.757	46.988	40.956
7	BULG	-6.023	.648	-.767	-11.499	1.237	-1.464
8	AUST	10.632	9.368	9.456	20.297	17.885	18.052
9	MAUR	-44.416	-47.293	-47.196	-84.793	-90.287	-90.102
10	JAPN	-7.951	-9.568	-.771	-15.178	-18.266	-1.473
11	ISRL	-13.475	-20.510	-29.007	-25.725	-39.156	-55.377
12	INDI	-78.509	-93.543	-110.938	-149.881	-178.582	-211.790
13	ECUD	-77.019	-87.553	-95.221	-147.036	-167.147	-181.785
14	CTIW	-24.500	-25.059	-25.519	-46.774	-47.841	-48.718
15	NZEA	33.577	27.798	23.149	64.102	53.068	44.194
16	ENGL	44.230	40.880	37.350	84.440	78.043	71.305
17	SWTZ	30.554	31.344	32.670	58.331	59.838	62.369
18	SWED	34.905	35.396	35.218	66.637	67.475	67.234
19	SPAN	-30.880	-32.680	-35.125	-58.953	-62.389	-67.057
20	POLE	-.756	-2.501	-4.820	-1.443	-4.774	-9.202
21	NORW	28.459	28.542	26.877	54.330	54.488	51.310
22	NETH	33.527	34.807	34.045	64.005	66.450	64.995
23	LUXB	254.912	306.813	328.133	486.651	585.734	626.435
24	ITAL	-14.697	-18.311	-21.636	-28.058	-34.958	-41.306
25	ETHP	-89.512	-102.829	-111.848	-170.886	-196.311	-213.528

Table 2, Continued

COUNTRY I.D.

		R			SM		
		1960 (U.S.=100)	1965 (U.S.=100)	1970 (U.S.=100)	1960 (U.S.=100)	1965 (U.S.=100)	1970 (U.S.=100)
26	YUGO	-29.389	-34.320	-30.226	-56.107	-65.520	-57.704
27	LEBN	-28.347	-31.977	-31.871	-54.117	-61.047	-60.845
28	KONG	-6.366	-10.094	-10.165	-12.154	-19.270	-19.406
29	VIET	-72.880	-82.621	-92.375	-139.147	-157.731	-176.352
30	DOMC	-66.058	-76.196	-82.594	-126.111	-145.466	-157.680
31	HAIT	-91.021	-101.036	-108.199	-173.768	-192.888	-206.562
32	MALT	-25.138	-28.030	-30.766	-47.992	-53.513	-58.736
33	NICR	-64.574	-73.600	-79.313	-123.278	-140.509	-151.415
34	SURN	-51.202	-55.288	-56.940	-97.749	-105.549	-108.704
35	TURK	-64.553	-68.755	-72.849	-123.238	-131.260	-139.076
36	URGY	-27.479	-32.888	-35.027	-52.460	-62.786	-66.870
37	ZAMB	-92.938	-102.069	-106.927	-177.426	-194.859	-204.133
38	ALGE	-77.973	-86.007	-88.137	-148.857	-164.194	-168.262
39	IRAQ	-47.203	-52.677	-52.956	-90.114	-100.566	-101.098
40	PAKT	-81.920	-91.423	-99.936	-156.392	-174.535	-190.788
41	RICO	.049	3.030	8.383	.094	5.784	16.004
42	MALY	-51.877	-52.357	-51.446	-99.038	-99.954	-98.215
43	PORT	-17.193	-16.347	-16.985	-32.822	-31.208	-32.426
44	HOND	-52.994	-50.910	-51.344	-101.170	-97.192	-98.020
45	THAI	-56.619	-62.582	-60.147	-108.092	-119.474	-114.827
46	CZEC	16.564	12.459	10.669	31.622	23.780	20.307
47	TRIN	-10.420	-11.194	-11.709	-19.892	-21.370	-22.355
48	LEIS	-38.001	-35.422	-34.526	-72.548	-67.623	-65.914
49	USOA	52.381	52.381	52.381	100.000	100.000	100.000
50	ELSV	-56.990	-65.152	-72.088	-108.800	-124.380	-137.622
51	UOSA	-10.668	-12.248	-12.800	-20.365	-23.382	-24.437
52	MEXI	-58.076	-58.983	-62.637	-110.872	-112.604	-119.580

Table 2, Continued

COUNTRY I.D.

		R 1960 (U.S.=100)	R 1965 (U.S.=100)	R 1970 (U.S.=100)	SM 1960 (U.S.=100)	SM 1965 (U.S.=100)	SM 1970 (U.S.=100)
53	CYPR	-5.387	-5.736	-8.203	-10.283	-10.951	-15.660
54	CEYL	-37.528	-34.515	-35.492	-71.645	-65.893	-67.758
55	CHIL	-39.292	-34.291	-27.509	-75.013	-65.465	-52.518
56	BRAZ	-45.363	-50.307	-48.123	-86.603	-96.041	-91.872
57	GUAT	-71.841	-78.111	-78.904	-137.152	-149.121	-150.635
58	COST	-47.995	-53.145	-53.795	-91.625	-101.459	-102.700
59	CANA	40.288	39.641	43.398	76.913	75.678	82.850
60	EGYP	-63.222	-59.800	-69.523	-120.697	-114.163	-132.726
61	BELG	31.414	38.574	45.226	59.973	73.642	86.340
62	HUNG	-6.928	-.880	2.049	-13.227	-1.679	3.911
63	AUSL	36.502	34.740	34.130	69.687	66.323	65.157
64	ARGT	-9.939	-8.030	-7.119	-18.974	-15.331	-13.591
65	SUDN	-82.666	-87.058	-88.329	-157.818	-166.202	-168.629
66	KENY	-80.648	-83.151	-84.978	-153.964	-158.742	-162.231
67	VENZ	-46.757	-48.600	-47.907	-89.263	-92.782	-91.460
68	GAMB	-69.411	-76.994	-82.901	-132.512	-146.984	-158.266
69	GUAD	-33.474	-32.954	-31.217	-63.905	-62.912	-59.596
70	BRUN	-5.214	-.490	3.646	-9.954	-.935	6.961
71	SKOR	-51.783	-54.864	-53.222	-98.859	-104.740	-101.605
72	PHIL	-71.684	-77.975	-80.253	-136.852	-148.862	-153.211
73	INDO	-84.543	-93.784	-98.410	-161.400	-179.041	-187.874
74	COLM	-67.676	-71.470	-72.382	-129.200	-138.442	-138.183
75	JAMC	-56.321	-60.233	-58.866	-107.521	-114.990	-112.381
76	GHAN	-76.184	-80.204	-80.086	-145.443	-153.116	-152.891
77	ROMN	-8.465	-11.625	-14.439	-16.160	-22.194	-27.565
78	ALBN	-30.197	-34.646	-31.996	-57.648	-66.142	-61.083
79	SAUD	-42.759	-48.138	-50.513	-81.631	-91.900	-96.434

Table 2, Continued

COUNTRY I.D.

		R			SM	
		1960 (U.S.=100)	1965 (U.S.=100)	1970 (U.S.=100)	1960 (U.S.=100)	1965 (U.S.=100)	1970 (U.S.=100)
80	JORD	-42.134	-50.145	-55.538	-80.437	-95.732	-106.027
81	IRAN	-42.489	-46.861	-48.548	-81.116	-89.462	-92.682
82	BURM	-85.950	-95.452	-98.440	-164.086	-182.227	-187.932
83	PERU	-50.518	-59.885	-60.671	-96.443	-114.326	-115.826
84	TUNS	-63.724	-69.901	-75.045	-121.655	-133.447	-143.268
85	UGAN	-90.179	-100.549	-110.359	-172.160	-191.957	-210.685
86	MORC	-77.141	-87.816	-93.430	-147.270	-167.649	-178.367
87	MADR	-75.229	-79.379	-79.378	-143.619	-151.541	-151.540
88	LIBR	-76.142	-87.673	-98.031	-145.362	-167.375	-187.150

TABLE 3

SPEEDS OF IMPROVEMENT IN THE LEVELS OF LIVING*

COUNTRY I.D.	ΔR 1960-1965 (U.S. 1960=00)	ΔR 1965-1970 (U.S. 1960=100)
1 IREL	+4.746	+12.229
2 GREC	+6.241	+12.574
3 GERM	+8.779	+16.973
4 FRAN	+5.969	+12.260
5 FINL	+5.565	+18.618
6 DENK	+9.416	+16.239
7 BULG	+12.007	+8.358
8 AUST	+5.050	+13.659
9 MAUR	+6.799	+7.305
10 JAPN	+6.564	+18.443
11 ISRL	+2.805	+5.227
12 INDI	-2.978	-5.898
13 ECUD	+1.467	+2.514
14 CTIW	+5.004	+5.492
15 NZEA	+3.494	+6.783
16 ENGL	+2.258	+7.661
17 SWIZ	+12.198	+22.785
18 SWED	+11.288	+21.275
19 SPAN	+6.216	+6.327
20 POLE	+3.354	+5.679
21 NORW	+11.767	+18.733
22 NETH	+10.179	+22.149
23 LUXB	+137.422	+278.917
24 ITAL	+4.785	+8.336
25 ETHP	-1.168	+1.694
26 YUGO	+3.530	+10.104
27 LEBN	+4.488	+6.286
28 KONG	+4.773	+6.113
29 VIET	+0.602	-1.560
30 DOMC	+1.033	+3.003
31 HAIT	+2.240	+4.629
32 MALT	+4.465	+3.029
33 NICR	+2.055	+2.589
34 SURN	+11.208	+4.772
35 TURK	+6.423	+5.716

*This table is derived from Table 2 by adjusting for the
fact that the levels-of-living indices (R) of the United
States for 1960, 1965 and 1970 respectively, are 100,
102.89, and 112.03 (where U.S. 1069 = 100).

Table 3, Continued

COUNTRY I.D.		ΔR 1960-1965 (U.S. 1960=100)	ΔR 1965-1970 (U.S. 1960=100)
36	URGY	+2.521	+3.723
37	ZAMB	+3.404	+5.136
38	ALGE	+3.280	+6.702
39	IRAQ	+3.406	+5.320
40	PAKT	+1.550	+1.057
41	RICO	+8.829	+11.740
42	MALY	+9.976	+8.340
43	PORT	+6.361	+7.489
44	HOND	+10.895	+5.992
45	THAI	+3.673	+7.722
46	CZEC	+3.590	+7.726
47	TRIN	+12.044	+10.940
48	LEIS	+11.302	+7.532
49	USOA	+8.017	+11.757
50	ELSV	+2.630	+1.202
51	OUSA	+5.539	+6.209
52	MEXI	+9.870	+3.861
53	CYPR	+6.894	+6.813
54	CEYL	+10.664	+4.606
55	CHIL	+13.359	+14.157
56	BRAZ	+4.494	+8.822
57	GUAT	+5.426	+7.479
58	COST	+4.945	+9.602
59	CANA	+10.891	+23.367
60	EGYP	+11.382	+0.322
61	BELG	+13.815	+30.139
62	HUNG	+13.087	+11.419
63	AUSL	+6.257	+9.788
64	ARGT	+7.983	+7.697
65	SUDN	+6.800	+6.531
66	KENY	+8.360	+5.739
67	VENZ	+10.670	+9.792
68	GAMB	+2.908	+1.881
69	GUAD	+9.860	+10.710
70	BRUN	+16.315	+17.349
71	SKOR	+6.134	+8.518
72	PHIL	+4.743	+5.593
73	INDO	+2.334	+3.839
74	COLM	+7.748	+7.196
75	JAMC	+8.143	+11.503
76	GHAN	+7.649	+7.740
77	ROMN	+2.825	+5.009
78	ALBN	+3.100	+7.094
79	SAUD	+4.727	+5.639
80	JORD	+1.419	+0.568

Table 3, Continued

COUNTRY I.D.	ΔR 1969-1965 (U.S. 1960=100)	ΔR 1965-1970 (U.S. 1960=100)
81 IRAN	+4.368	+4.238
82 BURM	+2.506	+4.803
83 PERU	+0.840	+6.208
84 TUNS	+4.800	+2.786
85 UGAN	+1.796	+1.680
86 MORC	+0.805	+4.045
87 MADR	+6.189	+8.608
88 LIBR	+0.648	+2.434

TABLE 4

A CLASSIFICATION OF ALLOCATION PATTERNS

Pattern	Country	1965 Popula- tion(mil)	1965 Per Capita GNP $	1960-70 Growth of Per Capita GNP %	Rel. Export Level	Trade Orient. (TO)	Prod. Orient. (PO)	Capital Inflow %	Income Shares Upper 20%	Lower 40%	Unit
1. Primary Speciali- zation	Tanzania	12	67	3.0	1.52	.05	.06	-.04	57.0	14.0	.48
	Uganda	9	83	2.2	1.28	.21	.14	-.01	47.1	17.1	.38
	Sudan	14	33	0.5	.96	.19	.08	.04	50.3	14.2	.43
	Ceylon	11	142	2.3	1.19	.32	-.04	.00	46.0	17.0	.37
	Sierra Leone	2	135	-0.5	1.23	.11	.14	.04			
	Zambia	4	179	4.6	2.36	.36	.16	-.17	57.0	14.6	.49
	Ivory Coast	4	179	4.8	1.37	-.04	.11	-.03	55.0	17.5	.43
	Iran	25	218	5.7	1.39	.48	.22	-.06			
	Iraq	8	249	2.6			.34	-.04	68.0	6.8	.61
	Malaysia	9	258	3.7	1.86	.31	.20	-.05	43.9	17.7	.36
	Saudi Arabia	7	271	6.3	2.30	.47	.47	-.42			
	Nicaragua	2	330	3.2	.99	.12	.12	.02			
	Venezuela	9	830	2.5	1.09	.90	.31	-.10	58.0	9.7	.52
TOTAL FOR 13 COUNTRIES		116									

TABLE 4
(continued)

Pattern	Country	1965 Popula- tion (mil)	1965 Per Capita GNP $	1960-70 Growth of Per Capita GNP %	Rel. Export Level	Trade Orient (TO)	Prod. Orient (PO)	Capital Inflow	Income Shares Upper 20%	Lower 40%	Unit
2. Balanced Normal Capital Inflow	Thailand	31	110	4.5	1.40	-.06	-.03	.01	57.7	12.9	.50
	Philippines	32	149	2.7	1.21	.13	-.05	.01	55.4	11.6	.50
	Syria	5	174	5.4	.89	-.03	-.07	.00			
	Morocco	13	179	1.5	.89	-.03	.02	-.01			
	El Salvador	3	240	1.8	1.03	-.01	-.01	.02	52.0	12.7	.45
	Guatemala	4	278	1.9	.65	.12	.07	.03			
	Peru	12	289	1.7	.72	-.06	.01	.01	60.0	6.5	.57
	Jamaica	2	420	2.7	1.24	-.06	-.07	.02	61.5	8.2	.56
	South Africa	18	552	3.4	1.46	.06	.05	.00	58.0	6.2	.56
High Capital Inflow	Ghana	8	155	0.3	.70	.03		.08			
	Costa Rica	2	360	3.1	.78	-.01	-.00	.10	50.6	14.7	.43
	Spain	32	572	6.4	.73	-.05	.02	.04	45.2	17.0	.38
	Greece	9	585	6.2	.34	-.03	.13	.13	49.5	21.0	.37
	Ireland	3	815	3.2	1.07	-.04		.09			
TOTAL FOR 14 COUNTRIES		174									

TABLE 4
(continued)

Pattern	Country	1965 Population (mil)	1965 Per Capita GNP $	1960–70 Growth of Per Capita GNP %	Rel. Export Level	Trade Orient (TO)	Prod. Orient (PO)	Capital Inflow	Income Shares Upper 20%	Income Shares Lower 40%	Unit
3. Import Substitution	India	481	84	1.3	.95	.19	-.06	.02	54.0	14.0	.46
	Bolivia	4	124	2.3	.73	.34	.01	.06			
	Ecuador	5	195	1.7	.94	.54	-.03	.00	73.5	6.4	.66
	Brazil	81	216	2.2	.68	.29	-.04	-.03	66.7	6.5	.61
	Colombia	18	228	1.8	.44	.30	.12	-.01	59.5	9.4	.54
	Turkey	31	244	3.3	.53	.32	-.08	-.01			
	Chile	9	419	1.4	.73	.35	-.02	-.01	56.8	13.0	.49
	Mexico	43	434	3.5	.64	.28	-.13	.00	65.8	10.2	.58
	Uruguay	3	497	-0.3				-.06	47.4	14.3	.42
	Argentina	22	787	1.6	.48	.67	-.01	-.01	52.0	17.3	.42
TOTAL FOR 10 COUNTRIES		697									

TABLE 4
(continued)

Pattern	Country	1965 Popula-tion (mil)	1965 Per Capita GNP $	1960-70 Growth of Per Capita GNP %	Rel. Export Level	Trade Orient (TO)	Prod. Orient (PO)	Capital Inflow	Income Shares Upper 20%	Lower 40%	Unit
4. Industrial Specializa-tion Normal	Kenya	10	95	3.4	1.72	-.21	-.12	-.01			
	Egypt	29	138	1.6	1.37	-.10	-.16	.02			
	China (Taiwan)	12	201	6.3	.78	-.57	-.11	.03	40.1	20.4	.32
Capital Inflow	Yugoslavia	20	415	4.5	1.30	-.56	-.09	.01	41.5	18.3	.33
	Hong Kong	4	512	8.7	2.34	-1.03	-.34	.00			
	Singapore	2	522	5.5			-.11	.04			
High Capital Inflow	Pakistan	114	84	2.9	.88	-.31	-.00	.06	45.0	17.5	.37
	South Korea	28	123	6.4	.64	-.69	-.00	.08	45.0	18.0	.36
	Tunisia	4	198	1.9	.82	-.30	-.12	.14	55.0	10.5	.30
	Portugal	9	361	5.2	.99	-.70	-.17	.05			
	Lebanon	2	446	1.3	.67	-.31	-.06	.21	61.0	13.0	.52
	Puerto Rico	2	936	5.9	1.97		-.08	.21	50.6	13.7	.64
	Israel	3	1,126	5.1	.62	-.28	-.10	.13	39.4	20.7	.30
TOTAL FOR 13 COUNTRIES		239									

Source: Chenery and Syrquin (1975), and this author.
Deviations from large and small country regressions.
Source: Chenery et al., (1974).
Additional Group 1 countries in 1970: Nigeria, Indonesia, Mozambique.
Additional Group 2 countries in 1970: Malagasy Republic, Cameroon.
Features that deviate from the criteria for each pattern.

TABLE 4
(continued)

Pattern	Country	Level-of-Living Index (SM) 1965	1970
1. Primary Specialization	Tanzania	-191.96	-210.69
	Uganda	-166.20	-162.23
	Sudan	5.89	67.76
	Ceylon		
	Sierra Leone		
	Zambia	-194.86	-204.13
	Ivory Coast		
	Iran		
	Iraq	- 89.46	- 91.68
	Malaysia	- 99.5	- 98.22
	Saudi Arabia	- 91.90	- 90.43
	Nicaragua	-140.51	-151.42
	Venezuela	- 92.78	- 91.46
2. Balanced Normal Capital Inflow	Thailand	-119.47	-114.83
	Philippines	-148.86	-153.21
	Syria		
	Morocco	-167.65	-178.37
	El Salvador	-124.38	-137.62
	Guatemala	-149.12	-150.64
	Peru	-114.33	-115.83
	Jamaica	-114.99	-112.38
	South Africa	- 20.38	- 24.44
High Capital Inflow	Ghana	-153.12	-152.89
	Costa Rica	-101.46	-102.90
	Spain	- 62.39	- 67.06
	Greece	- 66.02	- 64.13
	Ireland	- 28.29	- 30.95
3. Import Substitution	India	-178.58	-211.79
	Bolivia	- 67.15	-181.79
	Ecuador	- 96.04	- 91.87
	Brazil	-136.44	-138.18
	Colombia	-131.26	-139.08
	Turkey	- 65.47	- 52.52
	Chile	-112.60	-119.58
	Mexico		
	Uruguay	- 62.79	- 66.87
	Argentina	- 15.33	- 13.59
4. Industrial Specialization	Kenya	-158.74	-162.23
	Egypt	-114.16	-132.73
	China (Taiwan)	- 47.80	- 48.72
Normal Capital Inflow	Yugoslavia	- 65.52	- 57.70
	Hong Kong	- 19.27	- 19.41
	Singapore		
High Capital Inflow	Pakistan	-174.54	-190.79
	South Korea	-104.74	-101.61
	Tunisia	-133.45	-143.27
	Portugal	- 31.21	- 32.43
	Lebanon	- 61.05	- 60.85
	Puerto Rico	5.78	10.00
	Israel	- 39.16	- 55.37

TABLE 5

CORRELATION BETWEEN EACH OF THE 10 ALLOCATION INDICES AND THE TAXONOMIC DISTANCE
AND THE LEVELS-OF-LIVING INDEX FOR 1965 AND 1970.

	A1	A2	A3	A4	A5	A6	A7	A8	A9	A10
	- - - P E A R S O N C O R R E L A T I O N C O E F F I C I E N T S - - - -									
d 1965	.1450 (44) s=.174	-.8126 (44) s=.001	-.2470 (44) s=.053	-.0644 (42) s=.313	.1076 (41) s=.252	.3614 (38) s=.013	.0434 (39) s=.397	.1394 (32) s=.223	-.0974 (32) s=.298	.1280 (32) s=.243
SM 1965	-.2838 (44) s=.031	.7408 (44) s=.001	.4102 (44) s=.003	.1386 (42) s=.191	-.2059 (41) s=.098	-.2744 (38) s=.048	-.0082 (39) s=.480	-.2483 (32) s=.085	.1818 (32) s=.160	-.2304 (32) s=.102

A VALUE OF 99.0000 IS PRINTED IF A COEFFICIENT CANNOT BE COMPUTED

	A1	A2	A3	A4	A5	A6	A7	A8	A9	A10
d 1970	.1740 (44) s=.129	-.8106 (44) s=.001	-.2471 (44) s=.053	-.0421 (42) s=.396	.0933 (41) s=.281	.3496 (38) s=.016	.0426 (39) s=.398	.1386 (32) s=.225	-.1021 (32) s=.289	.1297 (32) s=.240
SM 1970	-.3333 (44) s=.014	.7437 (44) s=.001	.4081 (44) s=.003	.1194 (42) s=.226	-.1892 (41) s=.118	-.2573 (38) s=.089	-.0315 (39) s=.424	-.2393 (32) s=.103	.1723 (32) s=.173	-.2147 (32) s=.119

A VALUE OF 99.0000 IS PRINTED IF A COEFFICIENT CANNOT BE COMPUTED

REFERENCES

Baster, Nancy (ed.), Measuring Development: The Role
and Adequacy of Development Indicators, Frank
Cass, London, 1972.

Beckerman, W., International Comparisons of Real Incomes, OECD, Paris, 1966.

_____ and Bacon, R., "International Comparisons
of Income Levels: A Suggested New Measure,"
Economic Journal, Vo. 76, 1966, pp. 519-526.

Chenery, H.B., and Associates. Redistribution With
Growth, London, Oxford University Press, 1974.

Chenery, H.B. and Syrquin, Patterns of Development,
Oxford University Press, London, 1975.

Drewnoski, "Social Indicators and Welfare Measurement:
Remarks on Methodology" in Measuring Development,
Baster, Nancy (ed.), Frank Cass, London, 1972,
pp. 77-90.

Economic Council of Japan, Measuring Net National Welfare of Japan, Tokyo, Economic Research Institute,
1973.

Elliot, Charles, The Development Debate, SCM Press Ltd.,
London, 1971.

Food and Agricultural Organization, Various Yearbooks,
Various Issues, Rome.

Gostkowski, Z., "The Evolution of Developmental Gaps
Between Rich and Poor Countries,1955-65: A Method-
ological Pilot Study," International Social Science
Journal, Vol. 27, No. 1, 1975, pp. 38-52.

Hellwig, Z, "On The Problem of Weighting in International
Comparison," in Toward a System of Human Resources
Indicators For Less Developed Countries, Z. Gostkow-
ski (ed.), The Polish Academy of Sciences Press,
Wroclaw, Ossolineum, _____, "Procedure of Eval-
uating High-Level Manpower Data and Typology of
Countries by Means of the Taxonomic Method" in Toward
A System of Human Resources Indicators For Less De-
veloped Countries, Z. Gostkowski (ed.), The Polish
Academy of Science Press, Wroclaw, 1972, pp. 115-131.

Jain, Shail and Arthur E. Tiemann, "The Size Distribution of Income: A Compilation of Data," IBRD Development Research Center, Discussion Paper No. 4, August 1973.

Janssen, R., "Commodity Cushion," Wall Street Journal, March 24, 1976.

Lancaster, K., "A New Approach to Consumer Theory," JPE, Vol. 74, April 1966, pp. 132-57.

Nordhaus, W. and J. Tobin, "Is Growth Obsolete?" Fiftieth Anniversary Colloquium V, National Bureau of Economic Research, Columbia University Press, 1972.

Prinski, R., "Developing Controversy," Wall Street Journal, March 9, 1976.

Strotz, R., "Utility Tree," Econometrica, Vol. 25, April 1957, pp. 269-80.

United Nations, International Definition and Measurement of Levels of Living: An Interim Guide, United Nations, New York, 1961.

UNRISD, Studies in the Measurement of Levels of Living and Welfare, Report No. 70.3, Geneva, 1970.

United Nations, Demographic Yearbook, Various Issues, United Nations, New York.

Zapf, W., "Systems of Social Indicators: Current Approaches and Problems," International Social Science Journal Vol. 27, No. 3, 1975, pp. 479-498.

V
ECONOMIC GROWTH, POLICY AND INCOME DISTRIBUTION

William Loehr
University of Denver

One of the major realizations among development economists over the past five years has been that the dual goals of economic growth and economic equity may not be compatible. Considerable research has pointed to the increasingly unequal income distributions that accompany economic growth (Adelman and Morris, 1973; Chenery et al., 1974; Fishlow, 1972; Loehr, 1977). Many indicate the possibility of a trade-off between growth and equity (Adelman and Morris, 1973) while others (Ranis, 1977) point to a number of counterexamples where growth and increasing equity have proceeded apace. Given this increasing concern, international development institutions such as the World Bank have begun to shift their attention from activities which are purely growth-oriented to those which attempt to strike a balance between economic growth and equity (Chenery, 1977). Development plans of developing countries are now stressing the distributional aspects of development policy (e.g. Kenya, 1974) whereas only several years ago little mention of income distribution could be found in such documents.

The search is now on for the causes of declining equity in developing countries. Some researchers have singled out certain macro variables such as socio-economic dualism (Adelman and Morris, 1973; Kelly, Williamson and Cheetham, 1972) as leading to declining shares of income for the poor. Others look at specific policies in such areas as the fiscal system (McLure, 1975), agriculture (Berry, 1974; Tuckman, 1976), or technology (Tokman, 1975). Despite this intense effort by economists to discover the causes of increasingly unequal income distributions and to devise policies to offset present trends, there is little consensus as to causes. Policy has, therefore, been ad hoc, aiming for "solutions" which may not be solutions at all, but merely attempts to eliminate poverty in the short run in the hope that the developing countries will some day become more like the developed ones, when the distribution issue is less of a "problem."

Our task is to draw out the factors which have been linked both theoretically and empirically, with economic inequality and development. From these factors, specific areas for possible policy intervention are suggested and examined. Comparative case studies of eight countries will be developed so that the effects of the factors affecting inequality can be seen within the context of a specific development experience. Finally, policy areas will be examined which will be of concern to the international development community for at least the next decade.

THE RECENT EVIDENCE

Scholars concerned with income distribution through the early 1960s, generally found greater income inequality in developing countries than in developed ones and through cross section studies implied that as poor countries develop, incomes become more inequitably distributed. While the methods employed by most early analysts varied widely, several consistent hypotheses were advanced as explanations of the difference between developed and less developed countries (LDCs). Kravis (1960), Oshima (1962) and Kuznets (1963) would probably all have agreed that inequality and its positive relationship to growth among LDCs, could be explained in large part by one or all of several factors:

(1) The uneven distribution of human resources causes wide disparities in productivity and thus income. (2) There are barriers to economic mobility which are greater in developing countries than in developed ones. These barriers may take the form of open racism, restrictive legislation, unrealistic job qualifications, ignorance, tradition, etc. (3) The Economic Structure of a country may tend to concentrate income in a few hands. This may have to do with the ownership of property and wealth, location of specific resources such as minerals, etc. (4) The social and political organization of a country may not be conducive to a widespread sharing of income, and, (5) Dualism, an element of economic structure, may create a situation where there is an "automatic" tendency for income to become concentrated despite the fact that it may be accompanied by rapid economic growth. Not all of these factors could be expected to be operative at any one time across all samples of countries. In general, however, they are found in most of the literature dealing with income distribu-

tion which has appeared in the past fifteen years.

Considerable attention has been directed toward the idea that as countries move from very low levels of development toward higher levels, income at first becomes more inequitably distributed. After a "middle" development level is reached further growth is associated with increasingly equal distribution of income. This has come to be called the inverted "U hypothesis," where inequality first increases, then decreases with growth. Paukert (1973) finds a sharp increase in inequality (on the basis of Gini indices) as one moves from the lowest per capita GDP countries up to those in the $300-500 per capita range. This $300-500 range represents those countries of most extreme inequality. As higher per capita income levels are approached, inequality becomes progressively less.

It has also been observed that countries experiencing the most rapid rates of economic growth suffer from increasing inequality (Adelman & Morris, 1973). Fishlow (1972) and Wells (1974) point to the increasing inequality accompanying rapid growth in Brazil in the late 1960s, and Arndt (1975) finds similar trends in Indonesia. Trends toward greater inequality along with economic growth have been witnessed by Chenery et al. (1974) in many countries; in Argentina, Mexico and Puerto Rico by Weisskoff (1970) and in India by Swany (1967), though the latter case is not so clear cut (Kumar, 1974). Our survey here is by no means conclusive since it is a rather long list of investigators, using various methods, who have found inequality and growth anong LDCs to move together.

The findings of Adelman and Morris (1974) confirm the hypothesis that at the lowest levels of development, growth tends to increase inequality. Broadly speaking, in the poorest countries, growth works against the poorer segments of the population. The allocation of income to the poorest 60% of the population is best "explained" by the extent of socio-economic modernization and the expansion of educational services.[1] Over the entire sample the poorest 60% of the population received 26% of total income, but there appeared two subgroups where the share of the poorest 60% was relatively high (30-34%). One of these subgroups was characterized by a relatively low level of development accompanied by a predominance of small-scale or communal subsistence agriculture. The other was a subgroup of relatively well-developed countries where major efforts to improve upon

129

human resources had been made. Small income shares of the poorest 60% were most significantly related to sharply dualistic development processes. On the other hand, the upper 5% of income recipients receive about 30% of income on the average. The largest part of the variation in income of upper income groups is explained by the endowment of natural resources and the extent of government involvement in the economy. Countries where the share of upper income groups is relatively small tend to exhibit relatively intensive government participation in the economic environment as well as a relatively scarce supply of natural resources. Apparently the latter variable assumes importance because when resources are abundant they are more often than not, concentrated in the hands of a small class of businessmen, landlords, or expatriates.

Of the variables found important in the Adelman and Morris study, improvement in human resources and direct governmental economic activity seem to offer the greatest promise for greater equity in income distribution. While dualism was found to be an important explanatory variable, it, in itself, is not a policy variable. But policies can be devised (p.82) for widening the base for economic growth, e.g. credit can be made available to small entrepreneurs, technical services can be extended, etc.

It is not a forgone conclusion that, when considering all LDCs, as growth proceeds, inequity increases. Ahluawalia (1974) has found in a study of 65 countries that the growth rate of GDP was positively related to the income share of the lower 40% of income recipients suggesting that the dual objectives of growth and equity may not be in conflict. These results flowed from cross section regression analyses where income recipients were divided into three groups: top 20%, middle 40%, lower 40%, and their respective income shares were used as dependent variables. When the regressions were rerun separating countries by income level, it was found that the share of the poorest 40% did decline with growth up to the point where per capita income levels of about $400 were reached, and increased thereafter. Thus, there is consistency in the studies cited in that it tends to confirm the inverted "U hypothesis."

Work at the World Bank (Chenery et al., 1974) has turned up two variables related to the quantity and quality of human resources as most closely related to relative income shares. The level and availability of education was positively related to the income shares of

130

the poorest 80%. Primary school enrollment rates most significantly explained the share of the poorest 40% and rates of enrollment in secondary schools played a similar role for the middle 40% of income recipients. Population growth, on the other hand, bears a negative relationship with the share of the poorest 40% of income recipients and this effect seems "quantitatively substantial."

All of the above analyses rely upon cross-sectional studies for their conclusions. The paucity of data usually forces us to work with only one or two points in time for which data on income distribution have been collected. Few developing countries have even one year estimates which are reliable, let alone time series on income distribution.[2] Time series do exist, however, on some developed countries and at least one study (Roberti, 1974) does exist, involving Finland, Netherlands, Norway, Sweden, the U.S. and U.K. in the post war period. Roberti found that a time series of income shares showed in general that GDP per capita is negatively related to the shares of the fourth through eighth deciles and not related at all to the shares of the second and ninth deciles. These findings are consistent with other findings based upon cross section data for LDCs (Roberti, 1974; 631: Loehr, 1977).

Roberti's findings are consistent with those of Berry's (1974) study of Colombia. Since time series of income distribution data do not exist it was necessary for him to infer distributional changes from data on wages for groups of workers together with information on occupational structure over time. Overall from 1934-35 to 1964 both the top decile and the lowest deciles have experienced a slight reduction in their income shares. Meanwhile, gains accrued to the two deciles just below the top. Overall income distribution in Colombia became increasingly unequal from 1934-35 until the mid 1950s, whereupon it improved somewhat, corresponding to the increasing share of income accruing to non-agricultural workers. The idea presented by Adelman and Morris (1973: 1974) that poorer groups suffer an absolute deterioration in real income as growth proceeds receive some support from Berry's data in that real agricultural wages were observed to be below their 1935 level for almost the entire 1935-1964 period.

Policy Issues

It is evident that the empirical literature on income distribution in LDCs repeatedly hones in on given

sets of explanatory variables. While these do not all
appear in all studies, there is enough overlap among
the sets of variables found to be highly correlated
with income distribution, that several areas for policy intervention can be discerned.

Economic dualism was pointed out by early analysts
as a cause of deteriorating income equity in LDCs and
this finding has stood out in the recent work of Adelman and Morris (1973; 1974). It is particularly true
of countries in the early stages of development that
growth begins in the expansion of a very narrow modern
sector. This sector is often oriented around the exploitation of some abundant natural resource or some
other specialized economic activity. Development proceeds in a manner similar to that first described by
Lewis (1954) and then others who elaborated upon dualistic economic growth (Kelly, Williamson and Cheetham,
1972; Paauw and Fei, 1973). The impact upon income
distribution appears as a sharply declining income share
for the poorest 60% of the population with a concomitant increase in the share of the upper 5% (Adelman and
Morris, 1973: 178). Apparently these movements àre
simply due to the enclave nature of many early growth
efforts, which involve only a small part of the population. This effect wanes as higher development levels
are reached and growth becomes more broadly based.

It is not normally the case that dualism per se
can be considered a policy variable. Rather, it is a
condition which can be affected by a wide array of policies in such areas as credit, foreign trade, land tenure,
etc. Thus, rather than discussing dualism specifically
we will more often be interested in the implications of
policy for changes in dualism. Most policies are not
designed with dualism as a primary target, but many have
an impact upon it. It is this impact which we will
attempt to trace below.

Growth itself is the primary interest of many students of income distribution and thus considerable attention has already been directed toward it above. Again,
growth is not a "policy variable" in the normal sense of
the word since it is not normally the growth rate which
one would choose to adjust but rather the form of the
growth that occurs. Since growth can be achieved via
several policy packages it is these latter which attract
our attention here. In addition the consequences of
specific kinds of growth may change overall inequality
or impact adversely upon certain income groups. Again,
it is not the growth rate per se but the socio-economic

conditions that it creates which are the true objects of economic policy.

Some general policy areas are suggested by the literature on income distribution. Clearly, while growth and dualism per se are not policy variables there are a set of interrelated policy measures which do impact upon them and therefore upon income distribution. Some of these policies involve the stimulation of labor intensive growth and especially labor intensive exports. Removal of market imperfections in credit, marketing and technological diffusion as well as improvements in land tenure would fall withing this realm. There is also a set of policy relevant variable which appear to behave somewhat independently of growth and dualism and which have been observed to impact significantly upon income distribution. These we have placed under four categories: 1) human resources, 2) population growth, 3) intersectoral shifts, and 4) direct governmental economic activity.

Human resources seems to be one focus which may have productive policy payoffs. The data generally shows that basic education (either primary education or literacy) is related positively to the shares of the lowest income groups and that higher level education (secondary education) has a similar effect on middle incomes (Adelman and Morris, 1973; Ahluawalia, 1976). It can be argued that the upgrading of skills combined with economic growth which is labor and skill intensive is a pattern which is likely to lead to movements toward greater equity. Presumably a shift from unskilled, low paid labor to skilled, high paid labor leads to both a reduction in wage (skill) differentials and an increase in the share of wages in total output.[3] (Ahluawalia, 1976: 21). It is apparently reliance upon skills intensive, high employment industrialization which has allowed Korea and Taiwan to grow rapidly and achieve increasingly equitable income distributions simultaneously.

It can also be maintained that unlike other forms of capital, human capital is less prone to concentration. If income distribution is functionally related to capital concentration then reliance upon human capital rather than other forms is likely to stimulate greater equity. This is likely for several reasons (Ahluawalia, 1976):

1) Unlike physical capital, an expansion of the stock of human capital involves dispersing the investment across a wide cross section of the population.

133

2)   Whereas concentration of physical capital in
few hands is quite possible, there is a limit to
the human capital that can be emodied in one person.

3)   Human capital cannot be bequeathed across
generations.[4]

Population growth rates appear to be positively related to income inequality but the role of this variable is so poorly understood that no strong statements
can be made about it. Paglin (1975) however has explained how population growth rates can have significant
impact upon income distribution. His analysis refers
to the U.S.economy but it has general relevance to the
recent history of LDCs.

Paglin points out, as have others (Peck, 1974;
Dich, 1970) that there is an age-income profile for
most countries which shows young and old persons earning relatively low incomes, and persons in middle age
groups earning relatively high incomes. At any point
in time then, some inequality will exist simply because
not everyone is of the same age. It is well known
(Pitchford, 1974) that as population growth rates accelerate, there is a shift in the age profile toward
younger population members. For example, if the fertility rate among American women were raised from its
observed 2.3 live births (1970) to 4.0, gradually over
a 25 year period, the proportion of children (0-14 years)
in the population would rise from 28% (1970) to 36%.
If the age-income profile did not change, inequality
would appear to increase not because inequality within
any given age group has changed at all, but because
there are simply a larger number of young, low paid
persons.

The lesson is clear for developing countries. Many
have felt the medical revolution only recently, and
population growth rates are high. In those where population growth rates have recently accelerated, or where
they are still accelerating, we should expect inequality
to be increasing. In those countries, like Korea and
Taiwan that have recently reduced population growth
rates, we expect, and in those cases find, increasing
equity. Changes in population growth rates can only be
felt with a considerable lag since it takes years for
the children who are born today to become low paid workers sometime around the turn of the century!

Intersectoral shifts accompanying economic development were recognized by Kuznets (1963) as being cause

for expecting increased inequality. Oshima (1970) notes
that shifts from a rural to an urban focus for economic
activity, as economic growth proceeds, explain the changing income distribution better than growth itself. We
can generally observe in LDCs that inequality generally
tends to be greater in the urban (industrial) sector
than in the rural (agricultural), (Weisskoff, 1970;
Swamy, 1967). Rapid growth usually proceeds in a dualistic fashion such that growth in the industrial sector
is more rapid than growth in the agriculutural sector
(Adelman and Morris, 1973). In addition, rapid population growth and rural to urban migration occur. These
factors alone are enough to ensure that, ceteris paribus,
income distribution will become more unequal overall.

The inverted U shaped relationship between economic
growth and income inequality can be partially explained
by rural to urban migration (Robinson, 1976). An overall
measure of income distribution, G_T, is in some way a combination of two factors:

1) A weighted average of the inequality in the
rural and urban sectors, G_R and G_U respectively,
and,

2) The difference, D, between incomes in each
sector and the weight placed upon it. It is
possible that $G_R=G_U < G_T$ due to significantly
different average income levels between the two
sectors (i.e., a heavy weight placed upon D).
It is normally the case in most LDCs that $G_R < G_U$
and that D is substantial.

Inequality is then likely to move in three stages:

1) At early stages of development the primary
weight within G_T is on G_R, but as development
proceeds increasing weight is placed upon G_U
which is greater. This also causes the significance of D to increase and G_T rises.

2) G_T becomes greater than G_U due to the heavy
weight placed upon D in the aggregate measure.
Dualism may also cause the absolute level of D
to increase.

3) G_T falls and approaches G_U as society becomes
increasingly urbanized. G_R is weighed increasingly lightly and D falls in significance. An
associated factor here would be a shortage of
labor in rural areas, raising the marginal productivity of labor and thus rural incomes and
thereby reducing D.

135

Swamy (1967), in a study of inequality in India, was able to separate the increase in inequality into two parts: that attributable to intersectoral inequality (D) as opposed to intrasectoral inequality (G_R or G_U). He found that changes in intrasectoral equality 1951-1960 were small. No observable change took place in the agricultural sector while the income distribution in the non-agricultural sector became slightly more unequal. Only 15% of the overall increase in Indian income inequality could be attributed to changes in the intra-sectoral income distribution. The remaining 85% was as a result of the increased intersectoral inequality, i.e., shifts in population from the low inequality (agricultural) to the higher inequality (non-agricultural) sector. Weisskoff (1970) also examines the shift from agriculture to non-agricultural economic activities and finds overall inequality widening as a result.

Direct governmental economic activity can have an impact upon inequality. Most studies of fiscal activities show that these exert only mild redistributive pressures within most economies. Snodgrass (1974), for example, indicates that progressivity within the Malaysian fiscal system has increased noticeably since 1958. McLure (1975) indicates that overall, the fiscal system of Colombia exhibits mild progressivity. On the whole, surveys of general tax/expenditure incidence in LDCs (deWulf, 1974) indicate that upper income groups receive benefits from government expenditures which are a smaller portion of their incomes than are the benefits by low-income groups. Since most public expenditures provide public goods and services, almost insurmountable difficulties are encountered in evaluating tax and expenditure incidence.[5] Thus, care should be taken in interpreting most of these studies.

Stabilization policies seem to have been associated with sharply increased inequality. Arndt (1975) has analyzed post-Sukarno Indonesia and the stabilization and growth policies pursued there after 1966. With per capita income growing rapidly, the poorest income groups lost part of their relative share, but it is Arndt's judgment that they were at least holding their own in absolute terms. The severe stabilization program in Brazil, begun in 1964, also resulted in rapid economic growth (1967 and thereafter) and a deterioration in economic equity (Wells, 1974; Fishlow, 1972). The data presented by Wells (Table 8), however, indicate that the poorest decile of the working population could not possibly have been holding their own on an absolute

scale, since their relative share dropped by over 40%.
Informal reports from Chile are that current trends
are mostly along Brazilian lines. Unfortunately, the
cases cited present such a mixture of economic and
political confusion that few clear economic forces
can be observed.

At all but the lowest levels, direct expansion
of governmental participation in economic activity
and investment has an equalizing effect across all income groups with the exception of the very lowest
(Adelman and Morris, 1973: 195). Apparently, there
is an ideological correlate here in that those governments which play a relatively large role in the economy
also express a more socialist ideology than those that
do not.

Case Studies

Case studies which are adequate to explain the
relationship between the policy areas that we have outlined above and income distribution and growth, would
require more detail treatment, rather than sections
in a paper of this length. Nevertheless, we are of
the opinion that there is much to gain from placing
these policy areas side by side within the development
experience of real countries. Thus, in what follows
we will discuss income distribution and growth in
eight countries, orienting our discussion around the
policy areas rather than taking each country one at
a time. The price we pay for brevity is that coverage
may not be complete, i.e. not all countries are discussed regarding all policy issues. Since dualism is
not a policy area per se, the last topic discussed will
include how all policies together, impact upon dualism.

The Countries

Three main considerations led us to the choice of
the eight countries to be studied. First, since dualism has come out as a major factor related to income
distribution but is not a policy variable in and of
itself, we chose countries which are all of about the
same degree of dualism.[6] Dualism is such a complicated
collection of conditions that if it were not "controlled
for," any differences in inequality might be explained
by some simple reference to it. Also, in this way we
can more clearly refer to policies designed to affect
dualism without having the intervening problem of ex-
plaining distributional differences due to the level

of dualism.

Secondly, we wanted to choose countries for which there were fairly comparable readings on income distribution at two recent points in time. This is a rather severe limitation as one immediately sees upon examining the data compiled by Jain (1975). Only sixteen LDCs listed there met this criterion.

Thirdly, we wanted to represent a range of experience viz, income and growth. Thus, the countries that were chosen are as follows:

1) Rapid growth - increasing equity: Korea and Taiwan

2) Rapid growth - decreasing equity: Mexico and Brazil

3) Slow growth - increasing equity: Sri Lanka and Costa Rica

4) Slow growth - decreasing equity: Colombia and India

Growth and Inequality in Eight Countries

In the specific cases examined here there is no relationship which can be observed between growth rates and income inequality. Table one presents data on income inequality, expressed as Gini coefficients for two points in time, as well as growth rates in real per capita income over the same time span. Obviously the time periods were dictated by data availability. Growth rates reported for Brazil do not truly reflect the record of the 1960s there. Up until 1967, Brazil suffered from severe inflation and stagnation, with annual growth rates below 3%. Since 1967, growth has often hit 10%, averaging 7.8% in real terms from 1970 to 1975. Sri Lanka's growth rate for the 1963-69 period took a considerable dip below the already low rate of about 1% growth, 1953-63. During the latter period inequality was about constant in Sri Lanka. Indian growth continued slightly negative during the 1960s and inequality remained fairly constant during that time period. For South Korea we show only a three year span 1968-71. In most cases this would be inadequate to build the case that inequality was declining or that growth was rapid. In the Korean case, however, it is the general consensus that income inequality has

138

lessened substantially over the past twenty years and that the Korean growth record is one of the best among LDCs. Thus, a three year span is indicative of long-run trends.

Ranking the countries by level of GDP per capita does reveal the inverted "U"-shaped relationship alluded to above. The countries with lowest per capita GDP tend to have lower Gini coefficients, but in three of them, Korea, Taiwan, and Sri Lanka, the trend is toward increasing equity -- not decreasing as the U hypothesis would lead us to expect. Ranking by GDP may more simply reveal the difference between Latin American and Asian economies. The former tend to have greater inequality and higher development levels. India continues to be the exception, having the lowest GDP per capita, a high degree of inequality and an extremely poor growth record.

TABLE I

GROWTH AND INEQUALITY: EIGHT COUNTRIES

	Years of Observation #1 #2	GINI INDEX Year #1	GINI INDEX Year #2	Growth Rate in GDP per Capita Year #1 – Year #2	GDP per Capita in Year #2 (1970 dollars)
South Korea	1968 1971	.30	.27	8.8%	263
Taiwan	1953 1964	.58	.33	7.1	235
Mexico	1963 1968	.58	.61	7.9	638
Brazil	1960 1970	.60	.64	3.7	391
Sri Lanka	1963 1969	.47	.37	-1.2	170
Costa Rica	1961 1971	.52	.47	2.6	561
Colombia	1962 1970	.48	.56	2.0	409
India	1954 1964	.42	.47	1.6	97

Sources: Inequality data are from JAIN (1975). Growth and GDP
per capita data are from U.N. Yearbook of National
Accounts Statistics (various). To arrive at 1970
values implicit price deflations were used from Economic
Report of the President 1975.

Note: All GINI indices are calculated on the basis of household
data with the exception of Brazil and Colombia, which are
based upon the income of "Economically Active" populations.

An examination of the Gini index alone hides specific income groups, which may lose or gain in their relative position over time. Table two shows relative income shares at two points in time, for each country.[7]
We note that increasing inequality on the basis of the
Gini index does not imply that "the poor get poorer."
In Brazil, despite a rise in the Gini index, there was
a simultaneous increase in the share of income accruing
to the poorest 20% of income recipients which we refer
to here as the "poor." Apparently the increase in overall inequality was due primarily to the offsetting increase in the share of income going to the richest 10%,
which increased substantially. In the Brazilian case,
increased income shares going to the rich appear to
have come about by an erosion in the share of the percentile groups from 20 to 60. For convenience we refer
to this group as the "near poor."

TABLE II

INCOME SHARES OF SELECTED PERCENTILE GROUPS(In Percents)

	Years of Observation		Share of Poorest 20%	
	Year 1	Year 2	Year 1/Year 2	
South Korea	1968	1971	8.6	9.9
Taiwan	1953	1964	2.9	7.8
Mexico	1963	1968	4.4	3.7
Brazil	1960	1970	0.8	1.1
Sri Lanka	1963	1969	4.5	7.4
Costa Rica	1961	1971	5.7	5.4
Colombia	1962	1970	5.8	3.5
India	1953	1960	7.0	5.5

	Share of 20-60 %ile Groups (Near Poor)		Share of Richest 10%	
	Year 1/Year 2		Year 1/Year 2	
South Korea	29.7	31.1	24.2	23.3
Taiwan	16.4	29.1	45.2	26.1
Mexico	16.5	15.8	49.0	51.7
Brazil	16.8	14.7	45.0	50.3
Sri Lanka	22.9	25.3	36.9	29.6
Costa Rica	18.0	23.0	44.0	34.4
Colombia	19.8	17.5	39.2	44.1
India	24.0	23.7	34.9	38.9

Source: Jain 1975

141

In all cases here where economic growth has proceeded rapidly, the poor find themselves with increased
income shares, and undoubtedly increased absolute income levels.[8] Unfavorable growth records seem to be
associated with declining income shares for the poor
and in the cases of India and Colombia, the growth record and relative changes in income shares which have
occurred lead one to expect that absolute income levels
have declined. Sri Lanka is the only country with
growth difficulties where the share of the poor has increased, and in that case substantially.

Increasing inequality (Mexico, Brazil, Colombia
and India) is accompanied by a reduction in the share of
income accruing to the "near poor" and an increase in
the share of the rich. In India it appears that the
rich have been able to maintain their absolute income
levels despite slight declines in real GDP per capita
overall, and absolute income losses to other income
groups. In Brazil and Mexico growth has been so favorable that the absolute incomes of the near poor have
probably not declined but this group has apparently
gained little from that growth.

In each case where equity has improved (Korea,
Taiwan, Sri Lanka and Costa Rica) the position of the
near poor has improved as well, while upper income
groups receive smaller income shares. In the cases of
Taiwan, Sri Lanka and Costa Rica relative income share
losses for the "rich" were substantial, ranging from
-42% in Taiwan to -20% in Sri Lanka. The Korean "rich"
lost a small part of their share, but inequality is so
low in Korea in any event that little room exists for
further redistributions along the lines of those elsewhere. In all cases of increasing equity except Costa
Rica, the poor gain a larger proportionate increase in
income share than do the near poor. Costa Rica is the
only case here where the poor lose part of their share
despite increased equity.

The introductory remarks comparing the "poor" and
the "near poor" are disturbing. A very rough description of the poor would probably show them to be persons
living on the fringes of economic activity. They are
probably employed very infrequently, and when they are,
it is in occupations requiring extremely low skills.
The group might include very young or old persons as
well as those unfit -- perhaps for physical reasons --
for "regular" work. Their occupations might include
seasonal agricultural work, occasional unskilled manual
labor, scavenging, etc.[9] The "near poor", however, are

142

probably persons with "regular" jobs. They are the
working poor and are employed in unskilled positions
in factories, or farms, in services such as shoe
shining or running errands, etc. The "poor" benefit
from economic growth, probably due to the assortment
of odd jobs that spring up and the increased demand
for unskilled, informal services which accompany increased economic activity. The "near poor", the more
steady bulk of the unskilled work force, benefit little. When growth and increased equity occur, their
share increases least (Korea, Taiwan); when growth
and decreased equity occur, their share falls most
(Mexico, Brazil). Only in the case of slow growth
and decreasing equity are the near poor able to fare
relatively better than the "poor" (Colombia, India),
who find opportunities for casual work drying up
almost entirely. The near poor simply suffer a
smaller cut than the poor when slow growth and increasing inequality occur simultaneously. These
statements are largely impressionistic but nevertheless present a reasonable scenario of how relative
shares change.

Human Resources

One of the primary factors associated with income distribution is the quantity and quality of human
resources. We have already discussed some of the reasoning behind this and present in Table III some data on
education and literacy in our eight countries. We
presume that the period covered by these data (1960-
66) adequately reflect educational changes occurring
at about the same time as the income distribution
changes shown in Tables I and II. Highest levels of
both literacy and percent of the population in primary
school are observed in our increasing equity countries.
Mexico stands out as the only increasingly inequitable
country with high educational and literacy levels. Past
studies note a positive correlation between primary
school enrollments and the share of the poor and this
seems to be borne out by our data here.

Costa Rica provided a counter example in that despite the highest rate of literacy and primary school
enrollment, the poor have not maintained their relative
share despite increasing equity overall. This, however,
is not in contradiction with the other studies which
have been based upon cross-sectional data. Costa Rica
still has higher literacy and higher primary school enrollments and a larger income share for the "poor" than
any of our highly inequitable countries. Thus, the

cross-section here looks similar to other cross-sectional data collections. However, we are concerning ourselves
here with rates of change. Since Costa Rica has for some
time maintained almost universal primary education and
literacy, almost no changes in income distribution can
be expected due to the educational factor. Similar statements might pertain to Korea, Taiwan, and Sri Lanka.
Their literacy and primary educational data are consistent
with cross-sectional data but because of the already high
levels reached in these areas, little room for inducing
changes in income distribution can be expected via basic
education expansion.

TABLE III

LITERACY AND EDUCATION

	% Population In Primary School 1966	% Population In Secondary School 1966
South Korea	17.1	3.8
Taiwan		
Mexico	16.6	2.3
Brazil	13.0	2.0
Sri Lanka	15.9	7.5
Costa Rica	20.3	2.8
Colombia	13.3	1.5
India	10.0	3.8

	Rate Increase (1960-66) Primary Enroll.	Sec. Enroll.	% Literacy (1966)	Rate Lit. Improvement 1960-66 (%)
South Korea	6.1	8.1	72.0	1.4
Taiwan				
Mexico	7.0	25.0	71.0	8.1
Brazil	7.1	10.8	59.0	6.5
Sri Lanka	1.9	6.9	72.0	3.1
Costa Rica	7.4	7.6	85.0	2.9
Colombia	6.6	11.8	58.0	1.0
India	6.1	10.3	32.0	2.0

Source: Arthur Banks, Cross Polity Time Series Data
(Cambridge: MIT Press, 1971)

Rates of improvement in secondary education in Brazil, Mexico, Colombia and India hold promise for improvements in the share of the "near poor." Each of these countries saw the income share of that group recently eroded but apparently major efforts are being made to boost the availability of secondary education. Again, the behavior here is not inconsistent with cross-sectional data. Brazil, Mexico, Colombia and India have low secondary enrollment and relatively low shares for the near poor. What is disturbing is the fact that all four have put in the greatest effort to expand secondary education but have simultaneously witnessed a decline in the share of the near poor.

It is important to note that, when compared with other countries of the world with similar per capita incomes, Korea, Taiwan and Sri Lanka are particularly well endowed with high quality human resources. Despite their low income levels all are blessed with almost universal literacy and education. Educational levels in Korea are almost three times those of other countries at a similar level of development and Taiwan and Sri Lanka are not far behind (Adelman, 1974). One of the characteristics of the Korean and Taiwanese populations is their appreciation for education. Families in these countries are willing to devote a larger portion of their budget to education than families elsewhere. Thus, high levels of education have come about with less strain than occurs elsewhere, where education requires more public and less private support. In Sri Lanka during the 1960s, over one-half of all government expenditures were devoted to the improvement of human resources in the areas of education and health (Jayawardena, 1974). These extraordinary efforts to improve upon human resources would lead one to expect the relatively equitable distributions of income that are indeed found in these countries.

Population

It was our reasoning above that high inequality and high population growth rates seem to go hand in hand because of the relationship between the age distribution and the age-income profile. As long as there is an age-income profile as described by Paglin (1975) where middle aged people earn more than either the very young or the very old, and accelerating population growth rate should cause an increase in inequality due to the relative increase in the number of relatively young (poorly paid) people. It is not enough to say that population growth rates are high or low, because a constant growth rate

145

implies some equilibrium age structure. Changes in population growth rates imply changes in the age structure and thus changes in income distribution given some reasonable age-income profile.

In countries where population growth rates have peaked and are declining we would expect increasing equity due to an increasing population of relatively highly paid, middle-aged income recipients. We have collected data on the population growth rate record of the countries being examined here. In Table IV, each rate of growth refers to the compound rate over the decade preceeding the date indicated. For example, the 2.4% indicated for 1970, Korea, refers to the growth rate during the 1960s. Since population growth peaked in the 1960s in Korea, we would expect income to become more quickly equitably distributed for this reason alone, _ceteris paribus_.

We have circled the peak population growth rate for each of our eight countries. Compare the occurrence of the peak in each of our increasing equity countries with the period over which we are examining income distribution:

	Peak in Population Growth	Period of Improving Equity
Korea	1960s	68-71
Taiwan	1950s	53-64
Sri Lanka	1950s	63-69
Costa Rica	1950s	61-71

In each case, the period of increasing equity has followed the peak in the population growth rates and at least partially overlaps the following decline in population growth rates. In the countries where income inequality is increasing, population growth rates are now at their peak with the exception of Colombia. The data on inequality in Colombia, however, occur entirely within the years 1962-70 when the population growth rate appears to have peaked. Thus, the effect of the peak might not yet be reflected in the data.

Both Korea and Taiwan pursue publically supported family planning policies and these may be in part responsible for their success in growth with equity. The Korean program was begun in 1962 and by about 1970 involved one fourth of all married women aged 25-44 (McDougall, 1972). Population growth rates of 2.8% for 1960-65, were down to about 1.8% for the 1968-71 period. These data correspond very nicely to our hypotheses about population growth and income distribution.

146

TABLE IV

POPULATION GROWTH RATE, VARIOUS PERIODS

	Korea	Taiwan	Mexico	Brazil	Sri Lanka	Costa Rica	Colombia	India
1940		2.5	1.7	2.0	1.5	2.4	2.0	1.3
1950		3.0	3.0	2.6	2.2	3.0	2.5	2.1
1960	1.9	3.5	3.0	2.8	2.6	3.7	3.1	1.5
1970	2.4	3.3	3.3	2.8	2.3	3.4	3.3	2.1
1975	1.7	2.0	3.5	3.0	2.3	2.6	2.8	2.1

Source: Growth rates shown for 1970-1975 are from IMF International Financial Statistics; all others from Plato IV, a data bank and simulation program maintained at the University of Illinois and accessible at the University of Denver.

Note: Growth rates shown are compound rates over the period preceding the year indicated -- that is, over each decade and 1970-75.

Korean goals are to lower population growth to 1.5% during 1976 and thereby raise the economically active proportion of the population to 36% in 1976, compared to 32% one decade ago.

Little in addition to this can be said about the affect of population growth on inequality. No empirical studies have been done in developing countries which relate population growth to income distribution via the age-income profilè. There nevertheless appears to be more than adequate justification for increased research effort along these lines.

Intersectoral Studies

Rural to urban migration can be expected to cause increasing inequality overall if: 1) inequality is greater in the urban sector and 2) if the income gap between the two sectors is large. Table V shows this to be the case for our eight countries.

TABLE V

RURAL-URBAN INEQUALITY

	Year	Rural Gini (G_R)	Urban Gini (G_U)	Ratio G_U/G_R	Ratio of Urban Incomes to Rural Incomes
Korea	1971	.31	.34	1.06	1.87
Taiwan	1972	.29	.27	.93	1.22
Mexico	1963	.53	.47	.89	2.31 (a)
Brazil	1970	.45	.56	1.24	2.81
Sri Lanka	1969	.35	.41	1.17	1.72
Costa Rica	1971	.37	.39	1.05	1.85
Colombia	1970	.48	.55	1.15	2.32
India	1960	.37	.46	.24	1.97

Source: Jain (1975)
(a) From Weisskoff (1970).

Mexico and Taiwan are exceptions to what one normally expects in developing countries in that in both cases inequality is greatest in the rural areas. The other countries conform to the pattern of most LDCs where urban inequality is greater. All countries here are experiencing rates of urban growth which far exceed population growth.

All four increasingly inequitable countries (Colombia, India, Mexico and Brazil) show much larger income gaps than in those countries where inequality is decreasing. With the exception of Sri Lanka, the greatest differences in sectoral inequality are also found in the increasingly inequitable countries. In Sri Lanka, though the sectoral inequality difference is fairly large, the proportion of the population which is urbanized (20%) is fairly low and urban population growth slower than in the other countries. Thus, the relative differences in sectoral income distributions play a much smaller role in Sri Lanka than they play in other countries. In Brazil, for example, 60% of the population is urbanized and further urbanization is taking place at a rapid rate. In addition, the income "gap" in Brazil between rural and urban incomes is great. Thus, for this reason alone one would expect increasing inequality to show up in aggregate measures of Brazilian inequality.

Taiwan and Korea have been blessed with a set of circumstances which has allowed them to develop in an egalitarian way, without creating distributional problems between sectors. Both underwent a thorough land reform in the early years of independence. An agricultural base of small farmers, virtually all owner operators, ensured that income distributions in agriculture were to be more egalitarian than in other LDCs where land is concentrated in the hands of a few. In both cases the governments have been active in preventing the agricultural terms of trade from deteriorating, thereby maintaining a minimum difference between rural and urban incomes.

Somewhat less success in this regard has been seen in Costa Rica and Sri Lanka. Land has always been more or less equally distributed in Sri Lanka and during the 1960s Costa Rica engaged in programs designed to modernize the operations of small and medium sized farms. Both of these countries have been less successful than Korea and Taiwan in promoting import substitution in agriculture followed by export expansion based in part on agricultural resources. Sri Lanka has attempted to maintain

149

the agricultural terms of trade by public involvement in
food purchasing. Food subsidies serve the dual purpose
of maintaining agricultural prices and providing an input into the improvement of human resources. Sri Lanka
has encouraged import substitution in paddy and other
crops (which also benefits the balance of payments) by
guaranteeing prices, providing credit and encouraging
"green revolution" technology for small farmers. Costa
Rica has performed less well in these areas, maintaining
much greater concentration of land and much less agricultural diversity. Coffee and bananas still account
for about 60% of all Costa Rican exports.

Problems of agricultural productivity and land
distribution have not been successfully tackled in
Mexico, Brazil, Colombia and India. All continue to
be plagued by concentration of land in few hands, insecurity of land tenure and agricultural productivity performances which continually lag behind the rest of the
economy. Mexico has been making progress of late, but
much of it is due to the expansion of agribusiness and
exports of agricultural commodities which tend to serve
the interests of very large farmers rather than the
small farmer majority.

Direct Public Economic Activity

It would be impossible in a paper of this length
to adequately compare all possible policy combinations
which could be pursued across a set of eight countries.
We intend therefore to describe the major policy orientation of the countries of concern here and note similarities or differences. Most policies listed here
can be examined at length in other sources.[10]

In Korea and Taiwan, policy has not been conscious-
ly equity oriented. Rather, public policy there was
designed to stimulate economic growth, and the special
set of circumstances facing Taiwan and Korea allowed the
growth to advance rapidly and equitably. The element
which sets these countries apart from the others is
that they were egalitarian from the start. Following
Japanese occupation ending in 1945, both underwent reforms which created an egalitarian base upon which to
build. In Korea, land reforms in the late 1940s created
an agricultural sector of small farmers and eliminated
tenancy by 1950. Concentrations of physical capital
were partially eliminated when the Japanese were defeated.
Post-partition chaos and war wiped out most remaining
capital concentrations and eliminated most social distinctions. Similarly, Taiwan underwent a thorough land

reform following the departure of the Japanese. No major industrial concentrations existed and most physical capital that did exist was spread among many small businessmen and farmers, many of whom immigrated to Taiwan from the mainland.

Given this egalitarian beginning, policy in Korea and Taiwan aimed at achieving maximum growth based upon relatively free market forces and the efforts of small businessmen and farmers. Both countries quickly moved from an import substitution stage to a labor intensive, export promotion stage. The relatively abundant endowment of highly educated (given their income level) labor allowed labor intensive industrial expansion aided by maintenance of realistic exchange rates, credit at more or less market rates, etc.

Costa Rica and Sri Lanka are somewhat different from Korea and Taiwan in that they appear to have made a conscious effort to achieve greater equity by public policy. Neither country has been lucky enough to possess the egalitarian structures inherited by Korea and Taiwan but both have made efforts to bring it about. Of the eight countries being examined here, Costa Rica and Sri Lanka have by far the largest public expenditure per capita.[11] Sri Lanka's $40 per capita expenditure seems like a particularly heavy public commitment in a country where per capita income is only about $170 to begin with. In Sri Lanka growth efforts are concentrated in areas where small businessmen and small farmers are the primary beneficiaries. Import substitution has been encouraged but as yet neither Sri Lanka nor Costa Rica has been able to enter a period of rapid export expansion. In both countries social welfare programs are well developed and provide fairly comprehensive coverage to persons with low incomes. In Sri Lanka social welfare programs occupy about one-half of the public budget and apparently exert a considerable positive pressure on the real income of the poor. Costa Rica maintains one of the most well developed social welfare systems in Latin America, providing poor families with subsidized education, health facilities, etc.

Brazil, Mexico, Colombia, and India have pursued policies which involve much greater intervention in the market than has occurred in Korea and Taiwan. Neo-classical growth policies have led to attempts to stimulate growth primarily by physical capital formation. In Brazil, Colombia and Mexico, attempts to stimulate growth

151

and employment by raising aggregate demand have led to
serious distortions and have precipitated considerable
need for government controlled price regimes. The use
of such policies seems to have been justified by the
Keynesian ideas which were originally designed for developed economies in depression. During depression in
developed countries, however, factors of production
which are combined with capital are already in abundance
and need only be mobilized. These cooperating factors
have not often been present in Brazil and Mexico, and
thus attempts to stimulate capital formation and then
mobilize other factors of production through increasing
aggregate demand, have most often led to either open or
suppressed inflation. Policies have stressed capital
formation through protection against imports and either
directly or indirectly subsidized credit. The result
has been low levels of employment expansion and a degree of capital intensivity which seems inappropriate
given their relative factor endowments.

The contrast between Brazil and Mexico on the one
hand and Korea and Taiwan on the other is sharp. In
both, growth has been the primary concern and equity
changes simply followed. In Korea and Taiwan an egalitarian base combined with "letting the market work" has
brought growth and an improvement in an already egalitarian climate. Mexico and Brazil spring from a base
which is far from egalitarian. Despite the Mexican
Revolution, both have shown sharp inequality to begin
with, "letting the market work" would have created
greater equity. While some intervention in markets
was probably justified, the emphasis in Brazil and Mexico has probably been overly placed upon physical as
opposed to human capital. Growth and investment policies have implicitly assumed that human capital was adequate to the development task. When this has proven
not to be the case and skill bottlenecks have occurred,
the response has often been to increase capital intensity thereby increasing the productivity of the skills
that did already exist. The overall effect has been
to create employment "problems," to ignore comparative
advantages in labor intensive industrialization, and
probably to raise the level of dualism in both countries.

Development policy in India has proceeded in a much
more centralized fashion than in any of the other coun-
ries seen here. A series of five year plans beginning
in 1950 set the tone for Indian development policy which
in retrospect appears to have had two main thrusts.
The first and primary thrust was that of heavy public
investment in capital intensive industrialization.

152

Especially in the Second Plan (55-60), growth models a la Harrod and Domar held sway. It was reasoned that the poverty problem was so massive that diverting large amounts of public resources into direct poverty relief would prevent any significant amount of capital investment and probably not help alleviate poverty either. Heavy industrialization was supposed to provide the focus for rapid growth, generating capital for the future and eventually provide resources with which poverty could be attacked.

A secondary thrust was more intentional than actual. Stated policies emphasized that equity was to be achieved by a series of steps to be taken in tandem with industrialization. Land was to be redistributed and tenancy laws made more equitable. Educational opportunities were to be extended to all and resources made available to small businessmen. Most anlysts agree that those intentions have never been carried out on any substantial scale. Agricultural programs have tended to help large farmers disproportionately; education is primarily available to upper income groups. Overall, to the extent that action was taken on any of these fronts the relatively well off have benefited more than the poor. Bradhan (1974) and others point to the Indian power structure as being the main obstacle to equity oriented programs. Rich farmers, big businessmen, etc., have the power to make sure that they benefit first, before resources are to trickle down to lower income groups.

Overall, India has not successfully attacked any major poverty problems in a significant way. In addition, the capital intensive growth drive has stalled amid high costs, insufficient markets and bureaucratic obstacles. The strong centralized role played by the Indian government has placed about one fourth of the country's capital stock in public hands. Many of these public enterprises were inefficiently acquired and inefficiently run and thus are only able to operate behind very high protective tariffs, quotas, etc.

The Colombian experience has similarities to the Indian, in that political obstacles appear to hinder any attempt to provide greater equity. Agricultural land is particularly inequitably distributed in Colombia and little progress has been made in providing small farmers with access to land. Industrial development has not been approached in such a centralized manner

153

as in India, but overly capital intensive investments
with high costs, limited markets and need for protection have been common. It is not easy to separate the
business and governmental elite in Colombia and the
close cooperation between the two groups almost ensures
that little progress will be made in poverty oriented
development programs.

POLICY ISSUES AND CONCLUSIONS

    What we have come up with here is much like an
agenda for research. Economists and policy makers
have already declared income distribution to be a major concern in developing countries, occupying a status
similar to economic growth. The major issue of the
near future is how to achieve equity and growth simultaneously. The experience of those countries that
have promised growth now, equity later, has not built
confidence in their ability to deliver the latter. An
examination of the evidence linking equity and growth
combined with our case studies, suggest several areas
which may have productive payoffs in developing equity
oriented growth policies.

    The role of small enterprises in economic growth
and development is little understood. It is clear
that growth based upon the efforts of small businesses
and small farms can be rapid and equitable (Korea and
Taiwan). Sri Lanka and Costa Rica emphasize small economic entities in their development policies and have
increased economic equity, though their growth record
is not good.[12] The two major factors distinguishing
Sri Lanka and Costa Rica on the one hand and Korea and
Taiwan on the other is that the latter began their recent growth history with small enterprises already in
existence while Sri Lanka and Costa Rica have had to
take positive steps to encourage their development.
Also, Korea and Taiwan, given this structure, have relied much more upon market forces to promote economic
growth. In none of the cases of decreasing equity have
small enterprises been encouraged nor have they played
much of a role in economic growth.

    The issue then is the role of small enterprise in
equity oriented growth policy. We know very little
about what motivates small businessmen -- though some
work does relate to small farms. The growth potential
of small enterprises within a variety of economic
structure contexts is unknown. Obviously most LDCs
will be operating within a context where both large and
small businesses operate side by side and often in com-

154

petition. How this interaction is to occur and the policies required to promote growth with equity in this
context is an issue which is only now arising.

Continued or growing poverty is incompatible with
equity oriented growth. The rapid growth in Korea and
Taiwan has demonstrated that the poorest segments of
society can be helped by rapid growth. The Mexican
and Brazilian experience however indicates that the
"near poor" suffer -- if not absolutely, relatively.
This same "near poor" group also seems to suffer most
where economic stagnation lays a heavy burden on almost
everyone (Colombia, India). Policies must be devised
which help ensure that this "near poor" group, the
bulk of the unskilled or semi-skilled labor force,
benefit from growth or at least are not overly pena-
lized from lack of it. The "near poor" are after all
the basic work force upon which equitable growth must
rely.

Issues related to the protection óf the poor and
"near poor" cannot be answered at this time. Vague
references to growth which will somehow trickle down
to lower income groups (Mexico, Brazil) is not an adequate ingredient in equity oriented growth policy.
Poverty must be dealt with explicitly. Very little
is known about who the poor are and what their needs
are and thus, policies oriented toward them are difficult to devise.

Reduction in rates of population increase can have
favorable affects on equity as well as growth. It is
the record of the countries here and of those examined
elsewhere. Equity oriented growth policies will be
more difficult to carry out if population planning is
not an integral part of the policy set. At issue is
not whether population planning is possible but how it
is to be made palatable to a variety of political,
traditional and religious tastes.

Intersectoral shifts with balance between rural
and urban equity and growth must be maintained. Wide
gaps between rural and urban incomes (Mexico and Brazil)
make overall equity more difficult to achieve. Serious
attention must be paid to creating conditions in rural
areas which raise relative incomes there and help dis-
perse growing economic activity throughout each country (Korea, Taiwan, Sri Lanka). Policy measures
which are outside the traditional realm of agricultural
policy will probably have to be invented in the areas
of rural industrialization, geographically dispersed
industrial sites, etc. These could be combined with

measures designed to reduce economic dualism by making the rural economy a part of the urban/industrial one by use of such measures as export expansion based upon agricultural raw materials (Korea, Taiwan). Policies which only stress growth of urban industry, create wide intersectoral income gaps and have an adverse impact upon overall equity (India) even if growth is forthcoming (Mexico, Brazil).

Social welfare policies will continue as a policy issue area.

There has been little clear cut distinction between welfare policies which are required because the pattern of growth has created inequities and those that are true prerequisites to further growth with equity. If growth with equity can be achieved in the first place then welfare policies of the former type will be in little demand. Welfare policies which precipitate growth with equity are not now clearly separate from any others. Clearly there are welfare policies that exert a beneficial impact upon the quantity and quality of human resources (e.g. nutritional supplements for children, health care, etc.) and therefore likely to promote both growth and equity. Policy packages are not now clearly recognized and much more work remains to be done to introduce them to development policy makers.

We have not been exhaustive, either in our case studies or in the policies which could add to our ability to provide growth with equity. We have however drawn out some of the major policy issues related to this ability. Development policy within which growth and equity are equally weighted objectives is relatively new to development economists. We believe that increased attention to the policy issues mentioned here will help move us toward satisfying this concern.

[1]Adelman and Morris (1974) do not carefully define all
the relevant independent variables but they can
be found in their other work (1973, 1967).

[2]An examination of the data compiled by Jain (1975),
probably the most comprehensive data collection
to date, reveals only 27 countries for which
comparable data exist at two points in time.
Eleven of these are developed countries. By comparable data we mean data which stems from the
same sources and collected and "processed" in the
same way.

[3]This requires the assumption that a substitution of
skilled for unskilled labor can be made without
reducing the marginal productivity of the latter.
See Ahluwalia (1976:21).

[4]This is not to say that there is no relationship
between human capital embodied in one segment
of the population at one time, and the amount
embodied in future generations of the same segment.

[5]Public goods are those where (1) once provided, no
one can be excluded from consuming them and (2)
consumption of one person does not reduce the supply available to others. The classic example of
a "pure" public good is defense. However, rarely
are public goods "pure" in the sense of meeting
the definition precisely.

[6]Adelman and Morris (1973:1967) classify a large number
of countries on a dualism scale. All countries in
our sample, with the exception of Taiwan, were classified as being of "moderate" dualism. Taiwan
was classified as slightly less dualistic than the
others.

[7]The basis for the inequality calculations are house-
holds, except in Brazil and Colombia where data are
with reference to economically active populations.

[8]This is in sharp contradiction to Adelman and Morris'
(1973) opinion that rapid economic growth leads to
both a relative and absolute decline in incomes
of the poor.

[9]See Papanek (1975) for a description of the activities of the "poor."

[10]On Korea, Mexico, and Brazil, see Looney (1975); on Taiwan see Ranis (1977); on Sri Lanka, Karunati-lake (1971); Colombia, Berry (1974); India, Mellor (1976).

[11]In 1966 for example public expenditures per capita were:

Korea - $22	Sri Lanka- $40
Taiwan- not available	Costa Rica- $61
Mexico- $35	Colombia - $33
Brazil- $33	India - $17

See Banks (1971).

[12]Recent evidence is encouraging. The IMF reports that real growth in Sri Lanka and Costa Rica for the 1970 - 75 period occured at the annual compound rates of 2.4% and 3.7% per capita respectively (International Financial Statistics, Sept. 1976).

Adelman, I. (1974) "South Korea" in Chenery et al. (1974), pp. 280-285.

Adelman, I. and C. T. Morris (1973) Economic Growth and Social Equity in Developing Countries (Stanford: Stanford University Press, 1967).

Adelman, I. and C. T. Morris (1967) Society, Politics and Economic Development (Baltimore: John Hopkins Press, 1967).

Ahluwalia, M.S. (1974) "Income Inequality: Some Dimensions of the Problem," in Chenery et al.(1974).

Ahluwalia, M.S. (1976) "Inequality, Poverty and Development," Journal of Development Economics (forthcoming).

Arndt, H.W. (1975) "Development and Equality: The Indonesian Case," World Development 3:2 and 3 (February/March). pp. 77-90.

Bardhan, P. K. (1974) "India" in Chenery et al.(1974) pp. 255-262.

Berry, A. (1974) "Changing Income Distribution Under Development: Colombia," Review of Income and Wealth 20:3 (Sept. 1974).

Chenery, H. et al. (1974) Redistribution With Growth (London: Oxford University Press).

Chenery, H. (1976) "The World Bank and Income Distribution," A public lecture at the University of Colorado, April 22, 1976, to be published in Loehr and Powelson (eds.) Economic Development, Poverty, and Income Distribution (Boulder: Westview Press).

Dewulf, L. (1974) "Do Public Expenditures Reduce Inequality," Finance and Development (Sept. 1974), pp. 20-23.

Dich, J.S. (1970) "On the Possibility of Measuring the Distribution of Personal Income," Review of Income and Wealth 16:3, pp. 265-272.

159

Fishlow, A. (1972) "Brazilian Size Distribution of Income," American Economic Review Vol. LXII No. 2 (May, 1972), pp. 391-402.

Jain, S. (1975) "Size Distribution of Income: Compilation of Data," (Baltimore: The Johns Hopkins University Press).

Jayawardena, L. (1974) "Sri Lanka" in Chenery et al. (1974), pp. 273-280.

Karunatilake, H.N.S. (1971) Economic Development in Ceylon (New York: Praeger).

Keely, A. C., J. G. Williamson and R. J. Cheetham (1972) Dualistic Economic Development (Chicago: University of Chicago Press).

Kenya, Republic of (1974) Development Plan 1974-78 (Nairobi: Government Printer).

Kravis, I. B. (1960) "International Differences in the Distribution of Income," R.E. STAT. Vol. XLII No. 4 (November), pp. 408-416.

Kumar, D. (1974) "Changes in Income Distribution and Poverty in India: A Review of the Literature," World Development Vol. 2, pp. 31-41.

Kuznets, S. (1963) "Quantitative Aspects of the Economic Growth of Nations: Distribution of Income by Size," Economic Development and Cultural Change 11:2, Part II, (January), pp. 1-79.

Loehr, W. (1977) "Economic Underdevelopment and Income Distribution: Recent Empirical Observations," a paper presented at a Conference on Economic Development and Income Distribution Sponsored by the Institute of Behavioral Science, University of Colorado (Estes Park, Colorado, April 22-24, 1976) p. 38, to be published in Loehr and Powelson (eds.) Economic Development, Poverty and Income Distribution (Boulder: Westview Press).

Loehr, W. (1976) "Notes on the Measurement of Income Distribution," Working paper (February) p. 23.

Looney, R. E. (1975) Income Distribution Policies and Economic Growth in Semi-Industrialized Countries (New York: Praeger).

McDougall, I. A. (1972) "Republic of Korea: Economic Development and Major Policy Issues," U.N. Economic Bulletin for Asia and the Far East Vol. XXIII No. 1 (June), pp. 37-60.

McLure, Jr., C. E. (1975) "The Incidence of Colombia Taxes: 1970," Economic Development and Cultural Change 24:1 (October), p. 155-83.

Mellor, J. (1976) The New Economics of Growth (Ithaca: Cornell University Press).

Oshima, H. T. (1970) "Income Inequality and Economic Growth: The Postwar Experience of Asian Countries," Malayan Economic Review Vol. XV No. 2 (October, 1970), pp. 7-41.

Oshima, H. T. (1962) "The International Comparison of Size Distribution of Family Incomes With Special Reference to Asia," R.E. STAT., Vol. XLIV, No.4 (November), pp. 439-445.

Paauw, D. S. and J. C. H. Fei (1973) The Transition in Open Dualistic Economies (New Haven: Yale Univeristy Press).

Paglin, M. (1975) "The Measurement and Trend of Inequality: A Basic Revision," American Economic Review 65:4 (Sept.), pp. 598-609.

Papanek, G. F. (1975) "The Poor of Jakarta," Economic Development and Cultural Change 24:1 (October), pp. 1-28.

Paukert, F. (1973) "Income Distribution at Different Levels of Development: A Survey of Evidence," International Labor Review 108:2-3 (August/September, 1973), pp. 97-126.

Peek, P. (1974) "Household Savings and Demographic Change in the Philippines," Malayan Economic Review 19:2 (October), pp. 86-104.

Pitchford, J. D. (1974) Population and Economic Growth (Amsterdam: North Holland Publishing Co.).

Ranis, G. (1977) "Growth and Distribution: Trade-offs or Complements," a paper presented at a Conference on Economic Development and Income Distribution sponsored by the Institute of Behavioral Science, University of Colorado (Estes Park, Colorado,

April, 22-24, 1976), to be published in Loehr and Powelson, (eds.) <u>Economic Development, Poverty and Income Distribution</u> (Boulder: Westview Press).

Ranis, G. (1974) "Taiwan"; in Chenery <u>et al.</u>(1974), pp. 285-290.

Roberti, P. (1974) "Income Distribution: A Time-series and a Cross Section Study," E. J. 84: 335 (September, 1974), pp. 629-638.

Robinson, S. (1976) "A Note on the U Hypothesis Relation Income Inequality and Economic Development," <u>American Economic Review</u> Vol. 66, No. 3 (June), pp. 437-440.

Snodgrass, D. R. (1974) "The Fiscal System as an Income Redistributor in West Malaysia," <u>Public Finance</u> 29:1, pp. 56-75.

Swamy, S. (1967) "Structural Change in the Distribution of Income by Size: The Case of India," <u>Review of Income and Wealth</u> 13:2 (June), pp. 155-173.

Thirsk, W. R. (1972) "Income Distribution, Efficiency and the Experience of Colombian Farm Mechanization," Program of Development Studies Rice University, Houston, Texas, Paper No. 33 (Fall, 1972), p. 54.

Tokman, V. E. (1974) "Redistribution of Income, Technology and Employment: An Analysis of the Industrial Sectors of Ecuador, Peru and Venezuela," <u>World Development</u> Vol. 2, pp. 49-57.

Tuckman, B. (1976) "The Green Revolution and the Distribution of Agricultural Income in Mexico," <u>World Development</u> Vol. 4, No. 1, pp. 17-24.

Weisskoff, R. (1970) "Income Distribution and Economic Growth in Puerto Rico, Argentina and Mexico," <u>Review of Income and Wealth</u> 16:4.

Wells, J. (1974) "Distribution of Earnings, Growth and the Structure of Demand in Brazil during the 1960s," <u>World Development</u> 2:1, pp. 9-24.

Yap, L. (1976) "International Migration and Economic Development in Brazil," <u>Quarterly Journal of Economics</u>, Vol. XL, No.1 (February) pp. 119-137.

VI
EFFECTIVENESS OF SOCIAL WELFARE EXPENDITURES IN SOUTH AMERICAN COUNTRIES: SOME COMPARATIVE ISSUES

Joseph E. Pluta
Defense Resource Management Education Center

SIGNIFICANCE AS A MAJOR INTERNATIONAL ISSUE

The role of public expenditures in the development process remains an area that few economists and other social scientists have endeavord to explore. Especially lacking has been a systematic format for analyzing the effectiveness of public investment in human resources within developing countries of South America.[1] In a recent overview of Latin American expenditure policy, Musgrave criticizes UN budget accounts for excluding investment in human resources from their concept of public capital formation and argues for increased investment in human capital to improve the skills of low income groups.[2] While the extent to which education causes economic growth is currently open to some debate,[3] Musgrave maintains that in Latin America:

> Available resources are too limited in many cases to sustain both redistribution and growth policies. The solution, therefore, has to be through a redistribution-oriented growth policy. This is of importance especially with regard to investment in education and health.[4]

The size and growth of social welfare budgets in developing countries has prompted some interest among development economists despite their admission that such growth is frequently due to non-economic causes.

> ...No one can say for certain how far the growth of, say education or health expenditures in any given country is due to a government's desire to placate local opinion or to its wish to conform with or emulate practices in other countries. But there can be no doubt that the emergence of world interest in these matters has made for greater pressure on governments to increase their level of spending.[5]

163

Citing data for the late 1960s, Prest shows that central
government education expenditure averaged 17.7% of the
total budget in a sample of twenty-three developing
countries as compared to only 12.8% in a sample of
eighteen industrialized nations.[6] He further argues
that, despite rapid expenditure growth in recent years,
future demand for education expenditure will grow more
quickly in many developing countries.[7] However, Latin
American governments spend a smaller portion of their
GNP for education than other religions of the world including South Asia, the Near East, the Far East (Japan excluded), and Africa (South Africa excluded), all of
which have lower per capita incomes.[8] Nevertheless,
time series data reveal that education expenditures as
a percent of GNP have grown over the past two decades
in seventeen of nineteen Latin American countries.[9]

Although the central governments of Latin America
generally spend less for health than for education and
although expenditure on the former has grown less rapidly than on the latter, the emergence of nutrition, disease control, sanitation, and other health factors in
developing countries as major world issues has rekindled
interest in the level of health expenditure. Broad comparisons on global basis reveal that in 1973 public expenditure for health averaged $3 per capita in develop-
ing countries and $134 per capita in developed countries,
outlays for health care in developing countries were
less than one-fourth of military expenditure, and, however measured, health needs rose faster in developing
countries than available resources resulting in very little progress being made in health care.[10] Data for 1972
show that 40% of the population in Latin America received
"no effective medical care of any kind" despite the generally better health record there than in other developing
regions.[11]

While public finance economists have tended to focus
on the determinants of public expenditure growth and historical analyses of aggregate and functional expenditure
patterns,[12] relatively little effort has been directed
toward the effects of expenditure patterns especially
in the areas of education and health. Yet, many domestic
social programs in developing countries have been criticized heavily for their lack of effectiveness. Despite
the problems of measuring benefits in these areas, the
growth of outlays coupled with the persistence of social
problems suggest the need for application of cost-benefit[13]
and/or cost-effectiveness analysis[14] to determine the impact of public education and health programs. Such an
analysis would have important implications for development

planning and may provide guidance to policy makers in illustrating how traditional budgeting systems might be transformed into more effective mechanisms for the allocation of public resources.[15]

MAJOR CONCLUSIONS AND SUMMARY OF FINDINGS

In presenting data on public education and health expenditure for three South American countries (Brazil, Colombia, and Ecuador), this paper offers evidence that expenditure increases were accompanied by favorable results in terms of selected output measures of effectiveness while expenditure stagnation or cutbacks were accompanied by adverse behavior of such measures. Expenditure increases were apparently most effective for education in Colombia between 1950 and the early sixties and for health in Colombia during the late fifties and between 1968-72. Perhaps more revealing is the relative ineffectiveness of education expenditure in Brazil between 1961-71, in Colombia between 1964-72, and in Ecuador between 1963-70. The same result occurred for health expenditure in Brazil between 1961-70. The poor performance of effectiveness measures in recent years during periods of expenditure cutbacks or stagnation provides an argument for the necessity of increased education and health expenditure levels in these three countries as well as for qualitative improvement in existing programs. Regarding the latter, improvements in efficiency would be of special concern. Greater levels of effectiveness might be attained from alternative allocation or organization of resources.

Recommendations for increased expenditure in developing countries must face, in addition to political constraints, the tax level constraint which frequently inhibits the introduction of new programs since many traditional demands upon government already exist. It has been argued that "...tax levels in developing countries are kept down by the limited availability of taxable bases, while in developed countries, variations in the demands for government services are, in relative terms, more important as determinants of tax levels."[16] In response to the failure of Colombia's educational system to reach large numbers of people, for example, the recent Musgrave Commission Report[17] has recommended greater use of the property tax in financing primary education where there has been a relative underinvestment in public funds when compared with higher education.

In addition to pressures to resist tax increases, further constraints upon expenditure growth and effectiveness have been inflation (especially in Brazil where outlay increases must be substantial just to match price increases), political instability (most apparent in Ecuador but not a problem in Brazil since 1964), and opposition of the upper classes in all three countries to widespread sharing of the benefits of social programs. In a study of Colombia,[18] it has been argued that there is a tendency toward government inaction except during crisis when political stability itself appears threatened. Only then are income redistribution schemes and effective public social programs likely to be forthcoming. A further problem is that recent U.S. aid to all of Latin America has emphasized technical development to accelerate trade,[19] a priority which, despite its obvious importance, is likely to have little effect upon the development of human resources.

In three countries of this study as well as elsewhere, any decision to increase education and/or health expenditure will be accompanied by difficult political decisions on either which other areas of the budget to cut or whose taxes shall be raised to finance outlay increases. If such political decisions are made, there appears to be some evidence that increases in education and health expenditure are potentially effective.

ANALYSIS OF DATA AND IMPLICATIONS FOR POLICY CHOICES

Unless otherwise indicated, all fiscal data used in this study are for actual expenditures, not provisional or projected estimates. In addition, figures are for central government expenditure only since data for lower levels of government are very scant, highly suspect, and difficult to integrate with existing central government data. On the problem of obtaining data from decentralized agencies in Latin America, Wilkie has noted:

> ....in Costa Rica, each agency conducts
> its own audit and reporting generally is
> non-standardized....(and) various officers
> of the central government are in disagree-
> ment about how many agencies even exist;...
> in Mexico...the chief investigator who com-
> piled the authoritative but incomplete fig-
> ures on projected public sector investment,
> has remarked....that even with presidential
> authority he could not persuade many of

Mexico's several hundred autonomous
and semi-autonomous agencies to open
their files on projected amounts, let
alone <u>actual</u> expenditures.[20]

Since the role of decentralized governmental units in
education and health varies in Brazil, Colombia, and
Ecuador, it must be remembered that this paper is comparing the effectiveness of expenditures made only by
central governments.[21] Despite the analytical problems
of employing this type of format, it is the author's
intention to argue that the <u>approach</u> for judging expenditure effectiveness may be useful as better and more
detailed data become available.

While some effectiveness models for social programs
have been devised for use in developed countries, the
lack of disaggregated data, especially by agency, prevented their use in this study. However, it is felt
that the descriptive, historical analysis employed here
provided evidence which does not require the use of extensive modelling procedures.

Overview of Expenditure Levels

Table I provides some measures of central government
expenditure for education and health in Brazil. Figures
prior to 1961 are available only on an aggregate basis
for the sum of education and public health and are disaggregated thereafter. Between 1948 and 1971, total central government expenditure for both functions has rarely risen above 1% of GNP. Measured as a proportion of
the total central government budget, education plus
health outlays rose from 6.4% in 1938 to 9.3% in 1971
with considerable fluctuation during the period. The
index of real per capita education and health expenditure
shows a net doubling over the period from 1948 to 1970;
but during the latter half of the 1960s, the individual
indexes for education and health both fell. Table I also
presents the conventional elasticity coefficient, computed
on a yearly basis as the percentage change in education
(or health) expenditure divided by the percentage change
in GNP. In general, the elasticity coefficients for
both education and health were greater during the early
1960s than during the latter half of the decade.

Following the methods employed in the pioneering work
of Wilkie[23] and used later for Brazil by Maneschi[24], an
effort is made to link the data of Table I (and the following two tables) with each Presidential Administration.

TABLE I
PUBLIC EXPENDITURES FOR EDUCATION AND HEALTH[1], BRAZIL

Year[2]	$\frac{E}{GNP}$	$\frac{PH}{GNP}$	$\frac{E}{G}$[3]	$\frac{PH}{G}$	Index of $\frac{\overline{EP}}{pop}$[4]	Index of $\frac{\overline{PHP}}{pop}$	President[5]	E_E/GNP[6]	E_{PH}/GNP[7]
1938			6.4%				Vargas		
1939			6.1%						
1940			5.8%						
1941			5.6%						
1942			6.3%						
1943			4.8%						
1944			6.7%						
1945			4.7%						
1946			5.6%				Dutra		
1947			8.2%						
1948	0.8%		9.6%						
1949	0.9%		9.7%		100			2.12	
1950	1.0%		10.5%		130			1.40	
1951	0.8%		9.8%		153		Vargas–Cafe Filho	-0.19	
1952	0.8%		9.8%		133			1.11	
1953	1.0%		10.3%		120			2.14	
1954	1.0%		9.9%		143			0.99	
1955	0.8%		8.2%		150			0.16	
1956	0.8%		6.7%		126		Kubitschek	1.05	
1957	1.0%		8.9%		128			2.43	
1958	1.1%		9.8%		156			1.60	
1959	1.1%		10.8%		181			0.98	
1960	1.2%		10.8%		175			1.30	
1961					177			0.76	

E/GNP: 0.8% — 0.3%
E/G: 6.4% — 2.8%
Index of EP/pop: 119 — 52
PH/GNP: 0.8% — 0.3%
PH/G: 6.4% — 2.8%

168

TABLE I
(continued)

Year[2]	$\frac{E}{GNP}$	$\frac{PH}{GNP}$	$\frac{E}{G}$[3]	$\frac{PH}{G}$	Index of $\frac{Ep}{pop}$[4]	Index of $\frac{PHp}{pop}$	President[5]	E_E/GNP[6]	E_{PH}/GNP[7]
1962	0.8%	0.3%	6.8%	3.1%	140	63	Quadros-	0.97	1.08
1963	0.6%	0.3%	5.5%	3.2%	109	64	Goulart	0.52	1.00
1964	0.7%	0.3%	5.8%	2.5%	131	56		1.40	0.71
1965	0.1%	0.3%	9.0%	2.7%	193	58	Castello	2.46	1.23
1966	1.9%	0.4%	7.4%	3.3%	147	66	Branco	0.33	1.57
1967	0.8%	0.4%	7.2%	3.0%	141	60		0.87	0.67
1968	0.8%	0.3%	7.1%	2.5%	155	55	Costa e Silva	1.01	0.45
1969	0.9%	0.2%	6.2%	1.6%	170	44		1.19	0.07
1970	0.8%	0.2%	4.8%	1.1%	160	37	Garrastazu	0.53	0.14
1971[8]	0.7%	0.3%	6.5%	2.8%			Medici		

$\bar{X}_{61/62-69/70} = 1.03$ $\bar{X}_{61/62-69/70} = 0.77$
$\bar{X}_{48/49-60/61} = 1.22$

[1] Budgetary data for this table and those which follow taken from UN, Statistical Yearbook, selected issues. GNP, population, and cost of living deflator taken from IMF, International Financial Statistics, selected issues.

[2] Data for 1938-1960 are for the sum of education and public health since figures for these years are not available on a disaggregated basis.

[3] Education as a percent of the total central government budget.

[4] Index of real per capita expenditure, 1948=100. Prior to 1961, index is constructed for the sum of education and public health (both in real per capita terms). Disaggregated data for 1961-1970 are comparable to data for previous years, e.g. the index for the sum of E and PH in 1961=171 (119+52).

[5] Duration of term is intended to correspond to the first and last budget for which each executive was responsible.

[6] Expenditure elasticity for education.

[7] Expenditure elasticity for public health.

[8] Estimate

The purpose of such an exercise is to present an admittedly rough picture of budget proportions at the beginning and end of each President's term of office and to draw some conclusions regarding the influence each executive had on the structure of the budget.[25] Executive power in budget policy (and in economic policy, in general) is much stronger in South America than in industrialized countries such as the U.S. where a greater amount of "locked in" expenditure inhibits a new President's influence on the budget. In addition, political rhetoric in South America has for some time promised substantial investment in human resources. In light of both of these facts, it is believed that the analysis presented here will shed light on what the record has been. In Brazil, the aggregate figures for education plus health stayed relatively constant during the last eight years of Vargas' first term, rose considerably under Dutra, remained constant again during Vargas' second term completed by Cafe Filho, and saw a second marked increase under Kubitschek. During the 1960s, the only appreciable rise in the indexes for education occurred under Castello Branco. Under every other executive during the 1960s, Brazillian education expenditures stagnated. Public health expenditure also stagnated throughout the decade and were even cut back drastically under Garrastazu Medici.

Table II presents similar data for Colombia, although expenditure patterns in education reveal substantial growth especially when compared with the relative stagnation of expenditure in Brazil. Education rose from 0.5% of GNP in 1950 to 2.2% in 1971 and from 8.7% to 15.9% of the total budget over the same period. As a proportion of the budget, education in 1971 was over twice its 1938 level. Perhaps more impressive was the more than ninefold growth in real per capita education expenditures between 1948 and 1970. In addition, the mean elasticity coefficient for the 1950-1970 period was 1.62, with a higher proportion of figures greater than one occurring during the 1960s.

Table II also reveals somewhat erratic behavior in the pattern of Colombian public health expenditures. While moving from 0.7% of GNP in 1953 to 1.1% in 1971, health expenditure fluctuated throughout the period. A similar picture is given by the figures for health as a percent of the total budget. While this figure moved from 8.5% in 1953 to 7.8% in 1971, it was actually much lower during most of the period except for the start of the decade. The index of real per capita health expenditure fluctuated during the period before reaching twice its 1953 level in 1970. Depsite the unspectacular movement in these measures of health expenditure, the

TABLE II

PUBLIC EXPENDITURES FOR EDUCATION AND HEALTH, COLOMBIA

Year	$\frac{E}{GNP}$	$\frac{PH}{GNP}$	$\frac{E}{G}$	$\frac{PH}{G}$	Index of $\frac{E}{pop}$[1] 1948=100	Index of $\frac{PH}{pop}$[1] 1953=100	President	$E_{E/GNP}$	$E_{PH/GNP}$
1938			6.9%				Santos		
1939			7.0%						
1940			5.8%						
1941			5.7%						
1942			4.2%						
1943			4.2%						
1944			5.5%				Lopez-Lleras		
1945			6.1%						
1946			5.8%						
1947			5.5%						
1948			4.8%		100				
1949			5.9%		114		Ospina		
1950	0.5%		8.7%		139			0.16	
1951	0.4%		7.5%		128		Gomez	0.58	
1952	0.4%		6.0%		134			1.75	
1953	0.4%	0.7%	5.5%	8.5%	143	100		2.40	
1954	0.5%		6.5%		186		Rojas	0.16	
1955	0.5%		4.2%		184			1.86	-0.39[3]
1956	0.6%	0.4%	6.8%	5.0%	203	67		-0.05	-0.32
1957	0.5%	0.3%	6.6%	4.6%	170	53		4.92	2.23
1958	0.7%	0.4%	9.3%	4.9%	255	60	Lleras-Camargo	0.18	9.46
1959	0.6%	0.8%	9.5%	11.5%	237	127		2.15	1.83
1960	0.7%	0.9%	8.7%	10.3%	283	147		5.87	0.26
1961	1.2%	0.8%	10.7%	7.3%	448	135		0.29	-3.78
1962	1.1%	0.4%	13.6%	5.1%	438	72			

171

TABLE II

(continued)

Year	$\frac{E}{GNP}$	$\frac{PH}{GNP}$	$\frac{E}{G}$	$\frac{PH}{G}$	Index of $\frac{E\bar{p}}{pop}$ 1948=100	Index of $\frac{PH\bar{p}}{pop}$ 1953=100	President	$E_{E/GNP}$	$E_{PH/GNP}$
1963	1.3%	0.4%	13.6%	4.6%	495	74		2.04	1.49
1964	1.4%	0.4%	17.1%	4.8%	548	69		1.28	0.50
1965	1.3%	0.3%	16.9%	4.5%	550	65	Valencia	0.56	0.07
1966	1.3%	0.4%	15.7%	5.0%	542	77		1.07	2.28
1967	1.3%	0.4%	14.9%	4.9%	537	78		0.83	0.98
1968	1.5%	0.4%	13.3%	3.9%	642	83		1.94	1.06
1969	1.7%	0.8%	13.9%	6.1%	763	148	Lleras-Restrepo	2.40	7.01
1970	2.0%	1.0%	14.9%	7.8%	921	214		1.92	3.43
1971	2.2%	1.1%	15.9%	7.8%				1.80	1.35
1972[2]	1.7%	0.8%	15.7%	7.8%					
								X=1.62	X=1.72

[1]Population figures for 1950-1967 taken from OECD, National Accounts of Less Developed Countries, Paris, July, 1968.

[2]Estimate.

[3]Figure computed from data for 1953 and 1956.

mean elasticity coefficient for health over the 1953-
1971 period was still 1.72. However, here too the
figure showed a considerable amount of variability.

While education grew steadily under the administration of Lopez, Lleras, and Ospina, it fell under Gomez
and stayed relatively constant under Rojas before the
considerable increases under Lleras Camargo. These
increases were the result of the 1957 Constitutional
Reform which assigned a minimum of 10% of the national
revenue to education, improvements in salaries and
training for teachers under the Alliance for Progress,
and expansion of facilities for vocational education.
Under the rule of Valencia, growth in education expenditure was quite modest although it has begun to turn
upward in recent years under Llera Restrepo. Public
health expenditure was actually cut in half under Rojas
before considerable increases and then a downturn under
Lleras Camargo. More recently, public health expenditure stayed virtually consistent during the terms of
Valencia and began to turn upward under Lleras Restrepo.[26]

Data for Ecuador are available only from 1951 to
1971 and are presented in Table III. During this twenty year period, education rose from 1.1% of GNP to 2.8%
and from 15.2% of the total budget to 19.3%. During the
same period, the index of real per capita education expenditures more than tripled while, despite some variability in annual figures, the mean elasticity coefficient
was very high at 2.10.

Public health expenditure stayed relatively constant
as a percent of GNP and actually fell as a proportion of
the budget from 5.1% in 1951 to 2.8% in 1971. The index
of real per capita public health expenditure fluctuated
considerably over the period but failed to grow appreciably. Despite a mean elasticity coefficient of 1.45, a
larger number of annual figures, especially for recent
years, were inelastic rather than elastic.

Due to frequent changes in the Presidency, especially during the 1960s, it is difficult to organize the
data meaningfully for purposes of comparing executive
influence upon the budget. Table III reveals that the
longest terms of office to which data can be fitted are
the four year periods of Velasco Ibarra (1952-56) and
Ponce Enriquez (1957-60), and here figures do not indicate
noteworthy changes. It is unfortunate that data do not
extend back prior to 1951 since Galo Plaza Laso is generally credited with inaugurating a period of economic
and political stability. Therefore, the limited length

173

of time series for earlier periods coupled with general political instability in later years prevent detailed synthesis of executive tenure and budgetary patterns for Ecuador. However, one may suggest at this stage that a major constraint upon the effectiveness of social programs during the 1960s has been political instability.

Measures of Effectiveness

While Table III illustrates   general movements in expenditure patterns under each Presidential Administration, it remains to be seen to what extent increases in such expenditure have been effective. A number of hierarchies of effectiveness measures have been developed[27] which have largely focussed on the distinction between input measures used for administrative purposes and output of benefit measures. The data assembled for this study include both types of measures which may be distinguished in the following manner. Regarding education, the output measures presented below include national figures for the percentage of illiteracy, circulation of daily newspapers per thousand people, per capita newsprint consumption, number of books published, and number of books translated. The assumption is made that an increase in any of the last four of these indicates that a larger number of people are reading more and therefore putting their education to some use. Input measures include the number of teachers, educational institutions, and students enrolled as well as the student-teacher ratio. Increases in any of these may indicate something about effectiveness but have little meaning if there is no improvement in output measures. For public health, output measures presented include infant mortality, foetal and perinatal mortality, and the number of reported cases of selected diseases.[28] Input measures employed are the number of physicians, hospital beds, dentists, nurses, pharmacists, and hospital establishments as well as population per physician and population per hospital bed. It is hoped that the selection of multiple output effectiveness proxies avoids the problems of suboptimization and displacement of bad effects to other areas which are frequently noted in the literature.[29] Expenditure effectiveness in terms of the above measures[30] may be analyzed as follows.

Public Education Expenditures. Between 1948 and 1960 in Brazil, the aggregate figure for education plus public health (in Table I) rose slightly only during the late 1950s under Kubitschek. Because the figures are not disaggregated, it is difficult to comment on the effectiveness of education and public health during this

174

TABLE III

PUBLIC EXPENDITURES FOR EDUCATION AND HEALTH, ECUADOR

Year	$\frac{E}{GNP}$	$\frac{PH}{GNP}$	$\frac{E}{G}$	$\frac{PH}{G}$	Index of $\frac{Ep}{pop}$ 1951=100	Index of $\frac{PHp}{pop}$ 1951=100	President	$E_{E/GNP}$	$E_{PH/GNP}$
1951	1.1%	0.4%	15.2%	5.1%	100	100	Plaza Laso	-0.10	0.22
1952	1.0%	0.4%	13.5%	4.8%	93	97		5.30	2.22
1953	1.2%	0.4%	13.7%	4.2%	119	107		-0.37	1.20
1954	1.1%	0.4%	9.3%	3.4%	107	115	Velasco	6.00	2.29
1955	1.3%	0.4%	10.5%	3.2%	136	123	Ibarra	3.73	-1.53
1956	1.4%	0.4%	11.4%	3.2%	147	123		-0.69	0.34
1957	1.2%	0.4%	10.8%	3.3%	135	122		3.47	2.53
1958	1.3%	0.4%	12.4%	3.7%	144	127	Ponce	0.13	-8.87
1959	1.3%	0.2%	11.5%	2.0%	140	72	Enriquez	2.77	11.76
1960	1.5%	0.4%	11.1%	3.1%	162	133	Ibarra	3.14	-0.79
1961	1.7%	0.4%	11.9%	2.5%	184	117	Arosemena	3.02	4.72
1962	1.8%	0.5%	15.3%	3.5%	201	137	Monroy	2.45	2.77
1963	2.1%	0.5%	18.9%	4.5%	234	164	Military	0.86	0.33
1964	2.1%	0.8%	16.0%	3.6%	236	157	Junta	1.21	11.87
1965	2.1%	0.4%	16.2%	6.0%	241	266	Indabura	1.37	-4.03
1966	2.2%	0.4%	17.1%	3.4%	250	146	Arosemena	1.37	0.11
1967	2.3%	0.4%	18.2%	3.2%	266	137		4.60	0.29
1968	3.0%	0.4%	20.2%	2.4%	367	131	Gomez	1.22	-0.87
1969	3.1%	0.3%	20.1%	2.0%	372	110		0.40	2.88
1970	2.8%	0.4%	17.6%	2.6%	371	165	Velasco		
1971	2.8%	0.4%	19.3%	2.8%			Ibarra	$\overline{X}=2.10$	$\overline{X}=1.45$

[1]Estimate.

175

period. Between 1961 and 1971, however, education expenditure remained relatively constant as a percent of GNP, as a proportion of the total budget, and in real per capita terms, although there is some evidence of an increase in 1965 under Castello Branco (see Table I). Table IV presents measures of effectiveness for education in Brazil. Looking first at the output measures, illiteracy fell only slightly between 1960-72 after falling appreciably between 1950-60, the circulation of newspapers per thousand people and newsprint consumption per capita fell during the sixties after previously rising, and neither the number of books published nor the number of books translated was up substantially from the 1960 level. The less significant input measures reveal that the number of teachers, educational institutions, and students enrolled have all increased during the sixties while student-teacher ratios fell markedly between 1962 and 1970. The evidence appears to indicate that the Brazilian central government has not been spending money on education and the output measures of effectiveness have registered little, if any, improvement.[31]

On the other hand, one can argue that in Colombia the increase in education expenditures between, say, 1950 and the early 1960s was effective. Expressed as a percent of GNP, in real per capita terms, or as a proportion of the budget, education rose considerably during this period with the first two indexes more than doubling (see Table II). Table V provides measures of effectiveness for Colombian education. The percent of illiteracy fell from 37.7% in 1950 to 27.1% in 1964, per capita newsprint consumption rose, and there was a considerable increase in the number of books published annually. Circulation of daily newspapers per 1000 people was the only output measure that did not register an increase during this period. All input measures -- number of teachers, educational establishments, students enrolled, and student-teacher ratios -- showed improvement.

However, between 1964 and 1972, Table II reveals that Colombian education expenditures increased only slightly as a percent of GNP (and that only in recent years) and actually fell as a proportion of the budget (although rising in real per capita terms). During this period, illiteracy was not reduced, newsprint consumption per capita fell, few books were translated, and the number of books published annualy rose slightly. Of the output measures, only the per capita circulation of daily newspapers rose appreciably. Even the circulation of nondailies fell between 1967 and 1971.[32] In the input measures, however, the usual rise in the number of

teachers and students enrolled as well as improvement
in student-teacher ratios may be noted. One can conclude from the evidence on Colombia that education
expenditures since that time have produced no noteworthy improvements in the measurable output indexes of
effectiveness.[33]

While education expenditure in Ecuador was fairly
constant during the early 1950s, a major increase occurred in all three indexes between 1959 and 1963 (see
Table III). The effectiveness measures of Table VI
show a substantial decline in the illiteracy rate between
1950 and 1962 (44.3% to 32.5%) and slight increases in
per capita newsprint consumption and in daily newspaper
circulation per thousand people. Input measures again
show rises in the number of teachers, educational institutions, and students enrolled with a slight improvement
in student-teacher ratios. The increase in education
expenditure was less pronounced between 1963 and 1970
with slight increases as a percent of GNP and in real per
capita terms. Education as a percent of the total budget remained relatively constant over this period. The
output measures reveal that, while newsprint consumption
per capita increased somewhat, the percent of illiteracy
stayed constant between 1962 and 1972 and daily newspaper
circulation per thousand people actually fell.[34] Input
measures show increases in the number of teachers and
students enrolled and some improvement in student-teacher
ratios. While the evidence for Ecuador is less convincing
than for Brazil and Colombia, a case may still be made
that relatively noteworthy increases in education expenditure during the late fifties and early sixties were
more effective than modest expenditure increases during
the mid and late sixties.

Public Health Expenditures. Table I showed that public health expenditure in Brazil declined between 1961-
70 whether measured as a percent of GNP, as a percent of
the total budget, or in real per capita terms. In addition, the mean elasticity coefficient for health was
less than one during this period. Table VII presents
effectiveness measures for health in Brazil. During the
1960s when health expenditure declined, there were rather
large increases in reported cases of hepatitis, measles,
polio, and tetanus, an increase in malaria during the
mid sixties before reported cases declined, and numerous
cases of tuberculosis as late as 1968. Of those diseases
for which data are available, only the number of reported
cases of typhoid declined. All input measures, however,
showed improvement. It is not possible to draw strong
conclusions from infant mortality figures since only the

177

first and last figures did not improve mortality and
foetal and perinatal mortality in the State of Guanabara declined substantially during the late 1950s when
Kubitschek increased social welfare expenditure. Once
again, a case may be made that expenditure increases
were effective while expenditure cutbacks produced
adverse effects in terms of effectiveness measures.

A similar case may be made with regard to public
health expenditure in Colombia. Between 1956-60, health
expenditure rose substantially under Llera Camargo according to all three indexes (see Table II). The effectiveness measures of Table VIII show that between, say,
1956-61, both infant mortality and foetal and perinatal
mortality declined. Input measures during this period
show increases in the number of physicians and dentists
and improvement in population per physician. Reference
to Table II also reveals that, after initial declines
in the early sixties, all three indexes of health expenditure rose in the late sixties and early seventies.
According to Table VIII, infant mortality improved during
the sixties but foetal and perinatal mortality grew worse.
However, nine of thirteen diseases listed showed improvement in the number of reported cases during the sixties.
Although there is some mix in the evidence drawn from
input measures, effectiveness of health expenditure in
Colombia appears to parallel the general pattern developed thus far.

Table III presented evidence of either stagnation or
a decline in health expenditure in Ecuador between 1951-
59. The effectiveness measures presented in Table IX
reveal virtually no improvement in infant mortality between, say, 1950-59 and a worsening of foetal and perinatal mortality during the second half of the decade of
the fifties. All three input measures, however, show
improvement. Despite the increase in Ecuadorian public
health expenditure between 1961-65, expenditures when
measured over the decade as a whole stagnated. Table IX
indicates only modest improvement (especially when compared with Colombia) in infant mortality until the 1970s,
little if any improvement in foetal and perinatal mortality, a worsening in the number of cases of malaria and
leprosy, little improvement in rabies, but some evidence
of improvement in diphtheria, polio, tuberculosis, and
typhoid. For whatever value they hold, the input measures
show public health expenditure in Ecuador to be relatively
ineffective during the sixties. In addition, there was a
fall in the number of pharmacists and no noteworthy change
in hospital beds, population per bed, and number of dentists. The only input measures to register improvement

TABLE IV

MEASURES OF EFFECTIVENESS FOR EDUCATION IN BRAZIL

Year	Newsprint Consumption		Daily Newspapers			% illiteracy[1]
	1000 metric tons	per capita kilograms	No.	Circulation		
				Total	per 1000 pop.	
1935-39	52.3	1.4				
1946-50	81.6	1.6				
1950-54	134.1	2.5				
1955-59	196.5	3.1				
1948						
1949						
1950						50.5%(-13)
1951						
1952						
1953	146.2	2.6				
1954	161.1	2.8	217	2932	51	
1955	167.6	2.9	235	2975	50	
1956	175.9	2.9				
1957	222.5	3.6	290	3879	63	
1958	204.2	3.2				
1959	214.9	3.3				
1960	230.3	3.2	291	3837	54	39.4%(-17)
1961	211.1	2.9				
1962	198.4	2.6	264	4009	53	
1963	199.1	2.6	255	4213	54	
1964	184.3	2.3	227	2606	32	
1965	178.5	2.2				
1966	183.9	2.2	248	2764	33	
1967	204.9	2.4	241	3110	36	
1968	251.7	2.9	250	3250	37	
1969	223.2	2.5	257	3393	36	
1970	251.8	2.7				
1971	223.2	2.3	261	3498	37	
1972	228.2	2.3				35.0%(61-16)

TABLE IV
(continued)

Year	No. of books published	No. of books translated	Teachers 1000	Educational Institutions	Students Enrolled 1000	Student Teacher ratio[3]
1935-39						
1946-50						
1950-54						
1955-59						
1948					4498	
1949					4719	
1950					5029	
1951					5232	
1952					5390	
1953	3000				5676	
1954	3390		231	82189	6071	26.3
1955	3385	208	233	81161	5718	24.5
1956		395			5844	
1957	4659	541			7430	
1958		625			7910	
1959	5337	502			8320	
1960	5377	464	342	111064	8750	25.6
1961	3911	444	375	112685	9245	24.6
1962		18	404	116025	10159	25.1
1963	5133	730	450	122619	10698	23.8
1964	4812	416	498	131509	11659	23.4
1965		497			12234	
1966		629	744		13359	18.0
1967		92			14208	
1968			892		15432	17.3
1969	6392	786	1008		16270	16.1
1970		427	1134		17362	15.3
1971						
1972						

TABLE IV
(continued)

Source: Unless otherwise indicated, data in this table and in those
which follow taken from UN, Statistical Yearbook, selected issues
1956-73.

[1] % of adult population (over 15) unable either to read or write. First
number in parentheses indicates world rank (132 countries); second number indicates rank among the 23 nations of Latin America. 1972 figures
taken from Ruth Leger Sivard, World Military and Social Expenditures,
1974, New York: Institute for World Order, 1974, p. 22, Figures for 1950
and 1960 taken from Kenneth Ruddle and Kathleen Barrows (eds.), Statistical Abstract of Latin America, 1972, UCLA Latin American Center, Jan.
1974, p. 164.

[2] Data for this and subsequent tables taken from James W. Wilkie,
Statistics and National Policy, UCLA Latin American Center, 1974,
p. 192.

[3] Computed by dividing total number of students enrolled at all
levels (e.g. primary, secondary, vocational, etc.) by total
number of teachers at all levels.

TABLE V

MEASURES OF EFFECTIVENESS FOR EDUCATION IN COLOMBIA

Year	Newsprint Consumption		Daily Newspapers			% illiteracy
	100 metric tons	per capita kilograms	No.	Circulation		
				Total	per 1000 pop	
1935-39	6.3	0.8				
1946-50	14.3	1.3				
1950-54	17.3	1.5				
1955-59	22.8	1.7				
1948						
1949						
1950						37.7% (-9)
1951						
1952						
1953	17.4	1.4				
1954	19.0	1.5	33	728	59	
1955	21.0	1.7				
1956	28.0	2.2	37	778	60	
1957	23.2	1.8	37	740	56	
1958	20.9	1.5	36	797	59	
1959	21.6	1.6				
1960	34.1	2.4				
1961	37.3	2.6	32	799	55	
1962	45.6	3.1	37	847	56	
1963	39.6	2.6	26	781	52	
1964	41.7	2.4				27.1% (-10)
1965	45.3	2.5				
1966	52.0	2.8				
1967	48.7	2.5	25	1021	53	
1968	42.2	2.1				
1969	43.6	2.1				
1970	49.7	2.4				
1971	40.8	1.9	36	2369	109	
1972	40.8	1.7				27.0% (53-13)

TABLE   V
(continued)

Year	No. of books published	No. of books translated	Teacher 1000	Educational Institutions	Students Enrolled	Student Teacher Ratio
1935–39						
1946–50						
1950–54						
1955–59						
1948					840	
1949					835	
1950					905	
1951					986	
1952					1039	
1953					1176	
1954			44	16403	1252	28.5
1955	439				1378	
1956			53	18832	1477	27.9
1957			56	19278	1568	28.0
1958			61	20559	1722	28.2
1959			64	21510	1814	28.3
1960			75	22572	1956	26.1
1961			79	23901	2093	26.5
1962			86	25303	2290	26.6
1963			94	26521	2407	26.5
1964			100	27508	2625	26.3
1965	709		137		2737	20.0
1966			149		2956	20.0
1967			160		3212	20.1
1968			221		3385	15.3
1969		122				
1970		15				
1971						
1972	848					

TABLE VI

MEASURES OF EFFECTIVENESS FOR EDUCATION IN ECUADOR

Year	Newsprint Consumption		Daily Newspapers			% illiteracy
	1000 metric tons	per capita kilograms	No.	circulation Total	per 1000 pop.	
1935–39	2.0	0.9				
1946–50	3.4	1.1				
1950–54	4.8	1.4				
1955–59	6.4	1.6				
1948						
1949						
1950						44.3% (−13)
1951						
1952			24	167	50	
1953	3.4	1.0				
1954						
1955	7.4	2.0				
1956	5.4	1.4				
1957	6.3	1.6				
1958	6.5	1.6				
1959	8.0	1.9				
1960	8.6	2.0				
1961	7.8	1.8	24	251	56	
1962	7.6	1.7	27	240[1]	52[1]	32.5% (−12)
1963	8.8	1.9				
1964	9.7	2.0				
1965	11.0	2.2	23	241	47	
1966	12.4	2.3	23	241	45	
1967	11.3	2.0	23	241	44	
1968	12.3	2.2				
1969	16.7	2.3	25	250	42	
1970	16.7	2.7	25	250	41	
1971	16.7	2.7	22	283	45	
1972	16.7	2.5				32.0% (60–15)

[1]Circulation figures refer to 18 dailies only.

TABLE VI
(continued)

Year	No. of books published	No. of books translated	Teacher/1000	Educational Institutions	Students Enrolled	Student Teacher Ratio
1935-39						
1946-50						
1950-54						
1955-59					337	
1948					352	
1949					376	
1950					389	
1951					397	
1952			14	4175	440	31.4
1953						
1954			16	4628	512	32.0
1955					544	
1956			17	4996	562	33.1
1957					594	
1958			21	5754	636	30.3
1959					673	
1960			24	6145	698	29.1
1961			26	6334	752	28.9
1962			29	6603	806	27.8
1963			31		876	28.3
1964			42	7331	933	22.2
1965			46		1001	21.8
1966			49		1068	21.8
1967			52		1126	21.7
1968			57		1203	21.1
1969						
1970						
1971						
1972	32					

TABLE VII
MEASURES OF EFFECTIVENESS FOR HEALTH IN BRAZIL

Year	Infant Mortality per 1000[1]	Foetal and perinatal mortality per 1000[2]	Physicians[3] 1000	Pop. per physician[4]	Dentists 1000
1940-50	170.0				
1945-49	117.5				
1950-54	107.3	50.7			
1955-59	107.6	41.7			
1948	115.9				
1949	108.6				
1950	109.1		17.4	3000	11.0
1951	107.5				
1952	104.9				
1953	101.1				
1954	113.5		23.2	2517	15.5
1955	112.5				
1956	120.5				
1957	107.5	42.1			
1958	105.0		30.5	2154	
1959	94.4		27.1	2500	
1960	70.0	28.5	26.4	2700	
1961			20.2	3620	
1962			29.8	2483	
1963					
1964			34.3	2290	22.0
1965					
1966			39.7	2090	24.3
1967			35.5	2410	
1968					
1969			47.3	1953	26.6
1970			46.1	2028	
1971					
1972	94.0		53.0	1870	

[1]Deaths under one year per thousand live births. 1972 figure taken from Sivard, p. 22 and is for the entire country. All other data taken from UN, Demographic Yearbook, selected issues 1955-72. Figures for 1945-60 are for the state of Guanabara only. The figure for 1940-50 is an estimated average annual rate for the decade for all of Brazil.

[2]Number of late foetal deaths per 1000 live births. "Late foetal deaths" are those of at least 28 weeks gestation. Data for Brazil are for the state of Guanabara only. Reliability and comparability of these data and those in the tables which follow are known to be greatly affected by

TABLE VII
(continued)

Year	Pharmacists	Hospital beds 1000	Pop. per bed	Nurses	Hospital Establish-ments
1940-50					
1945-49					
1950-54					
1955-59					
1948					
1949					
1950					
1951					
1952					
1953					
1954	12202				
1955					
1956					
1957					
1958					
1959					
1960					
1961					
1962					
1963					
1964					
1965		232.3	350		2850
1966	8737	228.6	367	23.6	
1967		294.1	294	26.0	3238
1968		321.5	274		3397
1969	14026			28.0	
1970		354.4	264	32.7	3830

2(continued) incomplete or irregular registration of foetal deaths, and/or live births, and by variations in definitions. Data are taken from Ruddle and Barrows, p. 88.

3 1972 figure taken from Sivard, p. 18. 1962 figure taken from C. Paul Roberts and Takako Kohda Karplus (eds.), Statistical Abstract of Latin America, 1968, p. 110. 1959 figure is from Norris B. Lyle and Richard A. Calman, Statistical Abstract of Latin America, 1965, p. 41.

TABLE VII
(continued)

NUMBER OF REPORTED CASES OF SELECTED DISEASES[5]

	Infectious Hepatitis[6]	Malaria	Measles	Acute Poliomyelitis	Tetanus	Tuberculosis	Typhoid[7]
1960-64		72060					4965[8]
1965		110306	5325	541			
1966	808	108630	4432	562	1076		
1968	4439	79357	36220	1585	3097	39813	2722
1970							

[4]The figure for 1972 is from Sivard, p. 22.

[5]1963 data taken from Ruddle and Hamour, Statistical Abstract of Latin America, 1970, pp. 107-109; data for 1966, 1965, and 1960-64, taken from Roberts and Karplus, pp. 113-119.

[6]State of Sao Paulo only.

[7]Includes cases of paratyphoid fever. Data for Brazil are from the state of Guanabara only and capitals of other states and territories. Source: Ruddle and Barrows, p. 144.

[8]Data is for 1963.

188

TABLE VIII

MEASURES OF EFFECTIVENESS FOR HEALTH IN COLOMBIA

Year	Infant Mortality per 1000[1]	Foetal and perinatal mortality per 1000	Physicians 1000	Pop. per Physician	Dentists 1000
1920–24	104.8				
1925–29	132.8				
1930–34	119.7				
1935–39	115.7				
1940–44	152.0				
1945–49	141.8				
1950–54	113.3	15.0			
1955–59	100.9	15.5			
1960–64	89.9				
1946	150.4				
1947	139.7				
1948	136.1		3.2	3400	
1949	134.1				
1950	123.9				
1951	119.9				
1952	110.7		4.2	2800	2.4
1953	111.0				
1954	102.7				
1955	104.2				
1956	103.8				
1957	100.4	15.1	4.5	3118	1.5
1958	100.0				
1959	96.9				
1960	99.8	11.3	6.0	2400	1.7
1961	89.6				
1962	89.6				
1963	88.2	17.7	7.5	2270	3.4
1964	83.3	17.0			
1965	82.4	17.7	7.3	2470	3.4
1967	80.0	22.8			
1968	78.3	23.3	8.7	2221	
1969	70.4	24.2			3.4[4]
1970			9.5	2161	2.7
1971					
1972	76.0		11.0	2030	

189

TABLE VIII
(continued)

Year	Pharmacists	Hospital beds 1000	Pop. per bed	Nurses	Hospital Establish-ments
1920–24					
1925–29					
1930–34					
1035–39					
1940–44					
1945–49					
1950–54					
1955–59					
1960–64					
1946					
1947					
1948					
1949					
1950					
1951					
1952	2464			0.5	
1953					
1954					
1955					
1956					
1957					
1958					
1959					
1960		44.7^5	345		
1961					
1962					
1963	1213				
1964					
1965				5.1	
1966		46.0	400		647
1967		46.1	417	7.1	671
1968					
1969	1200			19.7	
1970		47.3	446		741
1971		46.2	472		773
1972					

TABLE VIII
(continued)

NUMBER OF REPORTED CASES OF SELECTED DISEASES

	Diphtheria	Gonococcal Infection	Infectious Hepatitis	Influenza	Leprosy	Malaria	Measles
1960-64	1021	47331		73266		21245	36756
1963							
1965	644	28955		90828		18888	43332
1966	800	37273		82155	990	22148	22243
1968	641	37273	641		246	14328	21890
1970							
1971							

	Acute poliomyelitis	Syphilis[6]	Tetanus	Tuberculosis	Typhoid[7]	Whooping Cough	Rabies
1960-64	215	10166			11971		137
1963	330	9789					
1965	489	16704	754	14617	9084	18095	
1966	261	16530	527	16206	7024	17614	
1968					6923		
1970		15399					
1971							43

191

TABLE VIII
(continued)

[1]1972 figure taken from Sivard, p. 22. All other data from UN, Demographic Yearbook.

[2]1972 figure from Sivard, p. 18; 1963 figure from Roberts and Karplus, p. 110; 1960 figure from Lyle and Calman, p. 41.

[3]1972 figure from Sivard, p. 22.

[4]Figure from Ruddle and Hamour, Statistical Abstract of Latin America, 1969, p. 125.

[5]From Lyle and Calman, p. 43.

[6]Data for 1963 and 1970 from Ruddle and Barrows, p. 144.

[7]Includes paratyphoid. 1963 and 1970 figures from Ibid.

TABLE IX

MEASURES OF EFFECTIVENESS FOR HEALTH IN ECUADOR

Year	Infant Mortality per 1000[1]	Foetal and Perinatal mortality per 1000	Physicians[2] 1000	Pop. per Physician[3]	Dentists 1000
1925-29	170.1				
1930-34	146.9				
1935-39	149.3				
1940-44	141.9				
1945-49	127.5				
1950-54	111.7	25.9			
1955-59	106.8	28.5			
1960-64	96.1				
1946	132.8		0.8	3500	0.2
1947	122.0				
1948	122.4				
1949	115.2				
1950	109.7				
1951	109.5				
1952	109.8		0.9	3800	0.2
1953	112.3				
1954	115.8				
1955	112.8				
1956	101.8				
1957	106.0	30.9	1.3	3023	0.4
1958	105.8				
1959	107.7				
1960	100.0	22.4	1.7	2600	0.5
1961	96.2				
1962	95.9		1.6	2800	0.5
1963	94.6	21.7			
1964	94.0	22.8	0.9	5290	0.5
1965	93.0	21.0	1.7	3030	
1966	90.4	17.8			
1967	87.3	19.1	2.0	2767	0.6
1968	86.1	19.3			
1969	91.0	21.4			
1970	76.6		2.1	2929	0.3
1971					
1972	76.0		2.1	3030	

193

TABLE IX
(continued)

Year	Pharmacists	Hospital beds 1000	Pop. per bed	Nurses 1000	Hospital Establish- ments
1925-29					
1930-34					
1935-39					
1940-44					
1945-49					
1950-54					
1955-59					
1960-64					
1946	246			0.1	
1947					
1948					
1949					
1950					
1951					
1952					
1953					
1954					
1955					
1956					
1957				0.2	
1958					
1959		8.8^4	475		
1960	517			0.2	
1961					
1962					
1963					
1964				0.03	
1965				2.2	
1966		13.0	410		174
1967		12.6	440		174
1968		12.5	260		177
1969		12.4	473		178
1970	46	14.0	434	3.7	199

TABLE IX
(continued)

NUMBER OF REPORTED CASES OF SELECTED DISEASES

	Diphtheria	Infectious Hepatitis	Leprosy	Malaria	Acute Poliomyelitis	Syphilis	Tuberculosis	Typhoid[5]	Rabies[6]
1960-64							5223	2945	
1963								3010[6]	16
1965								2171	
1966	176		179	4698	148		5930	2127	
1968	159	159	200	37475	52		6170	1981[6]	
1970						1402[6]	4560	2094	15
1971									

[1] 1972 figure taken from Sivard, p. 22. All other data from UN, Demographic Yearbook.

[2] 1972 figure from Sivard, p. 18.

[3] 1972 figure from Sivard, p. 22

[4] Data from Lyle and Calman, p. 43.

[5] Includes cases of paratyphoid fever.

[6] Data from Ruddle and Barrows, p. 144.

were the number of physicians and nurses.

Evidence shows, therefore, that in all three countries, increases in public education and health expenditure are accompanied by improvements in output effectiveness measures while stagnation or declines in expenditure are accompanied by a levelling off or worsening
of such measures. There appears to be little general
relationship between central government expenditure
changes and input measures of effectiveness. The latter
tend to rise over time and are probably as much a function of population growth as public sector spending.
While no direct cause-effect relationship has been established above, it appears reasonable from the standpoint of public policy to focus on obtaining better
proxy measures of outputs for various public programs.
Such measures attempt to indicate something about how
well expenditure levels have accomplished objectives
(such as reducing deaths from selected diseases) as
opposed to merely showing the quantity of inputs employed.

INNOVATIVE ASPECTS OF METHODOLOGY

Effectiveness analysis commonly distinguishes between input measures where inputs to the process are
counted typically for administrative purposes and output or benefit measures which focus on the result(s) of
the process. In the benefit/cost framework for education,
economic analysis has tended to emphasize means of reducing costs by adjusting input measures of effectiveness.
For example, because teachers' salaries constitute
such a large proportion of total costs in developing
countries, past proposals have stressed the necessity
of increasing teacher-student ratios as the major means
of holding down costs.[35] It is perhaps not surprising
that policy recommendations of economists have emphasized
areas where relatively good data exist -- on the cost
side and for input measures of effectiveness rather than
on the benefit side utilizing output measures.

Despite past and even present reliance on input
measures by policy makers, a shift in emphasis toward
output measures would enable more accurate evaluation
procedures based on cost, effectiveness, and efficiency
criteria. Collection of data within individual countries
on literacy levels and availability of various forms of
reading material within certain localities or provinces
and as the result of specific programs would permit a

more in-depth analysis than that attempted here. However, it is hoped that the method suggested above will be a useful procedure for policy makers interested in pursuing such evaluation. Nevertheless, some reservations to the preceding analysis must be noted.

Stronger conclusions could have been drawn and expenditure data for lower levels of government been included. Further, the level of aggregation of data rendered it impossible to judge effectiveness of specific programs, for example, the results of vocational or primary education alone. A third caveat might well be the whole question of the legitimacy of these effectiveness measures as opposed to others and the extent to which other variables might have influenced the behavior of those chosen here. However, all of these reservations involve data limitations; yet, fiscal data and effectiveness measures used here are the most readily available in standard sources and perhaps the best available for comparative purposes.

This paper has focussed upon those aspects of effectiveness which are measurable; yet, many non-quantitative issues merit consideration. For example, educators and education administrators are frequently bound by tradition and, therefore, do not thoroughly scrutinize the structure and performance of the system. Because of this, it has been suggested[36] that education expenditures often do not reflect current realities. Further, many issues regarding effectiveness are not considered here. Common failures of education in developing countries are huge drop out rates, especially in lower grades, and little or no effort within the educational establishment to educate dropouts in any way[37] as well as failure in vocational education. These problems are prevalent in Brazil, Colombia, and Ecuador but have not been incorporated into the quantitative picture presented here. There are obviously numerous socio-cultural problems pertaining to expenditure effectiveness in addition to economic ones. It is frequently argued, for example, that education in developing countries is modelled after Western standards[38] which may inhibit program effectiveness. While these and other socio-cultural issues may be inadvertantly obscured by the present analysis, their existence is recognized to be of paramount importance.

Despite these reservations, the approach employed in this paper represents at least a systematic attempt to evaluate the effectiveness of education and health expenditure. The procedure of relating multiple output measures of effectiveness to expenditure patterns over time adds perspective to the question of what such expenditure has attempted to accomplish, a question often answered incorrectly (or at least vaguely) by exclusive reliance on input measures.

As better data become available, future research must consider regional effects of expenditure policy, for example, to what extent public health services are better in northern or southern Colombia or in urban vs. rural areas.[39] The urban and regional bias to public social services in the three countries of this study is well known. For example, recently released data reveal that in the state of Ceara in the Brazilian northeast infectious and parasitic diseases are still responsible for 23.3% of all deaths, 70% of children are seriously underweight, and 69% of homes in cities and towns are without running water.[40] The distributional impact of benefits is not fully illuminated when national average figures are used.

The growth of social welfare expenditure in developing countries will continue to put increased pressure on public sectors to devise means of evaluating public programs and of making traditional budgeting systems more effective. It has been argued elsewhere that the design of such innovative instruments, while conforming to commonly prescribed standards of cost-benefit analysis, must also insofar as possible be consistent with specific constraints of the planning and budgeting environment within individual countries.[41] The historical experience of three South American countries should provide additional guidance along these lines to those budget analysts who might regard such factors as of minimal importance. It has further been emphasized that "cost-benefit analysis can be an intensive consumer of staff, information, and time," the result being that analysis itself "can be costly in terms of both resources and delays in program decisions."[42] While recommendations for new data gathering procedures must always face this constraint, there is little reason to believe that output measures for specific programs could not be gathered by existing personnel under existing institutional arrangements.

Finally, it is generally assumed that cost-benefits and cost-effectiveness analysis are distributionally neutral or at least "distributionally indifferent."[43] But such techniques have important implications for income distribution in the context of health and education programs. Although the effect of education and health expenditure on the distribution of income is not expli-

198

citly taken into account in this paper, judging effectiveness of education by literacy and availability of reading
material appears to employ criteria which show potential
gains for the poor. The same may be said for judging the
effectiveness of health expenditure by infant, foetal and
perinatal mortality as well as reported cases of selected
diseases. Incidences of infant mortality, diseases reported here, and illiteracy are typically greater among the
poor so that substantial improvement in these areas would
indicate at least that some poor are benefiting. Use of
the benefit-cost technique in social programs, therefore,
may provide a valuable tool for policy makers based upon
equity as well as effectiveness and efficiency criteria.

[1]Some preliminary discussion of this issue is offered in Frank T. Bachmura (ed.), Human Resources in Latin America, Bloomington: Indiana University Bureau of Business Research, 1968. But none of papers in this volume treat multiple output measures of effectiveness for public education or health expenditure.

[2]Richard A. Musgrave, "Expenditure Policy for Development," in David T. Geithman (ed.), Fiscal Policy for Industrialization and Development in Latin America, Gainesville: University of Florida Press, 1974, p. 179 and p. 181.

[3]See, for example, Marcelo Selowsky, "On the Measurement of Education's Contribution to Growth," Quarterly Journal of Economics, Vol. 83, No.3, August, 1969, cited in Ibid., p. 179, who argues that the rate of return on investment in education is high and frequently higher than on investment in so-called real assets. The opposing point of view is taken by O. Zeller Robertson, Jr., "Education and Economic Development in Latin America: A Causal Analysis," Inter-American Economic Affairs, Vol. 28, No.2, Summer, 1974, pp. 63-71, who argues that education does not cause economic growth.

[4]Musgrave, "Expenditure Policy for Development," p. 184.

[5]Alan R. Prest, Public Finance in Underdeveloped Countries, New York: John Wiley and Sons, 1972, p. 18.

[6]Ibid., pp. 22-23.

[7]Ibid., p. 122.

[8]John M. Hunter and James W. Foley, Economic Problems of Latin America, Boston: Houghton Mifflin, 1975 pp. 234-235. The significance of this statement must be modified somewhat in that some Latin American countries devote substantially more private resources to education than is the case in other developing areas of the world.

[9]Joseph E. Pluta, "Evaluating Public Education Programs in Sixteen Countries of Latin America and Africa,"

paper presented at the Southwestern Social Science
Association Meetings, Dallas, Texas, March 1977.
See also data from United Nations, Statistical
Yearbook, New York: Statistical Office of the U.N.
selected issues, and United States Arms Control
and Disarmament Agency, World Military Expenditures, Washington, D.C., selected issues. Brazil
and Nicaragua appear to be examples of countries
with stagnating education expenditure.

[10]Ruth Leger Sivard, World Military and Social Expenditures, 1976, Leesburg, Virginia: WMSE Publications,
1976, p. 17. For discussions of special problems
of health care in developing areas, see M.J.
Sharpston, "A Health Policy for Developing Coun-
tries," World Bank draft paper, July 1975; Alan
Berg, The Nutrition Factor, Washington, D.C.:
Brookings Institution, 1973; and Leonard Joy,
"Food and Nutrition Planning", Journal of Agri-
cultural Economics, January, 1973, pp. 1-20.
Portions of all three of the above are reprinted
in Gerald M. Meier, Leading Issues in Economic
Development, 3rd ed., New York: Oxford University
Press, 1976, pp. 496-518.

[11]Ruth Leger Sivard, World Military and Social Expenditures, 1974: New York: Institute for World Order,
1974, p.12.

[12]See, for example, Joseph E. Pluta, "National Defense
and Social Welfare Budget Trends in Ten Nations
of Postwar Western Europe", International Journal
of Social Economics, Vol. 4, No. 2, June 1977;
Pluta, "Growth and Patterns in U.S. Government
Expenditures, 1956-1972", National Tax Journal,
Vol. 27, No. 1, March 1974, pp. 71-92; Richard
A. Musgrave, Fiscal Systems, New Haven: Yale
University Press, 1969, esp. chapters 3 and 4,
James W. Wilkie, "Recentralization: The Budgetary Dilemma in the Economic Development of Mexi-
co, Bolivia, and Costa Rica", in Geithman, op.cit.
pp. 200-247; Dennis J. Mahar and Fernando A.
Rezende, "The Growth and Pattern of Public Ex-
penditure in Brazil,1920-1969", Public Finance
Quarterly, Vol. 3, No. 4, Ocotober 1975, pp. 380-
399; Allen C. Kelley, "Demographic Change and
the Size of the Government Sector", Southern
Economic Journal, Vol. 43, No. 2, October 1976,
pp. 1056-1066; Cyril Enweze, "Structure of Public
Expenditures in Selected Developing Countries:
A Time Series Study", Manchester School of Economic and Social Studies, Vol. 41, No. 4, December

1973, pp. 430-463; A. J. Mann, "Public Expenditure Patterns in the Dominican Republic and Puerto Rico, 1930-1970", Social and Economic Studies, Vol. 24, No. 1, March 1975, pp. 47-82; and Irving J. Goffman and Dennis J. Mahar, "The Growth of Public Expenditures in Selected Developing Nations: Six Caribbean Countries 1940-1965, Public Finance, Vol. 44, No. 1, 1971, pp. 57-74, as well as a number of earlier studies cited in the above.

[13]See, for example, United Nations Industrial Development Organization, Guidelines for Project Evaluation, New York: United Nations, 1972; Ajit K. Dasgupta and S. W. Pearce, Cost-Benefit Analysis: Theory and Practice, London: Macmillan, 1972; A. R. Prest and R. Turvey, "Cost-Benefit Analysis: A Survey", Economic Journal, December 1965; and Richard A. Musgrave, "Cost-Benefit Analysis and the Theory of Public Finance: Journal of Economic Literature, Vol. 7, No. 3, September 1969.

[14]E. S. Quade, Analysis for Public Decisions, New York: American Elsevier, 1975, and Thomas A. Goldman (ed.), Cost-Effectiveness Analysis: New Approaches in Decision-Making, New York: Praeger Publishers, 1967.

[15]Some effort in this area has been made. See John C. Beyer, Budget Innovations in Developing Countries: The Experience of Nepal, New York: Praeger Publishers, 1973.

[16]Joergen R. Lotz and Elliott R. Morss, "A Theory of Tax Level Determinants for Developing Countries", Economic Development and Cultural Change, Vol. 18, No. 2, April, 1970, p. 338. This position is also supported in Marian Krzyzaniak, "The Case of Turkey: Government Expenditures, the Revenue Constraint, and Wagner's Law", Growth and Change, Vol. 5, No. 2, April, 1974, pp. 13-19.

[17]Fiscal Reform for Colombia, Final Reform and Staff Papers of the Colombian Commission on Tax Reform. Richard A. Musgrave, President, edited by Malcolm Gillis, Cambridge: International Tax Program, Harvard University Law School, 1971. Excellent reviews which summarize the important recommendations on the expenditure side (as well as the tax side) include: Vito Tanzi, "Fiscal Reform for Colombia: The Report of the Musgrave Commission", Inter-American Economic Affairs, Vol. 26, No. 2, Summer, 1972, pp. 71-80,

and Carl S. Shoup, "Three Fiscal Reports on Colombia: A Review Article", National Tax Journal, Vol. 26, No. 1, March, 1973, pp. 59-63.

[18]David T. Geithman and Clifford E. Landers, "Obstacles to Labor Absorption in a Developing Economy: Colombia, A Case in Point", Journal of Inter-American Studies and World Affairs, Vol. 15, No. 3, August, 1973, p. 329.

[19]William C. Bunning, "The Nixon Foreign Aid Policy for Latin America", Inter-American Economic Affairs, Vol. 25, No. 2, Summer, 1971, pp. 31-45.

[20]James W. Wilkie, "On Methodology and the Use of Historical Statistics", Latin American Research Review, Vol. 5, No. 1, Spring, 1970, p. 91, footnote 5.

[21]The author would like to indicate his awareness of some of the problems posed by this type of analysis. Obviously, strict comparison of countries such as Colombia and Brazil is not possible because the units to be analyzed are not comparable. Because Brazil is a federation of states while Colombia is not, fiscal responsibilities differ in the two nations. For this reason, comparison of total expenditures, including the states and municipalities in the case of Brazil and departments and municipalities in the cases of Colombia and Ecuador, would yield a more meaningful and more complete comparison. As noted above, however, data deficiencies prevent this.

Even with the inclusion of disaggregated figures, many problems would persist. For example, all profits from lotteries in Colombia are given to the health sector. Are these resources to be considered public funding? In similar fashion, the role of church hospitals and social security in all three countries adds considerable complication to the analysis of health resource allocation. Further, involvement of decentralized institutes also differs from country to country. In one country, a given program might be carried out by a decentralized institute while in another the same function might be performed by the Ministry of Health. Even within a country, decentralized agencies are often shifted from one ministry to another or a division of the ministry may become a decentralized agency or vice versa.

In addition, more detailed data would have enabled closer scrutiny of the breakdown of expenditures. For example, how much goes for what kind of education (primary, secondary, etc.) and for whom is it intended? Similarly, inclusion of detailed private sector education and health data would have been useful. It is hoped that the citing of expenditure data problems in developing countries, if not collectively exhaustive, is at least representative.

[22]Samuel J. Mantel, Jr., et.a., "A Social Service Measurement Model", Operations Research, Vol. 23, No. 2, March-April, 1975, pp. 218-239 and P. H. Rossi and W. Williams (eds.), Evaluating Social Programs, New York: Seminar Press, 1972.

[23]James W. Wilkie, The Mexican Revolution: Federal Expenditure and Social Change Since 1910, Berkeley: University of California Press, 1970.

[24]Andrew Maneschi, "The Brazilian Public Sector", in Riordan Roett (ed.), Brazil in the Sixties, Nashville: Vanderbilt University Press, 1972, pp. 185-229. This study, however, utilized data which were not broken down by function.

[25]Unfortunately, a more general analysis of how "type of regime" or "instability" affected these expenditures is beyond the scope of this paper.

[26]For an excellent summary of health planning in Latin America with an emphasis on Colombia, see Dieter K. Zschock, "Health Planning in Latin America: Review and Evaluation", Latin American Research Review, Vol. 5, No. 3, Fall, 1970, pp. 35-56.

[27]See, for example, David R. Seidman, "PPB in HEW: Some Management Issues", Journal of the Institute of American Planners, Vol. 36, No. 2, May, 1970, pp. 168-178 and James S. Dyer, "The Use of PPBS in a Public System of Higher Education: Is It Cost-Effective?", Academy of Management Journal, Vol. 13, No. 3, September, 1970, pp. 285-299. Both of the above are reprinted in Fremont J. Lyden and Ernest G. Miller (eds.), Planning-Programming-Budgeting: A Systems Approach to Management, 2nd ed., Chicago: Markham Publishing Company, 1972.

[28]A problem in assessing information on health concerns use of "reported" data. If the data collection process improves, the results may be biased toward showing ineffectiveness of health efforts since a

larger incidence of disease is now reported. A
similar problem may exist in education since the
determination of literacy likely changed over
the period. While such methodological problems
may be important, the researcher has little
choice but to work with existing data and indicate awareness that these and other related
data problems exist.

[29]See, for example, Michael D. Maltz, "Measures of
Effectiveness for Crime Reduction Programs",
Operations Research, Vol. 23, No. 2, May-June,
1975, pp. 452-474.

[30]These countries are an exhaustive listing of those measures found in UN sources. Other measures (most
notably life expectancy) would have enabled a
more complete analysis, had data been available.
Some caveats regarding the measures used also
are in order. Infant mortality, for example,
may be produced by numerous factors such as nutritional deficiencies, low quality of the environment including water and housing, and low
educational levels. Therefore, expenditures and
changes within the agricultural sector may have
more impact in reducing mortality rates of children than certain "health" actions.
It is hoped that the problem of lags is
avoided by using rather long periods of evaluation. Effects of many expenditures are not
instant and often may not produce results until
years after the expenditure took place. This
is particularly true in education. Expenditures
on grade school, for example, will not have immediate effects in increasing newspaper circulation since children do not buy papers. Caution
must also be exercised in comparing the effects
of actions under different presidential terms.
Governments likely receive considerable benefits
of actions carried out by previous governments.
Finally, the construction of a single indicator combining the separate indexes might be an
alternative approach for evaluation. Such an
effort, however, probably would not be very
meaningful given the inherent subjectivity of
weighting schemes as well as the limited range
of measures for which data are available.

[31]However, some and perhaps all of these measures were
likely affected by increased censorship of reading material under the repressive military government as well as the Brazilian depression of the 1960s.

[32]See data presented in the three most recent issues of UN, Statistical Yearbook, 1971, 1972, and 1973.

[33]For an examination of the effect of education expenditure upon the distribution of income in Colombia, see Jean-Pierre Jallade, Public Expenditures on Education and Income Distribution in Colombia, World Bank Staff Occasional Paper No. 18, Baltimore: Johns Hopkins University Press, 1974. Jallade concludes that Colombian public education expenditure redistributes income from rich to poor and does so more decisively in urban than in rural areas.

[34]For a discussion of the ineffectiveness of planning efforts during the sixties in the area of education and manpower training, see Clarence Zuvekas, Jr. "Economic Planning in Ecuador: An Evaluation" Inter-American Economic Affairs, Vol. 25, No. 1, Spring, 1972, pp. 66-68.

[35]Prest, Public Finance in Underdeveloped Countries, p. 124.

[36]Burton C. Newbry and Kenneth L. Martin, "The Educational Crisis in the Lesser Developed Countries", Journal of Developing Areas, Vol. 6, No. 1, January, 1972, p. 156.

[37]Ibid., p. 157.

[38]This position has been argued recently in Frank J. Swetz, "Educational Crisis in Developing Nations: Alternatives", Journal of Developing Areas, Vol.8, No. 1, January, 1974, pp. 173-174.

[39]The topic of urban bias has been given considerable attention in recent literature. See, for example Roland H. Ebel, "Governing the City-State: Notes on the Politics of the Small Latin American Countries", Journal of Inter-American Studies and World Affairs, Vol. 14, No.3, August, 1972, pp. 325-346. Much has been written on the urban bias of social services in Peru. See James M. Malloy, "Peru Before and After the Coup of 1968", Journal of Inter-American Studies and World Affairs, Vol. 14, No. 4, November, 1972, especially p. 447 and p. 451; Frederick B. Pike, The Modern History of Peru, New York: Praeger Publishers, 1969, p. 292; and Charles W. Anderson, Politics and Economic Change in Latin America, Princeton: D. Von Nostrand Company, 1967, p. 251 and p. 254.

Recent attempts to examine the regional impact of education include George F. Patrick and Earl W. Kehrberg, "Costs and Returns of Education in Five Agricultural Areas of Eastern Brazil", American Journal of Agricultural Economics, Vol. 55, No. 2, May, 1973, pp. 145-153, and Robert F. Arnove, "Education and Political Participation in Rural Areas of Eastern Brazil", Comparative Education Review, June 1973, pp. 198-215.

[40]William R. Long, "Brazilian Northeast Battles Poverty", Monterey Peninsula Herald, January 4, 1976, p. 5B.

[41]Beyer, op. cit., pp. v-vi.

[42]Ibid., pp. 125-126.

[43]See, for example, James M. Buchanan and Marilyn Flowers, The Public Finances, 4th ed. Homewood, Illinois: Richard D. Irwin, 1975, p. 184. However, some theoretical work has attempted to take into account both efficiency and equity effects of expenditure programs. See C. F. Azzi and J. C. Cox, "Equity and Efficiency in Program Evaluation", Quarterly Journal of Economics, Vol. 87, No. 3, August, 1973.

VII
COMMODITY POWER AND THE INTERNATIONAL COMMUNITY

Rachel McCulloch
Harvard Institute of Economic Research
Harvard University

ANATOMY OF A DEBATE

Commodity Power

   After decades of low profile activity, trade in primary products has recently burst onto the front pages of newspapers throughout the world, beginning with the remarkable success story of OPEC, the Organization of Petroleum Exporting Countries, and continuing with the formation or revitalization of producers' associations for a wide variety of commodities, ranging from bananas to zinc. Along with these efforts to organize cartels on lines suggested by OPEC, developing nations have become far more outspoken in their demands for cooperation from the industrialized countries in obtaining better terms for their commodity exports. These demands are part of a call by the third world for the creation of "a new international economic order," amounting to a major redistribution of world wealth from the "rich" to the "poor" nations.

   Primary products were long regarded as the "poor relations" of world trade. While it was universally recognized that commodity exports accounted for a major share of the export earnings of most developing nations, the development strategies adopted by these nations amounted largely to attempts to raise incomes through emulation of the economic structures of the developed world -- rapid industrialization was seen as the key to rapid growth of national income. Commodity agreements (guaranteeing higher process and stabilization of export earnings) were sought, along with loan and grant aid, as a means of financing the industrialization viewed as essential to rapid growth.

   Industrialization is still a major goal of most economically backward nations, but OPEC's recent coup has resulted both in a change of emphasis and a change of attitude among the less developed countries (LDCs)

209

of the world. The success of OPEC in quadrupling the world price of oil provided a gratifying spectacle for an audience of developing nations. The OPEC venture aroused almost universal admiration in the third world, even among those countries which could ill afford the increased burden of higher costs for their imported fuels -- a greater burden than for the industrialized countries, where oil represented a much smaller fraction of total imports. OPEC had engineered a vast increase in its earnings <u>without</u> the assistance of the developed powers. Moreover, unlike those LDCs which had managed to raise national income through the traditional routes, the OPEC members had benefited from a process which was appealingly quick and easy. Commodity power, requiring little of the hard work and national sacrifices entailed by traditional development strategies, seemed to open a new and far more attractive route for other developing nations -- an opportunity to seize, rather than earn, a greater share of world income and wealth through concerted action.

The short-cut to development through commodity power is accorded both respectability and philosophical justification in the predominantly socialist perspective of third world leaders. The current confrontation of developed and developing nations is seen as a worldwide analogue of the class struggle between capital and labor. Just as the labor movement had succeeded in wrestling economic concessions from the unwilling capitalist class, so would the LDCs wrest their fair share of world wealth from the industrialized lands -- which had, after all, achieved their current affluence through centuries of oppression and exploitation. Furthermore, a doctrine which views third world poverty as the inevitable consequence of prosperity elsewhere avoids any need to scrutinize the results of past policies chosen by third world leaders themselves.[1]

New Militancy on Resources[2]

At a series of conferences during the past year, representatives of the "Group of 77" nonaligned nations (now actually numbering more than 100) have reiterated their call for "a new international economic order." With respect to trade in primary products, the specific demands are far from revolutionary: higher prices (preferably indexed to the prices of manufactured goods), guaranteed access to markets, and stabilization of export earnings. What is revolutionary in the thinking of the Group of 77 is the expectation that new trading arrangements for primary products will constitute a major channel for redistribution of wealth from the industrialized to the developing nations.

While OPEC's recent successes have provided an inspiring example for the rest of the third world, current attitudes represent the logical outcome of more than a decade of increasing group awareness among the LDCs. The 1964 United Nations Conference on Trade and Development (UNCTAD) provided the LDCs for the first time with a forum devoted exclusively to the full range of problems raised by the economic development process. Representatives of the developing nations led by Dr. Raul Prebisch formed an effective voting bloc, maintaining a unified position on all key issues. UNCTAD I, held at a time of generally falling prices for primary commodities, devoted considerable attention to the issues raised by developing country exports of primary products. One of the "general principles" embodied in the Final Act of the Conference has a decidedly familiar ring to those who have read accounts of more recent meetings:

> The expansion and diversification of international trade depends upon increasing access to markets, and upon remunerative prices for the exports of primary products. Developed countries shall progressively reduce and eliminate barriers and other restrictions that hinder trade and consumption of products from developing countries and take positive measures such as will create and increase markets for the exports of developing countries. All countries should cooperate through suitable international arrangements, on an orderly basis, in implementing measures designed to increase and stabilize primary commodity earnings, at equitable and remunerative prices and to maintain a mutually acceptable relationship between the prices of manufactured goods and those of primary products.

The Conference also supported "special action, both national and international, to deal with cases where natural products exported by developing countries face competition from synthetics and other substitutes." Indeed, examination of the Proceedings of UNCTAD I reveals that virtually every proposal regarding the organization of commodity trade now before the international community

was first suggested at least a decade ago. Even the
"integrated approach" of Secretary General Gamani Corea
of UNCTAD may be said to have its precursor in Chapter 6
of the post-war Havana Charter of the International
Trade Organization (ITO), which laid down a code of
general principles which were to apply to all commodity
agreements. (The ITO, designed as a counterpart to the
International Monetary Fund with responsibilities for
regulating world trade arrangements, aborted after the
United States Senate failed to ratify the Charter; as
a result, the General Agreement on Tariffs and Trade
(GATT) assumed many of the responsibilities which were
to have been carried out by the ITO.)

The list of specific demands which the third world
has presented at an unending succession of international
conferences -- including UNCTAD II and III in 1968 and
1973, the Sixth Special Session of the U.N. General Assembly in 1974, and even conferences devoted to such
topics as the environment and population, not to mention the numerous conferences called by the LDCs themselves to plan strategy for future conferences -- has
changed but little over the years. What has changed,
and what has changed even more rapidly since trade in
commodities emerged as a headline issue in 1973, is the
perceived balance of power between the industrialized
bloc and the third world. International commodity agreements, just a few years ago seen as a thinly disguised
form of aid to the less developed countries, have emerged
as a major element in a new bargain to be struck between
more nearly equal sides. This change in perceptions has
affected both sets of participants. The commodity exporters, impressed by OPEC's ability to shake the com-
posure of the developed nations, suddenly see themselves
as bargaining from a position of strength, rather than
begging favors from a sometimes benevolent despot. Likewise, the industrialized countries, profoundly disturbed
by recent events, are newly prepared for serious negotiations, now seen as perhaps the only means of preserving
the existing world order -- and their own position in it.
Even observers in the industrialized nations who view the
threat of "commodity power" as vastly overrated have advocated concessions on the issue of commodity trade in
order to give the LDCs a larger stake in international
order. Total defeat for the third world on this focal
issue, some fear, would provoke a continuing series of
increasingly destructive confrontations.

212

Conflict within the Industrialized Bloc

The rhetoric of recent international conferences, pitting poor nations against rich and developing against industrialized, masks very real conflicts of interest and of philosophy within the bloc of industrialized nations. By attitude as well as practice, leaders in the European Economic Community are more comfortable with the socialist concepts of central planning, stabilization of markets, and administered prices than are their counterparts in the United States. The Americans favor a move toward freer trade in agricultural products, so that these would be subject only to the same degree of restriction now accorded to trade in manufactured goods. Europeans, irked by U.S. championship of a free market philosophy in international trade issues, are quick to recall the formidable variety of interventions the U.S. applies to its own agricultural sector.

U.S. and European negotiators, meeting under the auspices of the General Agreement on Tariffs and Trade (GATT), have run into a basic difference of opinion with respect to international commodity agreements governing the prices of their agricultural products. The differences have emerged largely in the form of a procedural debate, with the Americans pushing to consider agricultural trade along with trade in manufactured goods, and Europeans demanding a separate look at the special issues raised by agricultural trade in an exclusively agricultural subgroup.

Practical issues lie behind the rift. For the United States, expansion of low cost agricultural exports is essential to a healthy future for its balance of trade. The Europeans, on the other hand, fear that efficient U.S. producers, if given freer access to the EEC market, will create severe adjustment problems for their own generally small and inefficient farmers. Thus the Europeans have a stake in joining the third world push for international commodity agreements to raise and stabilize the prices of many agricultural products, particularly those they themselves produce.[3]

Basic differences also separate the Europeans and Americans on the issue of economic assistance for the third world. In past years, the U.S. was the last developed nation to endorse the UNCTAD proposal for a Generalized System of Preferences, entailing reduced tariff rates intended to give developing nations an edge over industrialized competitors in penetrating the world market for manufactured goods. The European

213

Economic Community implemented a program along these
lines in 1971; the U.S., which finally adopted legislation allowing for such preferential access as part of
the comprehensive Trade Reform Act of 1974, included
provisions effectively excluding OPEC members from the
program -- a move deeply resented by Latin American oil
exporters, whose major market for manufactured exports
is the United States.[4]

Early in 1975, while the U.S. was still expressing
unqualified opposition to almost any sort of international commodity agreement, the European Economic Community was signing a major new trade and aid pact with
46 developing nations. Under the Lome Convention, EEC
members are committed to significant moves paralleling
some of those suggested in the UNCTAD integrated program, notably stabilization of export earnings for a
large number of primary products. However, recent
speeches by U.S. Secretary of State Henry Kissinger indicate a significant softening of the previous hard line.
In May 1976, Kissinger expressed U.S. willingness to consider international agreements covering the prices of
raw materials "on a case-by-case basis." This shift in
position came in response to a demand by OPEC members that
policies toward all raw materials be discussed along with
oil at any producer-consumer summit meetings. However,
the U.S. has remained adamant with respect to the third
world demand for indexation of raw material prices, a
proposal largely rejected by European leaders as well.

COMMODITIES IN PERSPECTIVE

The Problem of Instability[5]

Most primary products are characterized by low price
elasticities of supply and demand -- that is, amounts
supplied and demanded are relatively unresponsive to
changes in price, at least in the short run. Thus, even
modest disturbances in supply or demand conditions may
require relatively large price changes to "clear the
market." For most commodities, the business cycle in
the developed countries is the major factor determining
fluctuations of demand around its long-term trend.
Weather conditions are the most important source of short-
term supply disturbances for agricultural products, while
political upheavals may affect supply of both agricultural and mineral raw materials.

The price fluctuations produced by these factors represent part of the normal functioning of the market, signaling relative scarcity or abundance to producers and consumers, as well as inducing private inventory accumulation or decumulation to reallocate available supplies of storable commodities to periods of highest economic value. International action to depress fluctuations of price around a long-term trend implies a sacrifice of valuable market information and induced responses in return for greater ease in planning by producer and consumer interests. In some cases, international efforts to stabilize price may have the opposite effect, so that the costs of intervention are incurred without the possible benefit of more predictable outcomes. This is likely to occur when stabilization authorities are slow to recognize a long-term change in the market.

It is possible, however, to argue in favor of multilateral stabilization agreements on "second best" grounds. Because of the likelihood of some type of government intervention in times of unusually high or low prices, private stabilization activity is probably depressed below the level which would be justified by its social value. While it would be better still to limit the power of governments to engage in erratic regulatory activities in the first place, compensatory action in the form of stabilization activities may reduce the damage.

Commodity Trade and the Developing Nations[6]

Both the literature of economic development and the rhetoric of recent international conferences have dealt at length on the disproportionate dependence of developing nations on export earnings generated by primary commodities. This dependence can be seen through several measures. As Table 1 indicates, individual developing countries often depend on a single commodity export for a large fraction of total foreign exchange earnings, making that total highly vulnerable both to short-term fluctuations and long-term trends in the price of the export. The implications of this vulnerability depend upon the opportunities for reserve accumulation or external borrowing as means for smoothing fluctuations in export earnings around a trend, and for diversification into other products if the price trend is downward. However, virtually complete specialization in a primary product with a declining price trend may still represent the best economic use of a nation's

215

resources.

Table 2 shows that LDCs as a group supply a disproportionate fraction of primary products in world
trade. In 1973, the LDCs accounted for less than 1/5
of total world trade, but supplied more than 2/5 of
total world exports of "primary products in the broad
sense" as defined by UNCTAD (SITC 0-4). Even this summary statistic understates somewhat the degree of LDC
dependence on primary exports, since it excludes exports of slightly processed metals (SITC 68). The aggregate figure also includes trade in grains, in which
developed countries dominate, so that actual LDC dependence on non-grain primary exports is somewhat higher.

Despite the disproportionate reliance of LDCs on
primary exports, the developed countries still produce
by far the larger absolute share of these products.
Thus, the implications of higher commodity prices for
the distribution of wealth between the "rich" and "poor"
nations are not unambiguous. To the extent that a policy of artificially high commodity prices is used to
transfer wealth between consuming and producing nations,
the largest absolute share of the transfer would go to
certain developed nations rather than to members of the
third world. Furthermore, the poorest LDCs, which have
been made poorer still in the past two years by soaring
prices for imported oil and food, would suffer even
further from adoption of a general policy of high commodity prices. These poorest LDCs, mainly those without
oil, have recently been termed the "fourth world" group.
Increased flows of grant and loan aid, financed in part
by OPEC beneficiaries of high oil prices, have protected
these nations from the full impact of higher import costs.
A general policy of supported commodity prices would
necessitate still more concessionary financial flows to
these nations in order to maintain even their present
low standard of living.

Vulnerability of the Developed Countries

The oil embargo and subsequent dramatic increases
in the price of oil and many other internationally traded
commodities during 1974 stimulated a plethora of new
studies in the industrialized nations to assess their
dependence on imported raw materials. The degree of dependence varies significantly across commodities. As
shown in Table 3, developing nations account for a large
fraction of total world supply of some metals and of
tropical agricultural commodities, but a far smaller

216

fraction of other raw materials, including some important food crops. As well as growing a large share of grains, the U.S.S.R. is a major world producer of minerals. And among the noncommunist developed countries, the U.S., Canada, and Australia together account for a high proportion of many key commodities.

Among the major developed nations, the U.S. relies to a relatively small degree on imported raw materials, while the EEC imports a larger fraction of its raw materials and resource-poor Japan depends upon imports for virtually all its needs. According to a recent U.S. study by a White House task force,[7] imports make up 15% of total U.S. requirements of key raw materials, while the corresponding figures for Western Europe and Japan are 75% and 90%. In the past two years, the industrialized nations have intensified efforts to diversify import sources and have expressed renewed interest in maintaining stockpiles of those critical commodities which might be attractive targets for future embargo attempts. For many raw materials, substantial government and private stockpiles are already maintained.

Figures for current and projected imports of various commodities tell only part of the story, however. The actual amount obtained from each source and the total amount consumed each year both reflect a given history of past prices and expectations of future prices. A substantial increase in prices charged by foreign producers or in the threat of supply interruptions will automatically reduce dependence on foreign supplies, by reducing total consumption through substitution and by increasing domestic supplies from increased production and recycling. Thus, the actual dislocations which would occur in a given commodity market as a result of an important change in price or availability cannot be gleaned easily from summary statistics on present imports, but must take into account the price responsiveness of alternative supply and of demand.

On the other hand, theoretical possibilities of substitution in supply or end use often prove costlier than anticipated, in part as a result of the increased demand, which drives up the prices of required inputs. In the case of oil, substitute coal soared in price, while even a prolonged period of higher oil prices has not brought any significant supplies from oil shale or tar sands, previously seen as important alternative sources.

Less developed exporters of raw materials are keenly aware that consumer dependence may easily be eroded by development of new sources or substitutes. To this consideration some observers attribute the many delays inserted by LDC representatives into international proceedings on regulation of mineral recovery from the seabeds. And the UNCTAD Permanent Group on Synthetics and Substitutes, a subsidiary body of the influential Committee on Commodities, promotes research and development to delay the encroachment of synthetics into the markets for natural products.

Possibilities for Unilateral Action

Those who advocate a conciliatory policy in dealing with third world demands often argue that international commodity agreements are the only way to stave off formation of new cartels along the lines of OPEC in many other primary products. Although the alarmist furor over this particular threat has died down considerably since the prices of many raw materials dropped from their unprecedented high levels, some economists and public officials remain convinced that it is only a matter of time until the exporters of bananas, copper, iron ore, and mercury, among others, follow the OPEC lead.[8] In citing the many new producers' associations which have been formed in recent months, the cartel alarmists seldom mention the dramatic falls in raw material prices which have accompanied their efforts. Of course, it may be true that price declines would have been still greater in the absence of cutbacks engineered by these groups -- but the recent history of commodity prices hardly bears out their immediate threat for consuming nations.

Even if a producer group blessed by low short-run supply and demand elasticities and high concentration of production is temporarily successful in raising prices, the cartel is unlikely to maintain its position for long without assistance from consumers. However, temporary embargo-style supply interruptions may be used to disrupt the functioning of industrialized markets. Since the producing nations largely lack the foreign exchange reserves necessary to sustain a lengthy embargo, moderate stockpiles of vulnerable materials would further reduce the probability of such action.

Supply and demand conditions vary greatly among primary commodities, so that it is difficult to generalize about the probability of successful cartelization by producer nations. In assessing the threat posed by unilateral exporter action, it is useful to consider three specific and somewhat diverse commodities -- tin, coffee, and bauxite -- which have been the subject of varying degrees of producer control in the past. These three cases are described in the following sections.

Tin: A Durable Agreement[9]

The International Tin Agreement, which first went into effect in 1956 and has been renewed regularly since then, is worth examining as the sole example of a successfully functioning long-term international commodity agreement. The main objective of the Agreement is to moderate fluctuations in the price of tin. This has been accomplished through a buffer stock; tin is sold when the price reaches the established ceiling and bought when the price falls to the floor. Occasionally export quotas have been imposed on producing nations. However, with almost 80% of world production concentrated in just four countries, this has been relatively easy to administer. The buffer stock arrangement has been financed by compulsory contributions from producers (with some financing assistance from the International Monetary Fund buffer stock facility) and voluntary contributions from consuming nations.

Current members of the Agreement include seven producing countries -- Australia, Bolivia, Indonesia, Malaysia, Nigeria, Thailand, and Zaire -- which together account for most of the world's tin production. The 22 consuming nation members include the EEC countries plus Austria, Canada, Czechoslovakia, Hungary, India, Japan, Poland, Korea, Roumania, Spain, Turkey, U.S.S.R., and Yugoslavia. The only important consuming nation absent from the list is the United States. (The U.S. seems likely to join the Agreement in the near future.)

The Agreement's longevity may be attributed to a number of factors: its limited objective, with floor and ceiling prices adjusted in accord with market shift; its membership, which includes most important producers and consumers; and concentration of world production, which has allowed for the occasional successful use of export controls. But with many good substitutes available, tin is an unlikely candidate for an OPEC-style embargo or price hike.

The present Agreement is due to expire in June, 1976, and a new Agreement is now being negotiated under

219

the supervision of UNCTAD. Among changes contemplated are enlargement of the buffer stock and compulsory contributions from consuming nations. The UNCTAD Secretary-General has also suggested that the new Agreement include provisions for research to promote the consumption of tin (to be financed by consuming and producing countries jointly), measures to encourage processing in the producing nations, and multilateral supply and purchase agreements. These suggested additions are in keeping with the Secretary-General's own "integrated program" for commodities.

Coffee: Persistent Stabilization Efforts

Coffee is the world's largest tropical crop, amounting to about $5 billion annually. Low short-run supply and demand elasticities make large fluctuations a likely outcome in a competitive market. Accordingly, world coffee trade has been subject to stabilization attempts dating back to the beginning of the century. Among producers, Brazil dominates the world market with about 25% of total output. Columbia produces another 12%, Central American producers account for another 18%, and African exporters together produce about 30%. Among importers, the United States buys one-third of world imports, while Germany purchases about 10%.

Coffee trees take 12 years to mature, and trees require four or five years after planting to yield their first crop. The trees continue to produce for about 20 years. Hence short-run supply elasticity is quite low; small increases in yield may be achieved through variation in fertilization, cultivation, and picking. Weather is the major factor affecting short-run supply of coffee. In July, a Brazilian frost sent the world price of coffee up by 30¢ per pound.

Prior to 1930, Brazil attempted to control the world price of coffee unilaterally. Its success in maintaining relatively high and stable prices induced Colombia and the Central American countries to plant coffee; the expanded sources of supply, together with a sharp drop in demand accompanying the depression of the 1930s, spelled disaster for Brazil's one-country stabilization program. But before abandoning the effort, Brazil burned vast quantities of coffee.

In 1940, Brazil was joined by other Latin American exporters in forming the first international commodity agreement supported by an importing nation with no production of its own -- the United States. The agreement, which fixed both export and import quotas, remained in effect until 1948. Prices were not explicitly mentioned in the agreement and were set by the United States Office of Price Administration.

In the years following World War II, prices rose rapidly, inducing expanded planting in Latin America and Africa. When the new supplies began to appear, prices dropped sharply, and new attempts to control the world market were stimulated. An unsuccessful attempt by Latin American producers to stabilize the market was followed by the International Coffee Agreement, including both Latin American and African producers. Under this agreement, producing countries were assigned sales quotas, but these were set high relative to total import demand; furthermore, the agreement had no effective machinery for enforcing the quotas. A stronger agreement, including both major producing and consuming nations, went into operation in 1962. Export quotas were to be enforced by the major importers; in practice, collusion between producing and consuming nations to violate quotas tended to undermine this mechanism. Renewal negotiations in 1968 were complicated by the growing importance of soluble coffee, which was not the subject to the tax exporting nations applied to coffee beans. The Agreement finally collapsed in 1972, when members were unable to agree on new target price range and production quotas in a period of rising coffee prices.

A new coffee agreement between 41 producing countries and 17 consuming countries has been under discussion this year. In April, the United States proposed a plan which would include an internationally administered buffer stock and export quotas. However, the recent Brazilian frost, which has resulted in rapidly rising coffee prices, may complicate the negotiations.

These perennial attempts to stabilize the world price of coffee raise the question of just how successful the agreements have been in promoting price stability. Since World War II, price instability appears to have been greater during periods covered by the agreements than otherwise. However, at least one writer credits the agreements, and particularly the participation of the United States in their operation, with producing substantial financial transfers from the consuming to the producing nations, so that while stability was not achieved, artificially average high prices and revenues were successfully maintained.[10]

Bauxite: Another OPEC?

The International Bauxite Association (IBA), with ten members -- Jamaica, Surinam, Guyana, Guinea, the Dominican Republic, Haiti, Ghana, Sierra Leone, Yugoslavia, and Australia -- which together mine about three-quarters of total world bauxite output, is one of many commodity producers' organizations which have been formed or strengthened in emulation of OPEC's successful operations. The aim of IBA, as with the other producers' groups, is to increase and stabilize the price received for its exports. But of the new groups, IBA seems to be in the best position to force a substantial price rise, thanks to the concentration of a large fraction of world production in just a few countries.

Jamaica, which alone accounts for about 30% of world exports, has led the way with a formula which ties the tax on bauxite to the price of the aluminum it is used to produce. This gives exporters some degree of indexation for price changes; protection is far from complete, however, since aluminum prices fluctuate substantially relative to an index of all manufactured goods. The tax rate was increased severalfold in the process of implementing the new system. Other IBA members have also effected large increases in their own taxes. The approach of raising revenues through higher production or export taxes, rather than by direct attempts to cut output, closely parallels the technique which has worked so well in the case of OPEC. Despite the much higher taxes, consumers of aluminum will not see a comparable price rise in the finished product. In contrast to the case of oil, in which crude petroleum constitutes more than half of the cost of the finished product, bauxite makes up less than ten percent of the cost of aluminum ingot.

The long run prospects for IBA are less certain. As with any attempt to raise price through concerted action of producers, substitution possibilities are crucial to success or failure. Aluminum is the most abundant metal in the earth's crust, and bauxite is only one of many raw materials which can be used in making aluminum. While the vertically integrated aluminum companies are unlikely to abandon their large fixed investments in the IBA countries, extraction of aluminum from alternative ores will become attractive if the price of bauxite stays high. Some companies are already investigating the technology for substituting other raw materials for bauxite. Bauxite in non-IBA countries represents another possible avenue for diversification of raw material sources.

Another factor influencing the demand for bauxite in the long run is the market for copper, aluminum's most important substitute. CIPEC, the Intergovernmental Council of Copper Exporting Countries, has recently engineered cuts in exports by some members in an effort (so far unsuccessful) to push prices back to the high levels experienced in 1973. Joint action by IBA and CIPEC would be more effective than moves by either group alone, but the coordination required would be difficult to sustain even briefly.

PLANS AND PROSPECTS

Controlling Trade in Commodities

Whether control is exercised by a "cartel" of producing nations without the explicit or implicit support of consumers, or through an "international commodity agreement" duly signed both by producers and consumers -- and perhaps endorsed for good measure by an international organization such as UNCTAD -- the same basic objectives and techniques are involved, and the same market forces conspire to undermine the effort.

Control of trade in commodity markets is generally motivated by one or more of three related objectives: to raise average price (and revenue, when demand is "inelastic" -- relatively unresponsive to price changes), to stabilize price, or to stabilize revenue. Efforts to raise price, either through a cartel or a commodity agreement, usually mean a more stable price as well, at least during the effective life of the arrangement. In some cases, the arrangement itself induces a subsequent period of extreme fluctuations, owing to the natural response of potential suppliers to an unnaturally high price maintained for some period of time. Because the demand for most commodities is inelastic, at least in the short run, revenue and price move in the same direction, so that price stabilization also results in more stable flows of revenue for exporters. However, revenues may be stabilized without working through price, so that annual export

earnings are smoothed without resort to direct intervention in the market for the commodity itself. These
price and revenue objectives may be promoted through the
use of three basic tools: export controls, buffer stocks,
and import-export agreements between producer and consumer nations.

Export Controls. Export controls, which usually
work through quantity restrictions -- production or export quotas -- but which may also work through price
restrictions -- export taxes -- raise price by reducing
world supply. They work best when production is concentrated among a few countries and is centrally controlled
within those countries (diamonds provide the classic example of effective control of price through supply restriction) and when production cutbacks do not cause
severe internal dislocations in employment, as with
petroleum.

Where one or a small group of sellers controls a
large fraction of total production, only the production
of the dominant supplier(s) need be controlled directly;
the dominant supplier sells only the difference between
world demand at the target price and the amount that remaining sellers would normally wish to supply at that
price. As production from all sources responds to the
elevated price, however, the dominant supplier receives
a shrinking share of total revenues and thus may choose
to abandon the price umbrella, as Brazil did in the case
of coffee.

With many sellers of nonnegligible size, allocation
of export quotas becomes a major stumbling block in controlling total supply. Formulas based on cost or capacity considerations may yield temporary agreement, but
since each seller can produce additional amounts at
costs well below the prevailing market price, the incentives to exceed quotas are strong. Furthermore, even
where a capacity rule is used to set export quotas, new
producers will inevitably be attracted by a sustained
high price, resulting in a smaller share for the original group, whether the new entrants join the arrangement
or, worse, remain outside and produce freely.

Export taxes, which indirectly restrict quantity,
have been used successfully in the case of petroleum by
OPEC members. However, each member faces the incentive
to reduce the tax or to give other special treatment
which lowers the effective price charged. Export taxes
have also been used by some bauxite producers in an at-

tempt to raise world price.

Buffer stocks. Buffer stocks work by removing supply from the market when price is low and increasing total supply when price is high. Usually a floor and ceiling price are negotiated; market price at or below the floor triggers purchases by the buffer, while a price at or above the ceiling is a signal to sell to the market. The result is to moderate price fluctuations and, depending on the target prices set, perhaps also to raise average price. A buffering arrangement which succeeded in moderating price fluctuations might actually lower average price over time, to the extent that stable prices induce new suppliers to enter the market.

Most markets are "buffered" to some extent by private transactions of firms or individuals who expect to profit by buying low and selling high. Also, manufacturers requiring inputs of raw materials maintain inventories and will generally enlarge these stocks when price is viewed as unusually low, while depleting them when price is expected to fall from a current high. Private price stabilizing activity is probably also depressed by the likelihood that governments will intervene when price is unusually high. Thus, the full economic value of stocks maintained cannot be captured by a private holder, who will be forced to sell at a price below that which would clear the market during the shortage.

International buffers need not make a profit, but if they fail to at least cover costs, a source of funding is required. The ability of the buffer to moderate downward fluctuations or to resist a longer-term trend in price depends on the size of the fund available for buffer accumulation. Likewise, the size of the stock itself determines the extent to which the arrangement can moderate price rises in times of short supply. The International Tin Agreement, which uses a buffer arrangement, has succeeded to some extent in smoothing small price fluctuations, but has been unable to resist larger price movements.

A long-term buffer arrangement is unlikely to be successful unless floor and ceiling prices are changed frequently as market conditions alter. A buffer arrangement with the limited objective of smoothing price fluctuations by augmenting private transactions carries a far smaller price tag than a buffer intended to raise average price as well. In the latter case, continually

225

growing stocks and financing requirements are inevitable, and support for the arrangement may be difficult to maintain. A buffer stock and export controls may be used together to raise and stabilize a price. To the extent that they are effective, the export controls will reduce the total financial cost (and accompanying stock accumulation) which would be otherwise required to maintain the price through buffer purchases alone.

Import-export agreements. Importer-exporter contracts generally guarantee the seller a minimum price for a maximum volume of exports, while assuring the buyer of a minimum quantity at a maximum price. Prices may be prearranged or based on spot prices at time of delivery. Long-term contracts are a normal feature of private as well as government transactions in raw materials. In commodities with active futures markets, one or both parties to a long-term contract can eliminate price uncertainty through an appropriate side transaction. Problems entailed by the use of such agreements include the difficulty of negotiating mutually agreeable terms in the first place and of enforcing the terms once the contract is made. The sugar agreement which is part of the recently concluded Lome Convention is an example of an attempt to control commodity trade through importer-exporter commitments.

Revenue Stabilization. While techniques to control price have a stabilizing effect on export earnings as well, export earnings may be stabilized directly without intervention in the markets for the commodities which generate those earnings. Proceeds stabilization is a basic feature of the Lome Convention approach to commodities. The crucial element in revenue stabilization is definition of the norm from which deviations in proceeds are to be measured. The norm will generally be a weighted average of earnings, both past and possibly expected future, generated by a designated class of export transactions. The transactions may be for an individual commodity, for a group of commodities, or for all exports taken together. Countries with export earnings falling below the norm are compensated with loans, possibly on concessionary terms, or even grants, based on the amount of the shortfall. The required funding for such a plan depends on the terms on which compensatory payments are provided. If the funds are loaned at market rates, the plan should be approximately self-financing. Otherwise, external financing will be required.

Related Proposals. In addition to the basic elements described above, proposals for reform of international commodity arrangements have included a number of other features which would also affect prices or revenues received by exporting nations. Recent third world proclamations have stressed relocation of processing facilities for raw materials in the producing nations, accelerating a trend which has already had substantial impact on world trading patterns for primary products in recent years. Another proposal calls for establishment of special funds to be used by commodity exporters to diversify their production of primary products. (The International Coffee Agreement included compulsory member contributions to such a fund.) To address the problem of competition from synthetic substitutes, expanded research activity to improve productivity and quality in raw materials and to find new end uses has been urged. The indexation proposal, which would link the price of raw materials to those of manufactured goods, represents one possible formula for determining the target prices to be incorporated in international commodity agreements. The indexed price thus established would still have to be maintained through one of the three basic techniques described above.

Comprehensive schemes dealing with trade in commodities have already been adopted by the International Monetary Fund and the European Economic Community. In addition, Secretary-General Corea of UNCTAD has proposed a wider plan incorporating some features of those already in use; this "integrated approach" has the broad approval of third world representatives and will probably form the basis of future negotiations between the LDCs and the industrialized bloc at the special session of the United Nations in September and the UNCTAC session scheduled for next year. The indexation proposal, which is only a single element of a commodity plan, has not been officially endorsed by UNCTAD but has met with favor among LDC representatives and will probably continue to be the subject to heated debate in upcoming conferences. The following sections describe in detail the specific provisions of these arrangements and proposals.[11]

International Monetary Fund

The International Monetary Fund has three facilities which can be used by countries dependent upon raw material exports to offset fluctuations in export earnings. These include the regular IMF drawing facilities, compensatory financing, and buffer stock financing. In each case, a primary requirement for eligibility is balance of payments need. Hence, no assistance is available when fluctuations in the price or volume of one commodity export are offset by other factors in the overall balance of payments. However, eligibility is not limited to any specific commodity exports. Relief is provided on a loan, rather than grant, basis, with repayment normally scheduled within a three to five year period.

While the regular drawing facilities are open to all 126 IMF members, the compensatory financing and buffer stock financing are specifically designed to meet the needs of raw material exporters. With worldwide attention now focused on the problems of these nations, the IMF is undertaking a review of its commodity-related facilities. The U.S. has recently proposed a "substantial liberalization" of the existing facilities, including higher limits on total credit available to individual members.

Regular Drawing Facilities. The Fund's regular drawing facilities are available to members experiencing "temporary" balance of payments problems, regardless of cause. The amount of financing available through this channel depends upon the country's quota, which is a rough measure of its economic size. A country can freely obtain credit up to one-quarter of its quota. After that, stricter qualifications are placed on further borrowing, with the country required to demonstrate that it is following policies to eliminate the deficit. This would seem to raise some difficulties for the use of the regular drawing facilities to finance deficits arising from unanticipated fluctuations in export earnings induced by weather conditions or other world market phenomena not within the control of the individual country. The maximum financing available through this facility is 125% of the country quota. The regular drawing facilities are viewed as a source of short-term financing; interest is paid on the amount outstanding (currently at a rate of 4% to 6%), and countries normally agree to repay drawings within a three to five year period.

Compensatory Financing Facility. Compensatory financing is available to Fund members which experience export earnings below their normal trend value. This facility, which was established in 1963 and liberalized in 1966, is geared to the special problems of countries heavily dependent upon raw material exports, and is designed to assist those affected adversely by unexpected market developments, especially those arising from weather and natural disasters.

An export shortfall is determined relative to a five-year average centering on the year in question. Actual export earnings for the first three years are averaged with projected values for the two following years. These projections are developed by Fund experts, subject to two guidelines: the average of the two forecast years may exceed that of the two initial years by no more than 10% and should not be below the level for the current year.

In addition to establishing an export shortfall, several other conditions must be met in order for a member country to become eligible for compensatory financing. Most important, the country must have an overall payments need, so that if depressed earnings from one commodity are offset by high earnings from another, the country may be ineligible. The situation must be regarded to be of a short-term nature and largely due to factors beyond the control of the country itself. And the Fund may also require that the country institute some measures to improve its overall balance of payments situation.

The amount of financing available under this scheme is, as in the case of regular drawings, based on the member quota. Up to one-half of the quota may be drawn in all, with not more than one-quarter to be drawn in a given year. As with regular drawings, interest is paid, and repayments are made within three to five years. It is suggested that members make earlier repayments as export earnings resume their normal values. Use of compensatory financing does not reduce the member's access to the regular drawing facilities of the Fund.

Since the compensatory financing facility was established in 1963, 32 countries have made 57 drawings totalling about $1.25 billion. Outstanding drawings are equal to about half that total.

Buffer Stock Facility. This facility was established in 1969 to help member countries finance the cost of international buffer stocks associated with commodity agreements. The Fund imposes stringent eligibility requirements upon use of this facility, and to date funds have been used only for one commodity -- tin. The Fund requires that the commodity arrangement to be supported be "economically sound" and that the need for fund fi-

229

nancing be temporary. In particular, both producer and
consumer nations must participate in the arrangement,
and the buffer stock transactions must be designed to
balance out in the medium term. In addition to tin,
only one other commodity, cocoa, has been declared eligible for this type of financial support.

Terms for buffer stock financing are similar to
those for compensatory financing but slightly more stringent. Again, balance of payments need must be established. As in the case of compensatory financing, a
member may draw up to 50% of its quota, but there is no
limit on the amount which can be used within a one-year
period. Total drawings from the two facilities together
are limited to 75% of the quota. An important difference from the requirements for compensatory financing is
that the "gold tranche" (first 25% of the member's quota
of regular Fund drawings) must be used before any buffer
stock financing. Interest and repayment period are the
same as for regular drawings and compensatory financing,
but any distributions of cash from the buffer stock to
the member must be used to pay the member's outstanding
drawings from the buffer stock facility.

Since the buffer stock facility was established,
total drawings of only about $37 million have been made
by five Fund members participating in the International
Tin Agreement; most of that total has already been repaid.

Lome Convention

An export stabilization plan for twelve primary
commodities and a separate agreement on sugar are included among the provisions of the Lome Convention. The
Convention, a far-reaching agreement covering many aspects of trade and aid, was concluded in February 1975
at Lome, Togo, between the countries of European Economic Community and 46 African, Caribbean, and Pacific
(ACP) developing nations, following almost two years of
negotiations. The developing countries include those
covered by the earlier Yaounde Conventions of 1964 and
1969, as well as independent nations in black Africa
and the Commonwealth countries.

Stabex. Under the terms of the Convention, ACP exporters of twelve primary products are protected against
fluctuations in the proceeds from exports to the EEC.
Under the "Stabex" plan, developing countries will be-

230

come eligible for monetary transfers whenever their earnings from one year's exports to the EEC fall below a specified level. The twelve products covered by the agreement are peanuts, cocoa, coffee, cotton, coconuts, hides and skins, timber products, bananas, tea, raw sisal, and (the only mineral export) iron ore.

In contrast to the IMF facilities, which focus on fluctuations in overall export earnings, Stabex takes a commodity-by-commodity approach. To qualify for Stabex assistance, an ACP exporter must depend on one of the included products for a minimum proportion of its total export earnings. When proceeds of exports to the EEC for such a commodity fall below the average for a base period by a specified percentage (smaller in the case of the poorer countries among the 46), the country becomes eligible for a transfer from the Stabex fund. While the transfer is conditional on EEC approval, advances are to be virtually automatic. For the 34 least developed countries in the group, the funds received need not be repaid. Others received an interest-free loan, to be repaid (at least in theory) when export earnings rise. A total of about $490 million has been allocated to finance the operation of Stabex over a five-year period to begin (retroactively) in February 1975. The plan is likely to take effect early in 1976, after it is ratified by all nine EEC parliaments.

An interesting feature of Stabex is that no restrictions are to be placed on the use of transfers by the beneficiary governments. In particular, the funds need not be used to compensate producers of the primary product generating the transfer. If the government foresees a long-term decline in the prospects for that product, the funds may be used instead for general revenue purposes or to subsidize the development of a more promising export.

Sugar. A separate provision of the Lome Convention guarantees supply and purchase of fixed quantities of sugar, which currently accounts for 12 percent of total ACP food exports to the EEC. Under the agreement, each producing country is assigned a quota within an annual maximum of 1.4 million tons for the ACP group. ACP exporters will sell to the EEC at the same price paid to EEC producers. In contrast to the Stabex scheme, the sugar agreement runs for an indefinite period, but at least seven years. Cancellation by either side requires two years' notice.

231

UNCTAD Integrated Program for Commodities

In an UNCTAD report[12] released early this year,
UNCTAD Secretary-General Gamani Corea has proposed the
negotiation of an "integrated" program for commodities
which would apply uniform principles to most primary
products exported by developing countries. The integrated program is made up of five basic proposals:

> 1) Establishment of international buf-
> fer stocks for eighteen commodities,
>
> 2) Creation of an international fund
> to finance the buffer stock arrangement,
>
> 3) Negotiation of supply and purchase
> agreements by individual countries,
>
> 4) Compensatory financing to stabilize
> export earnings of producing countries,
>
> 5) Expansion of raw material processing
> activities in producing countries.

The "Corea Plan" has been endorsed by several conferences called by third world nations to plan their joint
strategy with regard to primary exports; the plan now
seems to be the major issue confronting the industrialized countries in their attempts to make peace with the
developing nations in the U.N. No single element of the
plan has any claim to substantial novelty. Almost every
international commodity agreement has used buffer stocks
to stabilize price. A large part of all commodity trade
is already covered by long-term private or government
contracts between suppliers and purchasers. Indeed,
some writers believe the vertically integrated multinational firm operations are advantageous mainly because
of their ability to eliminate some of the uncertainty
surrounding price and supply of raw materials. Compensatory financing arrangements are already available
through the International Monetary Fund and are central
to the recently negotiated Lome Convention. And elimination of the "cascaded" tariffs which discourage processing of raw materials in their country of production
has been widely advocated on grounds of efficiency as
well as equity by international economists for a number
of years. So the Corea plan is novel mainly in that it
attempts to use a single multilateral apparatus to operate simultaneously on a broad group of raw materials
produced in over 100 developing countries, rather than

following the more traditional commodity-by-commodity approach.

International Buffer Stocks. The Corea proposal identifies eighteen major commodities as suitable for stockpiling. These are wheat, maize, rice, sugar, coffee, cocoa, tea, cotton, jute, wool, hard fibers, natural rubber, copper, lead, zinc, tin, bauxite, and iron ore. According to the report, these 18 commodities account for more than half of all developing country primary product exports (excluding petroleum). Along with the expected tropical products, the list include several commodities which are exported mainly by developed countries -- e.g., wheat, corn, and wool -- but which are deemed important to developing countries both as importers and as exporters. Under the plan, stocks would be accumulated when their prices are at an agreed floor level and released to the market when prices moved above an agreed ceiling. Thus, "accumulated stocks would serve as an international reserve of foodstuffs and industrial raw materials which would help to assure an uninterrupted flow of world consumption and world industrial production...international stocks would be able to exercise a continuing stabilizing effect on world commodity markets, in the interest of both exporters and importers."

Financing of Buffer Stocks. The Corea report estimates the cost of acquiring the necessary stocks at $11 billion (of which grains account for $5 billion and sugar, coffee, and copper together account for $3 billion). The stock financing is to be undertaken through a "common fund" supported by both importing and exporting countries. There is also a suggestion that the fund might prove to be an attractive investment for oil-exporting nations. Given the volatile behavior of commodity prices over the past few years, the actual cost could be substantially higher or lower. The industrialized nations would undoubtedly be called upon to subscribe a large part of the common fund, and the distribution of this noneligible financial burden is likely to be a major source of dissension, both between the third world and the industrialized bloc, and within the latter.

Supply and Purchase Agreements. Since the avowed aim of the third world is to raise prices received for their commodity exports, it is likely that suppliers will have to be allocated export quotas which are a fraction of the amounts the countries would wish to supply at the elevated prices. This aspect is especially critical in view of the fact that developed countries, which supply

a large fraction of most of the included commodities,
may have higher supply elasticities than their developing counterparts. The industrialized countries, fear-
ful of further interruptions in their supplies of critical raw materials, would make purchase commitments,
matched by assured supply from exporting countries. In
practice, this part of the plan is apt to be troublesome. Artificially high stabilized prices will induce
buyers and sellers to make agreements outside the program, while in periods of scarcity available stocks are
likely to be insufficient to bridge the gap between
"guaranteed" supplies to purchases and export shortfalls.
Private long-term contracts in volatile markets, along
with freely operating futures markets, would probably
provide more security for both buyers and sellers at a
smaller cost. At present, likelihood of abrogation of
contracts by governments, as well as the virtual cer-
tainty of intervention in times of unusually high or low
prices, hamper the efficient operation of these normal
market safeguards.

Compensatory Financing. Under this proposal, automatic compensation would be provided whenever developing countries experience shortfalls in their earnings
from raw material exports. The compensation would be
in the form of loans, to be repaid when export earnings
exceeded normal levels. Under some circumstances, un-
paid loan balances would be converted into grants. This
provision thus parallels closely what the Stabex facility under the Lome Convention will do for a limited
group of countries and commodities.

Expansion of Processing. Industrialized countries
often apply low tariffs on imports of raw materials,
with successively higher rates assessed on more processed
forms of the same commodity. This "cascaded" tariff
structure results in extremely high effective rates of
protection to processing activities, so that developing country producers of raw materials find it unprofit-
able to process raw materials. In their programs to
modernize and industrialize, a number of countries have
attempted to promote processing prior to export. In
some cases, these programs have led to "negative value
added" -- the value on world markets of the processed
commodity is less than the world market value of the raw
material consumed. However, the higher transport costs
for unprocessed forms make it probable that processing
prior to export is efficient for at least some countries
and commodities. Thus, a decision by industrialized
countries to phase out tariff structures which discrim-

inate against imports of processed raw materials would be mutually beneficial. (The preferential tariff arrangements now in effect between many developed and less developed regions has already provided some stimulus to development of raw material processing facilities.)

Indexation of Export Prices

Perhaps the most controversial proposal to emerge during the current debate on international policy toward trade in primary commodities involves indexation of export prices -- tying the prices of primary exports to those of manufactured products developing nations import from the industrialized countries. Some oil exporters, notably Iran, have called for tying of oil prices to a general index of manufactured import prices, providing a kind of cost-of-living escalator for the exporting countries. In other cases, such as bauxite and iron ore, the suggestion is to link the price of the raw material to that of the finished product (aluminum and steel). In several recent speeches, United States Secretary of State Henry Kissinger has reaffirmed U.S. opposition to the indexation concept, on the ground that such a scheme would harm the poorest LDCs, which import substantial amounts of primary commodities. Spokesmen for other industrialized countries have also voiced strong opposition to indexation.

The proposal to index commodity export prices finds its roots in the well-established belief that there is a long-run tendency for the terms of trade to turn against countries exporting primary products. This view was popularized by Dr. Raul Prebisch, the first Secretary-General of UNCTAD and a leading figure in the quest by developing nations for more favorable terms for their primary exports. Proponents of the thesis argue that the demand for primary products tends to grow less than proportionally with incomes, so that an expanding world economy will spend relatively less on these exports and relatively more on the products of the industrialized countries, resulting in a tendency for the prices of raw materials to fall relative to those of manufacturers.

Empirical evidence had not lent clear support to a long-run adverse terms of trade movement, but neither has it conclusively demonstrated the opposite. Recent years have seen soaring prices for almost all raw materials, but the prices of some have already receded well below highs reached during 1973 and 1974. For example, cocoa had fallen to 66¢ a pound in July 1975, down from its 1974 high of over $1.30, but still well above the price of 32¢ it brought in 1972. For the period between 1963 and 1975-I, indices developed by the Statistical Office of the United Nations indicate that the average prices of beverages (coffee, tea, and cocoa) and of mineral ores kept pace with those of manufactured exports, while those of cereals and fats, oils, and oil seeds did somewhat better, and those of textile fibers lagged behind. (See Table 4.) A group of UNCTAD experts, commissioned by Secretary-General Gamani Corea to assist in evaluating the indexation proposal, reported in May they found no conclusive evidence that developing nations have suffered from adverse long-term price movements. However, even within the group of experts some dissent from this conclusion was expressed.[13]

Apart from its possible deleterious distributional consequences for the poorest developing nations, the underlying economic rationale of the indexation proposal is weak. Maintaining a relative price which is independent of supply and demand conditions can result only in shortages or gluts. Even in combination with a buffer stock arrangement, an indexed selling price must lead to constant accumulation unless world supply can be controlled through strictly enforced individual production quotas. Furthermore, it is unlikely that producers of raw materials experiencing strong world demand will agree to limit their price increases to those dictated by the indexation formula; were they to agree to do so, shortages would result.

Direction for the Future

In their desire to make peace with the third world, the industrialized nations will undoubtedly be tempted to accede to demands for international agreements which sacrifice economic efficiency for other ends. If widely adopted, such policies imply a lower rate of growth for the world economy and less total wealth available to be distributed or redistributed. Even those who advocate a major redistribution of wealth between rich and poor nations must come to realize the long-run implications of effecting these transfers through international commodity agreements. If developed countries accept a short-run solution which sacrifices productivity in quest of a world distribution of income deemed more equitable, the implied sacrifice of economic efficiency may soon leave all nations worse off. Traditional development strategies focus on means of creating new wealth through investment; commodity policies at best redistribute a given total.

A further consideration for negotiators is the impact of higher commodity prices on the internal distribution of income. Without any mechanism to provide compensatory transfers, a redistribution of world wealth through artificially supported commodity prices is likely to be a redistribution from the poor of the industrialized nations to the rich of the developing nations.

Stabilization of export earnings, with compensatory financing provided at mildly concessionary interest rates for the poorer nations, may be a desirable middle ground for compromise. While meeting at least some of the problems currently faced by third world commodity exporters, such a scheme would not imply uneconomic distortions of production or consumption of particular commodities. If an earnings stabilization approach is chosen, it is important that a moving average of earnings be used as the norm against which shortfalls are measured, so that there remains an incentive for producing nations to shift into primary commodities with the highest economic value. An expansion of the present IMF compensatory financing facility would appear to be the best means of implementing this approach.

With the current mood of nationalism and expropriation, as so eloquently expressed in the Charter of Economic Rights and Duties of States, adopted at last year's U.N. General Assembly session over the objections of most of the developed countries, private capital may soon become the truly scarce resource for the third world. Financial intermediation by international agencies such as the World Bank may be necessary to substitute for private investment flows which are likely to dwindle in coming years if the developing nations begin to implement the "rights" which they have legislated for themselves. But whether an agency like the World Bank can also serve as an intermediary for specialized skills and technology previously channeled to the LDCs along with private investment remains to be seen.

FOOTNOTES

This paper was prepared for the Section on Documentary Programs of Bavarian Radio and Television.

[1] See Daniel P. Moynihan's provocative article, "The United States in Opposition" Commentary, March, 1973; Irving Kristol expresses a similar point of view in "The 'New Cold War,'" The Wall Street Journal, July 17, 1975.

[2] The factual material in this paper is drawn from a variety of sources; in most cases I do not attempt to make specific attributions of particular pieces of information. For recent international conferences and negotiations, most of the information was provided by new accounts in The Wall Street Journal, Business Week, The New York Times, and The Economist. On some issues, more detail was available in articles appearing in the United Nations Chronicle, UNCTAC Monthly Bulletin, IMF Survey, Bulletin of the European Communities, and the West German monthly Intereconomics. UNCTAD documents, including the Final Act and Report of UNCTAD I and Proceedings of UNCTAD II, yielded the specifics of past proposals.

[3] "U.S., European Trade Talks Jeopardized by Differing Attitudes in Market Control," The Wall Street Journal, May 5, 1975.

[4] "U.S. Trade Law Angers Latin Lands," The Wall Street Journal, March 3, 1975.

[5] The economist's perspective on international trade in commodities is detailed in Harry G. Johnson, Economic Policies Toward Less Developed Countries (Brookings, 1967), and Trade, Aid and Development: The Rich and Poor Nations, by John Pincus (McGraw-Hill, 1967). The political factors in raw materials trade are examined in Stephen D. Krasner's "Structuring International Raw Material Markets," to appear in Gerald Garvey, ed., The Political Economy of International Resource Flows (Princeton).

[6]Data on production and trade in primary commodities
were drawn mainly from these sources: United
Nations Statistical Yearbook, 1974, various
issues of the United Nations Monthly Bulletin
of Statistics, various issues of the International Monetary Fund International Financial
Statistics, Commodity Yearbook, 1974, and
F.A.O. Production Yearbook, 1973.

[7]Details from Council Report No. 16, United States-
Japan Trade Council, March 12, 1975.

[8]See especially recent articles by C. Fred Bergsten,
including "The New Era in World Commodity Markets," Challenge, September/October 1974, "Commodity Power is Here to Stay," The Brookings Bulletin, Spring 1974, and "The Response to the
Third World," Foreign Policy 18, 1975. For
other perspectives, see Raymond F. Mikesell,
"More Third World Cartels Ahead?" Challenge,
November/December 1974; Ray Vickers, "Cartel-
izing Commodity Prices," March 6, 1975, A. Gary
Shilling, "Lessons of History for OPEC," March
10, 1975, and Everett Martin and Roger Ricklefs,
"Commodity Power: 'Third World' Presses to
Stabilize the Prices of Its Raw Materials,"
July 3, 1975, all in The Wall Street Journal.

[9]In addition to references previously cited, information about specific commodities was drawn
from several recent books: Alton D. Law, International Commodity Agreements (Lexington, 1975),
Raymond Vernon and L. T. Wells, Jr., Manager in
the International Economy (to be published in
October, 1975 by Prentice Hall), and Scott R.
Pearson and John Cownie, et. al., Commodity
Exports and African Economic Development (Lexington, 1974).

[10]Law, op. cit.

[11]Sepcific provisions of alternative commodity plans
are described at length in testimony before the
U.S. Subcommittee on International Trade, Invest-
ment and Monetary Policy of the House Committee
on Banking, Currency and Housing by Julius L.
Katz, Deputy Assistant Secretary of State for
Economics and Business Affairs, James P. Grant,
President of the Overseas Development Council,
Gerald L. Parsky, Assistant Secretary of the
Treasury, and Sam Y. Cross, United States Direc-

tor of the International Monetary Fund. Other
details are drawn from a July 1, 1975 memorandum
on commodity agreements prepared by William
Strawn for the Members of Congress for Peace
through Law and a June 21, 1975 report by Richard
S. Frank for National Journal Reports.

[12]TD/B/C.1/166, as quoted in UNCTAD Monthly Bulletin
No. 101, January 1975.

[13]"Summary of main conclusions," Expert Group on Indexation. For a criticism of the Group's analysis,
see Jonathan Power, "Of Raw Materials, Raw Statistics and Raw Deals," New York Times, August 31,
1975.

TABLE 1

DEVELOPING COUNTRY COMMODITY EXPORTS

ACCOUNTING FOR MORE THAN 20% OF TOTAL EXPORT EARNINGS

COUNTRY	EXPORT	% OF TOTAL EXPORT EARNINGS, 1975
Algeria	Petroleum	91
Bangladesh	Jute	53
Barbados	Sugar	42
Bolivia	Tin	41
	Petroleum	26
Burma	Rice	44
	Teak	22
Burundi	Coffee	87
Cameroon	Cacao	25
	Coffee	24
Central African Republic	Cotton	23
	Coffee	23
Chad	Cotton	65 (1974)
Chile	Copper	67 (1974)
Colombia	Coffee	42
Congo	Petroleum	54
Costa Rica	Bananas	27
Dominican Republic	Sugar	65
Equador	Petroleum	57
Egypt	Cotton	37
El Salvador	Coffee	33
Ethiopia	Coffee	31
Gabon	Petroleum	86
Gambia	Peanuts	92
Ghana	Cacao	54 (1974)
Guatemala	Coffee	25
Guyana	Sugar	50
	Bauxite & Alumina	32 (1974)
Haiti	Coffee	33

241

TABLE 1, Continued

COUNTRY	EXPORT	% OF TOTAL EXPORT EARNINGS, 1975
Honduras	Bananas	21
Indonesia	Petroleum	74
Iran	Petroleum	97
Iraq	Petroleum	99
Ivory Coast	Coffee	24
Jamaica	Bauxite & Alumina	68
	Sugar	21
Jordan	Phosphates	41
Kuwait	Petroleum	93
Liberia	Iron Ore	75
Libya	Petroleum	100
Malawi	Tobacco	42
Malaysia	Rubber	37
Mauritania	Iron Ore	82
Mauritius	Sugar	85
Morocco	Phosphates	47
Nicaragua	Cotton	25
Nigeria	Petroleum	93
Panama	Bananas	21
Philippines	Sugar	26
	Coconut products	20
Rwanda	Coffee	63
Saudi Arabia	Petroleum	100
Senegal	Phosphates	26
	Peanuts	21 (1974)
Sierra Leone	Diamonds	54
Somalia	Bananas	20 (1974)
Sri Lanka	Tea	49
Sudan	Cotton	46
	Peanuts	22
Syria	Petroleum	69
Togo	Phosphates	76 (1974)
Tunisia	Petroleum	51
	Phosphates	20 (1974)

TABLE 1, Continued

COUNTRY	EXPORT	% OF TOTAL EXPORT EARNINGS, 1975
Uganda	Coffee	76
Uruguay	Wool	23
Venezuela	Petroleum	95
Western Samoa	Copra	57
	Cacao	26
Zaire	Copper	66 (1974)
Zambia	Cooper	90

Source: International Monetary Fund, International Financial
    Statistics, December, 1976.

TABLE 2

LDC EXPORTS OF PRIMARY COMMODITIES, 1973

(MILLIONS OF U.S. DOLLARS)

COMMODITY CLASS	EXPORTS TO / EXPORTS FROM	WORLD	DEVELOPED MARKET ECONOMIES	EEC	USA	JAPAN
Total trade (SITC 0-9)	World	572,650	408,560	240,580	69,960	34,460
	All LDCs	108,790	81,430	34,560	21,520	14,960
	Africa	20,360	16,650	11,390	2,190	1,030
	America	29,060	22,130	6,810	10,970	1,570
	Middle East	27,030	20,180	10,690	1,270	5,060
	Other Asia	31,300	21,540	5,380	6,960	7,020
	OPEC	42,650	34,300	16,650	6,570	6,870
Food, beverages, and tobacco	World	76,960	54,570	31,670	8,860	5,570
	All LDCs	20,640	14,980	6,950	4,380	1,660
Cereals (SITC 041-045)	World	15,670	7,060	4,070	36	1,870
	All LDCs	1,750	760	485	4	140
Crude materials except fuels; oils and fats (SITC 2 + 4)	World	57,950	44,340	22,280	5,200	10,010
	All LDCs	17,720	11,950	5,270	1,700	3,480
Oil seeds, nuts and kernels (SITC 22)	World	4,900	4,120	2,330	71	1,110
	All LDCs	1,170	1,000	680	63	145

TABLE 2, Continued

(MILLIONS OF U.S. DOLLARS)

COMMODITY CLASS	EXPORTS TO / EXPORTS FROM	WORLD	DEVELOPED MARKET ECONOMIES	EEC	USA	JAPAN
Textile fibres (SITC 26)	World	11,470	7,590	3,880	240	2,060
	All LDCs	3,200	1,790	910	64	500
Crude fertilizers and minerals (SITC 27)	World	4,160	2,940	1,600	420	335
	All LDCs	1,370	820	350	185	140
Metalliferous ores and metal scraps (SITC 28)	World	11,220	9,340	3,920	1,290	3,070
	All LDCs	3,710	3,250	1,100	610	1,220
Animal and vegetable oils and fats (SITC 4)	World	3,740	2,630	1,820	245	155
	All LDCs	1,330	1,030	690	185	39
Mineral fuels & related materials (SITC 3)	World	63,100	50,320	23,460	10,660	8,100
	All LDCs	43,040	34,800	15,580	7,890	6,790
	OPEC	37,820	31,240	15,310	5,780	6,180
Primary commodities (SITC 0-4)	World	198,010	149,230	77,410	24,540	23,680
	All LDCs	80,800	61,730	27,800	13,970	11,930

Source: United Nations Statistical Office, Monthly Bulletin of Statistics, July 1975.

TABLE 3

MAJOR PRIMARY COMMODITY PRODUCERS

COMMODITY	MAJOR PRODUCERS, 1974	OUTPUT AS % OF WORLD TOTAL	
		TOP 4 LDC PRODUCERS	ALL LDCs
Agricultural			
Cocoa	Ghana, Nigeria, Ivory Coast, Brazil, Cameroon, Equador	69	100
Coffee	Brazil, Colombia, Ivory Coast, Angola, Uganda, Guatemala	55	100
Corn	U.S., China, Brazil, U.S.S.R., South Africa, France, Yugoslavia, Mexico, Argentina	18	36
Cotton	U.S.S.R., U.S., China, India, Pakistan, Turkey, Brazil	32	63
Jute	India, Bangladesh, China, Burma, Nepal, Thailand	93	100
Peanuts	India, China, U.S., Senegal, Sudan, Nigeria	55	86
Rice	China, India, Indonesia, Bangladesh, Japan, Thailand	67	92
Rubber, Natural	Malaysia, Indonesia, Thailand, Sri Lanka, India, Liberia	85	100
Soybeans	U.S., Brazil, China	30	32
Sugar	U.S.S.R., Brazil, India, Cuba, U.S., France, Mexico	28	32
Tea	India, China, Sri Lanka, Japan, Indonesia, Kenya	67	89
Wheat	U.S.S.R., U.S., China, India, France, Canada	20	30
Wool	Australia, U.S.S.R., New Zealand, Argentina, South Africa, China	14	18

246

Table 3, Continued

OUTPUT AS % OF WORLD TOTAL

COMMODITY	MAJOR PRODUCERS, 1974	TOP 4 LDC PRODUCERS	ALL LDCs
Mineral			
Bauxite	Australia, Jamaica, Guinea, Surinam, U.S.S.R., Guyana	42	53
Copper	U.S., U.S.S.R., Chile, Canada, Zambia, Zaire	32	37
Iron Ore	U.S.S.R., Australia, U.S., Brazil, China, Canada	24	35
Lead	U.S., U.S.S.R., Australia, Canada, Mexico, Peru	18	29
Petroleum	U.S.S.R., U.S., Saudi Arabia, Iran, Venezuela, Kuwait	36	63
Tin	Malaysia, U.S.S.R., Bolivia, Indonesia, Thailand, Australia	62	77
Zinc	Canada, U.S.S.R., U.S., Australia, Peru, Mexico	18	27

Sources: U.N. Yearbook of Industrial Statistics, 1974; U.N. Statistical Yearbook, 1975; F.A.O. Production Yearbook, 1974; Commodity Yearbook, 1976.

247

TABLE 4

EXPORT PRICE INDICES
(1963 = 100)

	Weight in Index	1975-I	High	
All Primary Products	100%	291	302	(1974-IV)
Food	44%	246	265	(1974-IV)
Coffee, Tea, Cocoa	8%	197	219	(1974-II)
Cereals	13%	258	292	(1974-I)
Agricultural Non-Food	32%	202	228	(1974-I)
Fats, Oils, Oil Seeds	6%	243	307	(1974-I)
Textiles	10%	154	214	(1973-I)
Minerals	24%	485	487	(1974-IV)
Metal Ores	5%	207	224	(1974-II)
Fuels	19%	564	571	(1974-IV)
Manufactured Goods	100%	204*	204	(1974-IV)*

*1974-IV is latest date available.

Source: Statistical Office of the United Nations, Monthly Bulletin of Statistics, June 1975.

248

TABLE 5

COMMODITY EXPORT PRICES, 1961-1975

	1961	1962	1963	1964	1965	1966	1967	1968
CACAO (Ghana)	21.36	19.89	21.04	22.32	17.51	16.46	23.08	23.46
COFFEE (Brazil)	31.72	29.67	28.98	38.44	39.62	34.31	31.83	31.71
COPPER (Chile)	28.90	29.36	29.10	31.52	35.19	49.05	58.06	47.19
GROUNDNUTS (Nigeria)	8.16	7.65	7.41	7.86	8.71	8.91	8.24	6.91
JUTE (Pakistan)	283	199	189	195	228	238	251	218
LEAD (Australia)	7.80	6.70	7.56	11.37	13.94	11.81	10.29	9.86
RUBBER (Malaysia)	26.53	25.13	23.71	22.28	22.43	21.56	18.11	17.11
TEA (India)	57.50	55.63	56.53	56.55	55.71	52.78	53.57	48.37
TIN (Malaysia)	108.1	110.5	110.1	148.2	172.1	159.1	145.2	139.4
WHEAT (U.S.)	1.77	1.81	1.79	1.80	1.63	1.69	1.74	1.68
WOOL (Australia)	55.0	55.4	64.7	68.3	57.1	61.8	55.4	52.7
ZINC (Canada)	9.96	9.05	9.70	12.02	12.46	12.11	11.13	10.94
LDC Import Price Index (1961 = 100)	100	101	101	102	103	103	104	103

249

Table 5, Continued

	1969	1970	1971	1972	1973	1974	1975-I
CACAO (Ghana)	30.11	34.66	26.24	23.82	32.97		
COFFEE (Brazil)	32.89	44.26	33.88	42.73	52.68	57.51	50.61
COPPER (Chile)	61.49	56.96	49.01	44.45	70.78		
GROUNDNUTS (Nigeria)	8.64	9.46	11.27	12.36	13.23	16.24	
JUTE (Pakistan)	236	233	240				
LEAD (Australia)	9.71	13.35	10.94	12.93	17.49	48.89	23.47
RUBBER (Malaysia)	22.21	18.98	15.56	15.30	28.51	34.66	
TEA (India)	43.34	44.62	45.82	45.61	42.60	49.20	
TIN (Malaysia)	151.3	162.1	154.0	165.9	205.0	333.2	
WHEAT (U.S.)	1.64	1.58	1.68	1.74	2.94	4.67	
WOOL (Australia)	52.5	44.5	36.2	53.7	138.8	118.6	87.0
ZINC (Canada)	11.22	11.94	12.37	15.44	21.26	34.13	36.78
LDC Import Price Index (1961 = 100)	105	108	114	137	195		

Source: International Monetary Fund, International Financial Statistics, various issues. Unit values are derived from trade statistics of exporting country listed, in each case the major world exporter in 1963. Values are U.S. dollars per 100 pounds, except jute per short ton, and wheat per bushel. Import price index is derived from U.S. dollar prices.

250

VIII
INTERNATIONAL INTERDEPENDENCY AND WORLD WELFARE

Elias H. Tuma
University of California, Davis

THE PROBLEM

In its Programme of Action for the Establishment of a New International Economic Order of May 16, 1974, the United Nations General Assembly devoted a large section to the "Fundamental Problems" facing the international community. First among these was the problem of raw materials. The Assembly passed resolutions regarding sovereignty over natural resources, trade, prices, and the processing of these resources by the producer countries.[1] The number and variety of these resolutions indicate the sustained significance of natural resources and raw materials to the developing countries, and the problems facing them as a result. Probably these problems will still loom large years hence unless new measures are taken and seriously implemented. Most of the resolutions passed by the Assembly and most of the national policies in practice are political in nature and tend to commit the producers of the raw materials to continued dependence on the buyers of their products and to a relatively weak position in the negotiations and agreements resulting therefrom.

Continued dependence and vulnerability of the raw material producers are inherent in the economic order which has prevailed in the capitalistic and non-socialist economies. The developing producer countries continue to produce raw materials and primary goods for the benefit of the developed countries, on the assumption that a market economy based on trade and comparative advantage would be the most efficient and welfare-inducing system to all concerned. These assumptions, however, may be questioned on several grounds: (1) The market approach has not worked efficiently, as suggested by the need to take measures to correct inequities and inefficiencies. There are no examples in history to show that free trade and the market approach would be advantageous to all parties, or that they would reduce the gap between the trading countries. The British economy was a great beneficiary of free trade, being the first to develop and the most advanced technological-

ly for many decades. Ironically, that advantage from
free trade has been interpreted as the "imperialism of
free trade" against which the later developers have re-
belled.[2] (2) The market approach and comparative advantage work only if the trading parties begin from a level of relative equality, with no party dominating the
market; only if full mobility of both inputs and outputs were possible; and only if national and political
boundaries were rendered irrelevant. In other words,
freedom of trade and comparative advantage recognize
no political boundaries or national biases, which is
contrary to the facts.

The policy to encourage specialization in primary
products has been influenced frequently by assessing
development and change in quantitative terms only. Yet,
there is a qualitative aspect that has been given little
attention, namely: the production and export of primary
commodities does little to induce technological advance
or technical evolution of the producer country. This
tendency has been illustrated by regressing the structure of production on the per capita GNP. As income
increased the percent of production in the form of primary product declined, as would be expected in the process of development and change in the structure of production. However, in the absence of development, the
primary product share remained high and the composition
of the export basket primary oriented.[3] Thus, by con-
centrating on the production of primary commodities and
since there is no built-in mechanism for the lag to
disappear, the gap between the industrial and the non-
industrial primary-producing countries would tend to
increase, contrary to the spirit of comparative advantage and perfect freedom of trade.

The problem has another dimension which has been
somewhat slighted. Raw materials and primary commodities
are not all of equal significance in the relations between nations, contrary to the purely economic view that
measures every value by the number of dollars expended
to acquire it. Certain commodities are "strategic" and
require special treatment. In some of these cases the
price elasticity of supply may be zero and supply would
be forthcoming only by agreement or by exchanging other
strategic items, almost like a barter trade. In such
situations, the economic tools and comparative advantage
or free trade theory becomes helpless.

Finally, it is often forgotten that economic power
implies (or could imply) international political power.
Trade has been recognized as a political instrument of
national power for a long time. Mercantilist thought

considered trade a positive instrument to enhance state and national power, while in the modern "imperialist" context, trade has been regarded as a mechanism for domination.[4] The mechanism by which power may be accumulated involves the securement of supplies, the <u>supply effect</u>, and the securement of a share of other countries' wealth, the <u>influence effect</u>.[5] The influence effect prevails when a country can use the trade with another as a means of securing certain advantages otherwise unattainable.[6] Hence, while advocating freer trade relations and comparative advantage specialization, few people are willing to admit that the acceptance of specialization may mean the acceptance of a given pattern of distribution of power and dependence between nations, which may be altered only by changing the pattern of specialization and the structure of production and commodity trade. In other words, it is political economy, rather than economic analysis, that best explains international trade. Economic analysis <u>per se</u> not only ignores important aspects of the problem, but also tends to be misleading as a result.

These various misconceptions have often led to the mistaken belief that if only the producers of primary products were given a higher price for their commodities, assured of a market for their output, and allowed to buy the finished goods they desired from the industrial countries, all would be ideal: the primary producers would develop, prosper, and be fully independent. The opposite has been true: the producers of primary products who have exported raw material have remained underdeveloped, poor, and highly dependent. Even the producers of strategic resources who exported in raw form have remained underdeveloped and, except for a few oil producers, poor, and overly dependent on the buyers of their goods for the badly needed revenue and for the specific imports they needed. Although the buyers have also become dependent on the producers of strategic resources, the mutual dependence has not been symmetrical and the producers have found themselves at a disadvantage.[7]

Another misconception has been the widely-spread belief that interdependence between nations has been on the increase and hence a balancing mechanism has been evolving.[8] It is rarely recognized that interdependence, to be constructive, must involve units with varying specialties and needs but with relatively equal capabilities. The absence of such equality on one hand, and the high similarity between the different national units in the present international community, have rendered a "myth" the apparent interdependence in the world, thus

obscuring the real situation.[9] It is particularly
interesting that some observers explain the asymmetry
of interdependence as a result of "vulnerability" of
the actors, rather than as a cause of it.[10] One
might consider asymmetry and vulnerability as results
of the same causes.

Findings and Policy Implications

These various conditions of dependence and instability in the relationships between producers and
consumers of the strategic raw materials are the focus
of analysis in this study. Our findings and tentative
conclusions may be summarized and illustrated as follows:

(1) The assumptions on which current policy has
been based may be challenged and the options available to the producer countries may be shown to be more
numerous than has been thought to be the case. It
may be suggested that once political economy has been
introduced as the tool of analysis -- meaning the interdependence between economics and politics -- and
once the warranted and relevant assumptions have been
identified, the relationship between the producers
and consumers of the strategic and other raw materials
may be rehabilitated and rendered viable, stable, and
fairly predictable.

(2) Interdependence may be better understood in
the context of political economy, in which case power
and vulnerability become equally significant characteristics of control over strategic resources.

(3) The current relationship between producers
and consumers of strategic resources is one of dual
dependence and dual vulnerability, rather than of viable interdependence; hence, this relationship is unstable and unviable. Most recent national and international policies have tended to sustain this unstable
relationship by reinforcing dual dependence and one-
sided dependences.

(4) Viable interdependence between producers and
consumers of strategic resources is feasible, though
is would entail a cost in the form of loss of power,
but also gain in the form of loss of vulnerability.

(5) Structural change is basic to viable interdependence. In a nutshell, the structural change should
accomplish the following: a) Increase the ability of the

resource producer to utilize more of the resource
domestically, such that the country's dependence
on the raw material exports would be curtailed; b)
increase the country's ability to produce and trade
on the market finished and semi-finished products
based on the resource; c) the country would be able
to trade and bargain from a relatively equal technological and economic position; and d) the country
would become less vulnerable to the severe market
fluctuations or the changes in the politics of the
consumer countries than has been the case.

(6) The degree of success and the magnitude
of changes depend on the resources, the country's
dependence on the given resource, its backwardness
technologically and economically, and the political
determination of its leaders to achieve viable interdependence. In all cases, however, certain principles
must be observed: Earnings from the export of the
strategic raw resource should not be much higher than
the capability of the country to absorb capital investment; capital investment should be in industries
that would utilize the resource as well as satisfy
national and international demand for the finished
and semi-finished product based on it; investment
should be planned with more advanced techniques in
mind to reduce the backwardness and dependence of
the country on others; to the extent possible, the
resource exchange should be tied to the exchange
of other strategic resources that are lacking in
the country, including scientific and technical
knowledge; and to be effective, structural change
must gradually achieve high industrial levels including the ability to produce the machinery, not
just to operate it. To observe these principles
would bring about a more viable interdependence and
possible harmony between the producers and consumers
of the resource.

(7) The dependence of the oil producers illustrates the above observations. The proposed structural changes may also be illustrated with reference
to oil; policy implications will follow. The economy
of Iran as a producer of oil has been used to illustrate.

Iran, the largest, population-wise, of the OPEC
members, uses less than 10 percent of its oil output
domestically.[11] The problems, potential changes and
the results are shown diagramatically in Figure 1.

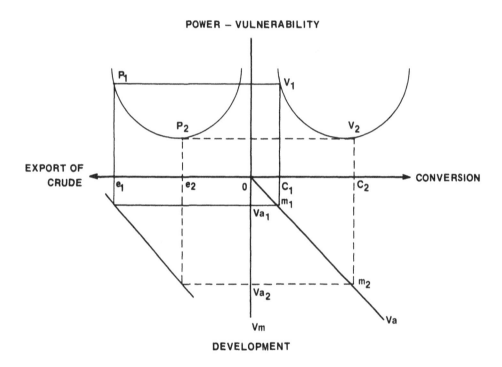

FIGURE 1

VIABLE INTERDEPENDENCE: IRAN

This diagram has been derived systematically, as shown in the Appendix, and is based on the discussion of the next section.

Iran processes a small percentage of its crude oil
or about 11 percent. The rest in exported in crude
form; roughly these are equivalent to Oc_1 on the conversion axis and $Oe1$ on the crude export axis respectively. Accordingly, Iran is highly vulnerable, at
level v_1 because of the small conversion. But Iran
is also powerful because of the consumer dependence
on its crude oil exports as in p_1. Such a position,
however, contributes little to development in the form
of value-added, technological change, or employment,
as shown on the value-added axis, the impact being
Ova_1, which corresponds to v_1, p_1, e_1, c_1. As long
as these patterns of use and trade continue, instability and backwardness are bound to continue. The converted crude is consumed primarily in the form of gas-
oline, kerosene and jet fuel, and fuel oils which are
used in industrial production. The total quantity of
all these amounted to only 4.5 percent of the crude
oil produced in 1974. Given other derivatives and
petrochemicals, the estimated 11 percent of crude oil
used domestically seems reasonable.[12] Though the data
on the value-added and employment and development impact are vague, it is apparent that the impact has
been limited, as in Va_1, since the processing has been
mainly in the form of refining which is highly concentrated, capital intensive, and dependent on machinery
produced abroad.[13]

Iran depends on the export of crude, as in e_1, and
earns large sums of money that should serve development
well. The use of these funds, however, tends to have
a limited effect on the economic structure of the country. Iran earned about 18 billion dollars from oil in
1974/5, which was a great jump over the previous annual
earnings of $5 billions in 1973/4, or $1.3 billion in
1970/1. The sudden increase in earnings had a shock
effect on expenditure and development planning. Iran
allocated roughly 71 percent of its oil revenues to
Plan Organization, the agency responsible for development on behalf of the state. The allocation of funds,
as classified by Plan Organization is biased toward
development (80-88 percent), and the rest for non-deve-
lopment projects. Of the development expenditures,
14-19 percent are allocated for industry and mines.[14]

This allocation pattern suggest a great commitment
to the idea of development. At the same time, it is
apparent that a large part of the expenditure is on
imports of finished and semi-finished capital and con-

257

sumer goods. Machinery and parts for assembly plants form the bulk of the industrial imports. Steel mills are built by foreign outfits on contract. Except for a modest beginning in the production of spare parts, there is no attempt to build machinery in Iran.

Iran has gone farther in undermining the impact of its oil revenues on development by contracting with foreign firms for the construction of schools, hospitals, and even houses, though local facilities should be capable of these undertakings. The expenditure on nuclear generators, so far in advance of any danger of running out of oil, seems most unwarranted. Better planning of the exploitation of oil fields would be more efficient than exporting crude oil in order to earn revenues which in turn are recycled into foreign economies in return for nuclear generators to produce energy -- which could have been produced with the use of oil in the first place. This is especially peculiar since Iran does not have uranium, nor the technology, nor the skill needed to operated these generators and maintain them. In many ways, Iran is utilizing its natural gas in the same fashion: export in raw form, low conversion, and a limited impact on the structure of the economy. Dual dependence and vulnerability continue as a result.

To achieve viable interdependence with the consumers of Iranian oil, a new pattern must evolve. Iran might increase its conversion of oil to Oc_2 or roughly up to 60 percent of its crude output; that would reduce its vulnerability to v_2; reduce its exports of crude to e_2, with the option of exporting finished products, and thus increasing the value-added to Ova_2. The process of development, employment, technical know-how, and viable interdependence would then become a reality. Can this change be implemented?

Given its pattern of investment and expenditure on consumption and non-productive imports, Iran would fare better if it were to cut its crude oil exports by half, and redirect investment into industries that would consume energy, create employment, and raise the level of technology rates commensurate with the ability of the country to absorb capital productively. For example, while producing petrochemicals, it should be possible to build factories that make the machines for the petrochemical industry. While the purchase of arms may seem unnecessary, the making of arms would have multiple effects: the security effect and the economic development and viability effects; Israel offers the best example in that respect. Iran is a major buyer of agricul-

tural machinery and motorized equipment. To invest in
the making of such machinery would utilize strategic
resources, save on foreign exchange, reduce dependence
on the outside, make it possible to build machinery
better suited for the environment, and radically reduce the technical gap between Iran, as an LDC oil
producer, and the DC oil consumers. As a spillover,
Iran might even attract back the skilled people that
have emigrated and thus restore a strategic resource,
the loss of which has often caused a bottleneck in the
process of development and the achievement of a viable
interdependence. Many other areas of investment may
be suggested. The main argument is that once Iran
has embarked on this redirection of investment, Iran
can begin to speak of a partnership and a viable interdependence with the developed oil consumers.

The above results and policy implications have been
obtained by examining the role of strategic resources,
the pattern of utilizing them in the history of the
developed countries, and by examining the policy options available to the producers and consumers of strategic resources. The analysis has also been demonstrated diagramatically in the appendix. These topics are
treated below in that order.

STRATEGIC RESOURCES AND FORMS OF DEPENDENCE

A primary product or resource is a raw material
which has been subjected to little or no processing
of any sort. It has little value added to it in the
form of processing, usually requires relatively simple
technology, except in extraction and conveyance, and
its production and export leave a limited impact on
the technology of the country. The linkage, forward
and backward, associated with processing and finishing
are missing; hence, the impact on employment tends to
be limited accordingly.

Whether a resource may be considered primary or
processed is a matter of degree and therefore its impact in the economic environment, on incomes, employment, technology, and trade would be gradated accordingly. Yet, here too there is arbitrariness since
a product may be considered fully processed for one
purpose and only half processed for another. Flour
is fully processed grain for home baking, but it is
semi-finished for those who wish to buy bread.

Value adding, and hence conversion, by definition, leave an impact on the levels of employment, output, income, and trade. It is also possible that value adding would enhance the use of skill and technology beyond the level of primary production, in which case the impact on capital consumption, human and otherwise, would be positive. Whether these effects may be expected with conversion is an empirical question since it is conceivable that conversion may be accomplished with the same skills and technology as primary production.

A resource or product may be considered strategic if it has a relatively low price elasticity of supply and a relatively low elasticity of demand. However, the resource supply and demand elasticities may be low as a result of exogenous or non-economic considerations. For example, it may be difficult to acquire jet fighters by varying the nominal price because the supply of jet fighters is dependent on political decisions and hence the supply is apparently price-inelastic. A product or resource may be economically strategic with little or no political significance. Opium poppy is such a product: it is economically strategic in Turkey, but it has no political significance, unless it were to be used as an instrument of warfare. On the other hand, some resources may be politically strategic though of no direct relevance in economic terms, especially if the relevance has been reduced by institutional arrangements; uranium may be such a resource. Most strategic items, however, are relevant to both economics and politics. An economically strategic resource would usually command monopolistic benefits and prices; a poltically strategic resource would command favorable terms in international agreements.

Resources may become strategic or cease to be so by various means which influence the supply and the demand for the resource, both in the short run and in the long run. The discovery of new resources of substitutes, and changes in technology would affect the elasticity of supply in the long run. Changes in taste and new technologies may affect the demand in the long run. In the short run, however, price or income variations may be the major influences on supply and demand, although international agreements and planning could distort these elasticities even in the short run. What makes a resource strategic is that long run measures to secure more or to demand less of it may be costly, uncertain, and too far away in the future, while failure to secure the resource in the short run could have grave effects on employment, income, and national security. This happens as the economy becomes structurally dependent on a given resource, whether it is a fuel, a raw material, or an engineering skill that is in demand. The more dependent an economy is on a resource, the more strategic in one economic situation or system of production but not in another. Hence, resources may be considered strategic according to their elasticities of supply and demand, the number of economies to which they are strategic and the degree of structural dependence on the resource these economies have.

A natural resource, however, may be technologically strategic and yet command neither economic nor political power. Natural rubber may be one such resource. A given resource may be indispensable for an industry but that industry may be expendable, in which case neither would the resource command monopoly prices nor would the country use poltical or military power to secure it. Thus, strategic resources may command economic and/or political significance to the extent to which they are scarce, structurally indispensable, and are demanded by an industry that is regarded strategic and relatively indispensable, either because of its quantitative or qualitative impact in the national economy.

The role of strategic resources in international relations reflects the economic and political power they command. A resource commands power (relatively high prices) if it is strategic, control over its supply is concentrated, and its demand is diffuse or little concentrated. Given the low elasticities characterizing a strategic resource, concentrated control confers monopolistic powers on the controllers allowing them to change monopolistic prices. However, such control may be offset and the economic powers diluted if the demand is also concentrated and capable of generating monopolistic control; the countervailing monopsony power could reduce the impact of monopoly, but not abolish it. The price finally "agreed upon" would reflect the degree of balance between the monopoly and monopsony forces. If the producers of the resource have monopoly power, but the consumers have no monopsony power, the latter would become dependent on the former and would have to pay the price dictated by the producers. This is <u>one-sided dependence</u>. However, if the consumers also have power and can reduce the market for the resource at will, we may speak of <u>dual dependence</u>.

As long as we limit the analysis to consumers and producers, we can confine the analysis to economic power. However, once national boundaries are introduced and producers and consumers are identified as political entities, power begins to play a part and the strategic resource begins to command both economic and political powers, to the extent to which control over its supply and demand are concentrated in the hands of a few (or single) countries. This is the situation represented by international cartels that are backed by national power. Here we would have one-sided dependences or a dual dependence of countries, as producers and consumers of the resource.[15]

Thus, it becomes necessary to consider not only power but also vulnerability of the producer and the consumer of the strategic resource. Power has been defined as the ability to secure benefits or to have performed what would not be secured or performed in regular market situations.[16] In contrast, vulnerability means the loss of potential benefits or the obligation to perform acts otherwise not performed as a result of manipulation of the strategic resource by another party.[17]

It is possible, however, that a country may have power without being vulnerable, as happens when a country controls a major part of the demand or supply of the resource, but the resource-related sector represents only a small percentage of the national economy. In contrast, a country may be vulnerable without having the power; this happens when the resource-related industry is significant in the national economy but the supply or the demand are only a small percentage of the total supply or the demand for the resource.

Power and vulnerability accruing from the control over the supply of or the demand for a resource in the international context and influenced by several considerations: country size, wealth, level of technology, determination, will to act as a monopoly or a monopsony, and the ability to back the decision to act with moral or military power.[18]

The size, wealth (endowment) and level of technology work in unison to determine the degree of power that can be mustered by the controller of the resource supply or demand. The size of the country (or group of countries) and its wealth would affect the ability of that country or group of countries to stand the pressure and offset the dislocations that might be caused by interruptions in the supply of the resource, without suffering

much economic loss or decline. Together with the level
of technology, these characteristics would affect the
extent to which resource-generated dependences can be
overcome or manipulated by military power. On the other
hand, the ability to maintain group control over supply
or demand (united front) and the recruitment of moral
support to prevent military action by the opponents would
render a resource-generated power a real force in negotiating the benefits.

In the extreme case, a relatively large, wealthy,
and highly developed country might be able to forego
the resource-generated benefits altogether without suffering any serious effects; this is possible whenever
exchange of the resource is mainly to enrich the quality
of life, rather than to sustain it. In this case, the
dependence generated by the resource exchange is neutral
and relatively power- and vulnerability-free. On the
other hand, a large, wealthy economy may opt to be self-
sufficient and utilize its own resources and isolate
itself as much as possible. In such a situation, only
a residual dependence would prevail and the power of
either party to the relationship would be minimal.

It is, however, unlikely for the producers of a
resource to adopt either extreme by exporting the total
resource as a primary product, or by being autarkic for
a long time. In either extreme there would be instability and conflict in international relations. Conflict
would be especially likely if the terms of the transaction were to be suddenly changed or unilaterally modified.
Let us see why neither situation is stable.

To export a strategic raw material or primary product as the main use of the resource gives the producer
power over the consumer such that extra benefits may
accrue as a result, as the buyer becomes dependent on
the resource supply. At the same time, as the producer
becomes dependent on the resource revenue to pay for
the imports that are in demand, the prospective buyer
acquires power over the seller. This two-way impact is
what has been described as power and vulnerability.
To the extent to which the buyer and the seller are on
equal levels of power and dependence (vulnerability),
the interdependence may be harmless; bargaining and
negotiation between equals would facilitate transaction.
However, in the event that the two parties are not of
equal power or vulnerability, the relationship between
them could be unstable and dangerous: the less powerful
may try to improve the terms, while the more powerful
would try to delay change, and any move by either party
is liable to be viewed with suspicion and distrust by

the other. Dual dependence, therefore, may be interpreted as dual power and dual vulnerability: both
parties would have power over each other and both
would be vulnerable to each other's decisions.

Total self sufficiency in the use of the resource
is also unstable but not necessarily dangerous. First,
unless the local market is large, the benefits of the
resource endowment would be lost. Second, it is hardly
possible for any country not to exchange goods and
services with other countries willingly for any length
of time. Hence, if no isolationism, then it would be
fully justified to use the resource to maximum advantage.
Third, if the resource is indeed strategic, the isolationist producer country would become a target of envy
and a potential target of attack from the outside. It
is therefore an unstable relationship with the outside
world for any country to become totally isolated.

However, the producer country may choose to export
no primary products and concetrate on processing and
exporting semi-finished and finished goods only. But
unless that country is willing to purchase goods and
services from the outside, it is unlikely that it will
find a market for its product. And if a market did
exist, the result would be virtually complete specialization and a high degree of dual dependence, which has
been shown to be unstable.

The only viable option is for both producers and
consumers to become interdependent in a viable relationship. By viable is meant stable, beneficial, and self-
sustaining. Interdependence would be built into the
structure of the respective economies and therefore would
be anticipated and taken into account in policy determination.

Viability in international politics has been defined
as "the ability and the willingness of one party to destroy or eliminate another." A party that cannot be destroyed as an independent source of decisions is said to
be "unconditionally viable." Conditional viability prevails when destruction is refrained from, either because
it does not pay to do so (secure conditional viability)
or because good will dominates (insecure viability).[19]
Our definition implies another dimension, namely the built-
in structural interdependence that removes the need to
make a decision to destroy or to refrain from destroying
the opponent. Under viable interdependence, the economic
structure would preclude the freedom of decision-making
regarding destruction of the other party, unless the
structure itself were to be in danger of self destruction.

To achieve viability, it is necessary to reduce vulnerability of each of the interdependent parties, establish feasible and efficient production and exchange structures, and reduce as much as possible the technological and power gaps between them. Trade agreements and price changes in favor of one party or the other might reduce instability in the short run. However, such arrangements are good only as long as the respective parties want them to be so, and any change of attitude would be a threat to the existing relationship. To avoid this instability and create viable interdependence, it would be necessary to modify the use of the strategic resource in favor of processing or conversion and hence in favor of a more diversified trade basket. Is it possible to achieve viable interdependence through structural change? Has it prevailed in the history of the modern economies? Are the developing countries capable of resource conversion to an extent that is consistent with viable interdependence between them and the consumers of their strategic resources?

Viable interdependence is conceptually possible. Its empirical feasibility will be treated next.

Patterns of Resource Utilization

The above questions may be explored under the following assumptions: (1) The producers of strategic resources are interested in the development of their economies. (2) Processing of resources -- conversion -- is positively related to development. (3) Export is a function of expected import; the more imports expected, the more it is necessary to export in order to maintain a positive balance of trade. Imports, however, are a function of expected development; the stage of development, and the capacity to absorb imported capital.[20] Given these assumptions, it follows that the producer of strategic resources would seek a balance between conversion and the sale of raw material such that the export earnings would pay for the needed capital imports. To maintain such a balance, production of raw materials would be planned to permit the full utilization of the conversion capacity and to earn enough foreign exchange to pay for imports. Any other policy is bound to influence the price in favor of the party that has more power relative to the other. The policy of resource use balance leads to a balance of power as well, such that the interdependence becomes viable, and neither party would wish to upset it.

COAL:

FIGURE 2

DOMESTIC UTILIZATION OF COAL, AS PERCENT OF SUPPLY
(Output + Imports) ÷ Output x 100

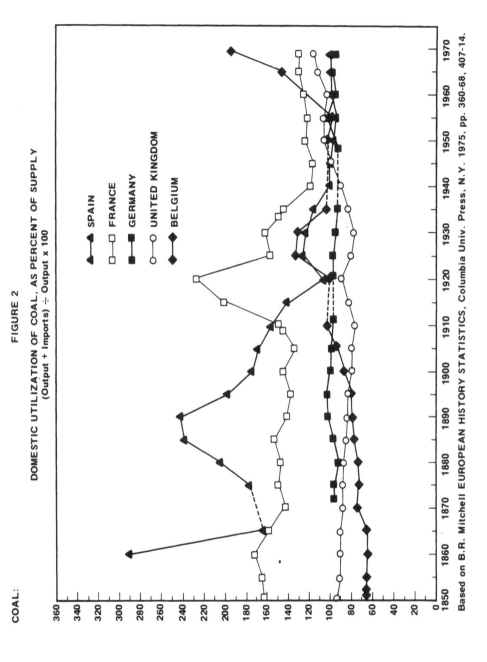

Based on B.R. Mitchell EUROPEAN HISTORY STATISTICS, Columbia Univ. Press, N.Y. 1975, pp. 360-68, 407-14.

IRON ORE:

FIGURE 3

DOMESTIC UTILIZATION OF IRON ORE SUPPLY
(Output + Imports) ÷ Output x 100

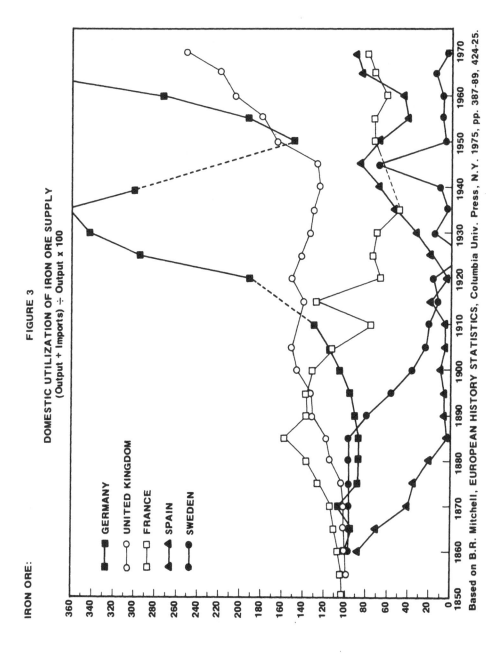

Based on B.R. Mitchell, EUROPEAN HISTORY STATISTICS, Columbia Univ. Press, N.Y. 1975, pp. 387-89, 424-25.

267

The producers of strategic resources have not always behaved according to these principles because they have often found themselves either in an enviable power position, or in a subdued inferior position they could not come out from. The early developers, such as Western Europe and the United States, have occupied power positions and thus have escaped being merely suppliers of strategic resources in raw form, as has been the fate of the less developed backward economies. The European producers of coal, for example, have invariably used a large percentage of their output in domestic sectors, as Figure 2 shows.

Belgium, the lowest relative user of domestic produced coal, nevertheless consumed 66 percent of the available supply in 1850, but has continued to increase its consumption relative to output, reaching 183 percent in 1969. The United Kingdom which is a major producer of coal has always consumed more than 75 percent of its output, while Germany has consumed more than 90 percent of its output. At the same time, there is little evidence that developed countries exported a large percentage of any strategic resource they are endowed with in raw form.

A similar picture may be drawn for iron ore, shown in Figure 3.

Both Germany and the United Kingdom have continued to be major consumers of their own iron ore output. This is equally true of France as a major producer of iron ore up to 1915, after which domestic use stabilized at a lower rate. In contrast, Spain, a major producer, was a modest consumer of its iron ore. Unitl the late 1930s, Spain consumed less than a third of its iron ore output. It is more important to notice, however, that Spain's consumption/output ratio actually began to rise as development accelerated in the last thirty years. The only contradictory evidence comes from Sweden, where the consumption/output ratio began to decline sharply after the beginning of the twentieth century. While development and growth of industry remained high in these years, it is' evident that the output of iron ore increased even more, thus causing the ratio to decline, as the output per capita of iron ore represented in Figure 4 suggests.

At the same time, Sweden's specialization in high quality steel production may have reduced the relative quantity of domestic use of iron ore in favor of quality.

The data on petroleum in the early years are not easily available, but we have information that seems to

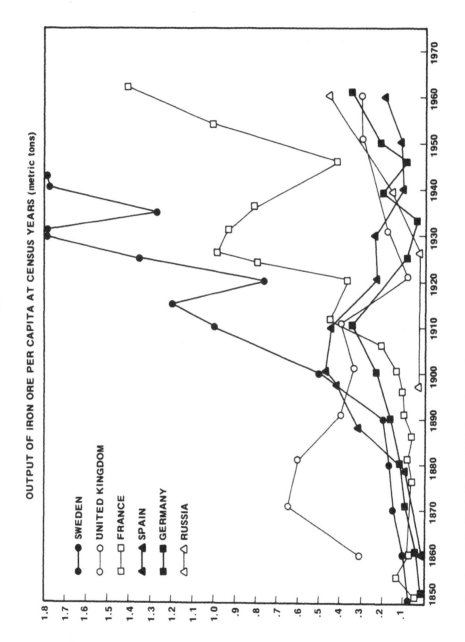

FIGURE 4

OUTPUT OF IRON ORE PER CAPITA AT CENSUS YEARS (metric tons)

SWEDEN
UNITED KINGDOM
FRANCE
SPAIN
GERMANY
RUSSIA

Based on B.R. Mitchell, EUROPEAN HIST. STATISTICS, Columbia University Press, N.Y. 1975, pp. 387-89, 19-24.

TABLE I

DOMESTIC PRODUCTION AND IMPORT OF SELECTED METALLIC ORES
AND CONCENTRATES, 1968

WEST GERMANY	Production	Imports	Percent of Imports in Total Supply
Bauxite	...	1,978	100
Copper (copper content)	1.32	382	97
Lead (lead content)	52.44	135.5	72
Zinc (zinc content)	117.48	100.7	46
Iron Ore	6,444	39,644	86
UNITED KINGDOM			
Bauxite	...	442	100
Copper (copper content)	...	484	100
Lead (lead content)	3.7	49	93
Zinc (zinc content)	...	166.7	100
Iron Ore	13,944	17,534	56
FRANCE			
Bauxite	2,712	335	11
Copper (copper content)	...	269	100
Lead (lead content)	26.4	80.4	75
Zinc (zinc content)	21.8	189.6	90
Iron Ore	55,236	5,017	8
JAPAN			
Bauxite	...	2,450	100
Copper (copper content)	119.9	236	66
Lead (lead content)	62.9	78	55
Zinc (zinc content)	264	409.2	61
Iron Ore	5,430	68,143	93
UNITED STATES			
Bauxite	1,692	12,618	88
Copper (copper content)	1,093.2	507	32
Lead (lead content)	326.4	78.4	19
Zinc (zinc content)	480	495.7	51
Iron Ore	86,508	44,646	34

Sources: United Nations, Monthly Bulletin of Statistics (January,
1973). Charles L. Kimbell, "Minerals in the World Economy,"
in Bureau of Mines, U.S. Department of Interior, Minerals
Yearbook 1969, vol.4.

From: Yuan-Li Wu, op.cit., pp. 12-13.

TABLE II

WORLD ENERGY PRODUCTION AND REGIONAL BALANCES
1925-67

	Production (million metric ton coal equivalent)		Percentages of World Production		Ratio of Production to Consumption[1]	
	1925	1967	1925	1967	1925	1967
North America	779	2,114	49.7	34.4	1.04	0.95
Western Europe	532	540	34.0	8.8	1.03	0.46
Oceania	16	46	1.0	0.7	1.03	0.69
USSR	27	1,124	1.7	18.3	1.07	1.14
East Europe	65	365	4.2	5.9	1.18	0.94
Communist Asia	23	255	1.4	4.1	0.95	1.00
Middle East	8	764	0.5	12.4	3.32	11.24
Japan	33	61	2.1	1.0	1.08	0.24
Other Asia	31	141	1.9	2.3	1.11	0.92
Caribbean	34	383	2.2	6.2	2.98	3.04
Other Latin America	6	68	0.4	1.1	0.45	0.69
North Africa	0.3	200	---	3.3	0.10	10.00
Other Africa	13	84	0.8	0.1	1.22	1.09
WORLD	1,567	6,143	100.0	100.0	1.06[2]	1.04[2]

[1]These ratios of production to consumption indicate whether a region has an export to import balance in energy, and by what proportion North America, for example, exported 4 percent of its production of all types of energy in 1925, but by 1967 it had shifted to importing, on balance, 5 percent of what it consumed. (These regional balance figures are not equivalent to total international trade since some trade is among countries of the same region.)

[2]World consumption figures are less than production because bunkers (fuel for ships) are excluded from national consumption data, and for unexplained discrepancies.

Source: Joel Darmstadter, "Energy in the World Economy," Development Digest, vol. X, #3, July 1972, p. 11.

support the above observations. The USSR has consumed most of its oil output over the years. Even after petroleum production has been revolutionized in the last few decades, Soviet Russia has expanded its domestic use of oil to become an importer as of 1950. Rumania, one of the early developers of the oil industry, consumed about two thirds of its output until the mid 1920s, after which the ratio declined temporarily, only to rise again to a level commensurate with industrialization growth in the country.

The same pattern of resource use continues to characterize the industrial raw materials and fuel, especially those which are exhaustible. These resources, mostly mineral, exist in both developed and developing countries. The minerals that seem to relatively strategic for one country or another include bauxite, chromium, copper content, lead content, zinc content, and iron ore, cobalt, mercury, nickel, tungsten, asbestos, industrial diamonds, quartz, platinum, tin and oil. Table I shows the potential dependence of five industrial countries on foreign supply of some of these minerals. In most cases the five most industrialized countries depend on imports for more than 50 percent of the total supply, and far more so with respect to energy, as Table II shows. According to these data, all the developed countries with the exception of the USSR were net importers of energy in both years 1925 and 1967, even though the United States, Western Europe and Japan were major producers. In other words, the major developed countries utilize all the resources they produce in domestic industry as well as all the imports. It is obvious that they emphasize conversion of these resources as an integral part of development, and they depend on imports because they derive economic benefits in the form of low costs or the conservation of their own resources. The United States, for example, is potentially self-sufficient in the production of manganese, bauxite, iron ore and copper; yet in 1972 the United States imported 95 percent of its manganese supply, 88 percent of its bauxite (1968), 28 percent of its iron ore, and 18 percent of its copper supply. The picture is only a little less glaringly so in the case of chromium, cobalt, mercury, nickel and zinc.[21]

While the ratio of consumption or domestic use to total output may indicate the degree of independence potential or self-sufficiency with respect to a given resource, the form of usage would be suggestive of the degree of development and change in the economic structure. The use of distribution, no doubt, reflects the level of income in society, the degree of automation and industrialization, as

272

suggested by the data on the use of energy. Recent estimates indicate that the U.S. industry consumes 40 percent of all energy consumed in the country, roughly 20 percent is consumed by each of household, commercial transportation, and commercial activities, agriculture and government. Thus, about 80 percent of all energy is consumed in other than household activities in one of the most industrialized societies.[22] The pattern of distribution in other countries shows that over a long period the early developers, especially Belgium and the United Kingdom, have used a large percentage of their hard coal in industrial production. Coke ovens and thermo-electric plants have been the major users.[23] It is of particular interest to note the developed countries also utilized a large part of the processed products they converted the raw resources into. Germany has usually consumed more than 80 percent of the steel and wrought iron it processed in the making of finished products. Sweden consumed 60 to 75 percent of the steel and wrought iron, and France consumed 90 percent. It is true that Spain, though underdeveloped, also consumed most of its steel output, but its output was a very small percentage of the iron ore it produced, in contrast with the developed countries.[24] In summary, then, it appears that the developed countries utilized most of their output of strategic resources in domestic use and consumed most of the finished products based on these resources.

Resource Utilization and Policy Options in Developing Countries

In contrast, the developing countries which are endowed have tended to produce the raw material but not consume it. They export it in raw form and leave the conversion and processing to others. The obvious reason for their behavior is that they have neither the capital nor the skills for conversion; and their own markets are relatively limited. Thus, underdevelopment sustains and feeds on the concentrated effort to produce and export raw material, including the strategic resources. For example, in 1971 the Philippines produced 115 thousand short tons of chromium but consumed none of it domestically. Bolivia produced 27,441 long tons of tin but consumed only 80. Malaysia produced 74,253 long tons and consumed only 270. The rest was exported to be processed and re-exported by other countries.[25]

The trend has not changed and it can be illustrated in other natural strategic endowments: The endowed countries produce and export in raw form if underdeveloped; they produce, process, and then export or consume in finished form

273

if they are developed. These observations are evident in the case of copper, tin, bauxite, aluminum, iron ore, lead and zinc.[26]

This trend may be seen most conspicuously in oil production and use, as in Figure 5. Only Venezuela approaches 25 percent use of its oil supply; but in all countries the ratio of domestic use to output has declined as output per capita of the resource has gone up, thus remaining highly consistent with the traditional pattern.

It is true that a high percentage of the domestic oil use is in the form of fuel oil which indicates industrial and manufacturing activity. The overall utilization, however, is far below what the experience of the developed nations shows as commensurate with development.[27]

The impact of this division of labor has been of concern to the developing countries for a long time because of the potential changes in the terms of trade and their high dependence on those products for revenue. The developed countries, however, have only recently become concerned, especially after the formation of OPEC and its eventful success in controlling the price of oil. Since then interdependence has become a common topic of discussion and policy study. The developed countries, especially the U.S., have sought to reduce their dependence on foreign supply. Elaborate policy statements have been formulated identifying the options available. Table III summarizes these options as they relate to various classes of countries from the standpoint of the United States. The sets of options that are most relevant in this context are those relating to the less developed countries, LDCs, and the Resource Producers. It is interesting that no options are identified for situations in which an LDC is also a resource producer. Option 2, for example, indicates that the United States would avoid conflict by having less dependency with LDCs and with resource producers, even though there may be a cost in the latter case. In contrast, Option 3 suggests that increasing dependency would be undesirable with LDCs but very desirable with resource producers. In other words, the United States should avoid interdependence unless the resource supply is at stake.

These options seem rational from the point of view of the United States -- a large rich, highly developed and powerful country. In general they would apply to other rich and developed countries, especially if they are also relatively large. But these options are not rational for the LDC resource producer country that wishes to develop. The LDC resource producers would need to

274

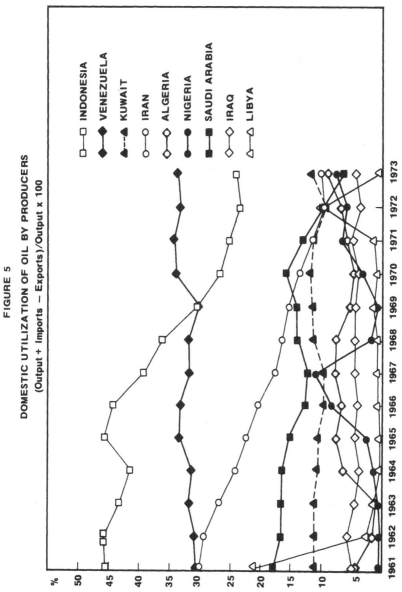

FIGURE 5

DOMESTIC UTILIZATION OF OIL BY PRODUCERS

(Output + Imports — Exports)/Output x 100

INDONESIA
VENEZUELA
KUWAIT
IRAN
ALGERIA
NIGERIA
SAUDI ARABIA
IRAQ
LIBYA

Based on U.N. Stat. Office, Stat. Papers, Series J, WORLD ENERGY SUPPLIES, 1976.

take a different perspective in analyzing these relations. Table IV summarizes various options of interdependence from the point of view of the developing endowed countries.

The LDC resource producers have had experience with options 1,2, and 3a in the case of oil. For many years they left it to the market mechanism and buyers and sellers transacted unencumbered by regulation or restriction. The result was perceived as economic imperialism, with one class of countries remaining underdeveloped and dependent on the sale of raw material for the foreign exchange they needed. The inequality or asymmetry of dependence between buyers and sellers has seemed to be worsening in recent years, despite the commodity agreements introduced to guarantee acceptable prices for the parties concerned. Commodity agreements may have helped to reduce serious price fluctuations but did not have much impact otherwise. Worse still, commodity agreements often entailed waste of capacity and product. For example, acreage limitations resulted in keeping the land idle; "surplus" output was dumped in the sea or destroyed to avoid dumping on the market; yet food was in short supply in various parts of the world. Furthermore, these agreements did not affect the production process or the structure of the economy; dependence and underdevelopment continued. In fact, commodity agreements have often favored the developed countries as major producers of the resources in question. Nevertheless, commodity agreements are still promoted to stabilize prices and incomes accruing from strategic raw materials and resources.[28]

The first major departure from these trends came with the oil cartel, beginning in 1960 but more seriously and effectively since 1973 when OPEC fully controlled the price of oil on the international market. Though previous attempts had been made to monopolize the marketing of resources, success came when the producers became politically independent, the third/fourth worlds became conspicuous and outspoken, and oil became strategic enough to command power. For a while Option 3a seemed to be most effective in restoring to the LDC resource producers the power they had lost and the means to become rich and modern. Now, a few years later, it is apparent that such has not been the case. Option 3a has created antagonism between the LDC producers and the LDC consumers of oil because the sudden increase in prices put a severe burden on their budgets and development plans. It has also antagonized the DC consumers enough for them to threaten, though unsuccessfully, to combat with an oil monopsony. On more than one occasion, the DC consumers have threatened with economic weapons, such as withholding the sale of strategic commodities, or with military power.[29] It is apparent that they are still trying to create a united front to influence the demand for oil. It is apparent also

TABLE III

U.S. Relations

Optional U.S. With
Strategies

	Allies	Communists

1. Reduce Risks
  a. Improve political
     relations
	ALWAYS USEFUL	

b. Coercion	Not applicable	Counterproduct- ive
c. Internationalize	COULD LESSEN STRAINS ARISING FROM ASSYMETRIC DEPENDENCY	
2. Lessen Dependency	Reducing level of mutual dependency, if high, should reduce strains	Not applicable now (excessive <u>future</u> depen- dency would be undesirable)
3. Increase Mutual Dependency	Danger of producing overload in current atmosphere	Current U.S.- Soviet strate- gy, based on persuasive logic
4. Autarky	HISTORICALLY COUNTERPRODUCTIVE	

5. Manipulate Asymmetry
   Through Linkage
   Strategies
	Theoretically pos-
	sible to gain eco-
	nomic advantages
	by threatening in-
	security or with-
	holding exports,
	but chancy
		Unproductive

277

TABLE III
(continued)

U.S. Relations
With

Optional U.S. Strategies	LDCs	Resource Producers
1. Reduce Risks a. Improve political relations	ALWAYS USEFUL	
b. Coercion	Decreasingly Applicable	Not efficacious
c. Internationalize	COULD LESSEN STRAINS ARISING FROM ASYMMETRY DEPENDENCY	
2. Lessen Dependency	Would avoid unwanted intervention consequences and reduce tensions	Desirable, through product substitution, alternative energy sources, lessened consumption, diversification of supply
3. Increase Mutual Dependency	Undesirable in terms of lessening U.S. involvement	Very desirable to balance relations better, increase stake in stability of flows
4. Autarky	HISTORICALLY COUNTERPRODUCTIVE	
5. Manipulate Asymmetry Through Linkage Strategies	Theoretically possible to gain economic advantages by threatening insecurity or withholding exports, but chancy	Unproductive

Source: Alker et al., vol. 1, p. 80.

278

TABLE IV

INTERDEPENDENCE POLICY OPTIONS

LDC Resource Producer Strategy/Relations with Resource Consumers

OPTIONS	LDC	DC	Effects on LDC Resource Producer
A. Continued Interdependence			
1. Free Market exchange	Share underdevelopment	Face monopsony effects	Exhaust resources without development
2. Internationalization	COMMODITY AGREEMENTS		TENUOUS
3. Cartel (monopoly) with			
a. Uniform prices	Antagonism and economic burdens	Conflict -- face monopsony	Unstable relationship
b. Discriminatory prices favoring LDCs	Envy and new layer of interdependence	Antagonism and rise of new alliances	Unstable
B. Reduce Interdependence			
4. Reduce supply and control prices	Antagonism and poverty	Antagonism and threat of retaliation	Unstable
5. Change Structure			
a. Reduce supply and become self-sufficient	ANTAGONISM WITH POSSIBLE DEVELOPMENT		Isolationism
b. Reduce supply of raw material and increase supply of processed derivatives; no price control	Join forces	Restructure; more equal bargaining and less conflict	New power and trade distribution; development viable and stable

279

that the LDC producers cannot continue to depend on this
option much longer because the consumers are now aware
of the strategy and are prepared for it much better than
they were previously.[30]

Option 3b was an attempt to relieve the LDC consumer
of the unexpected price rise burden, but it was replaced
by direct aid or loans to offset the price increase, rather
than apply discriminatory pricing. Various DC consumers
were presumably willing to negotiate separate deals to
assure the flow of oil, though such deals were directed
more toward commodity exchange than to pricing.

So far these various options, which would continue
interdependence in the traditional sense, have failed in
still another way. The impact of the new oil wealth on
development has been limited because of the pattern of
expenditure the producer countries have followed in dis-
pensing the oil revenues.[31]

According to available estimates, the oil exporting
countries (OPEC) spent about 44 billion dollars of their
$100 billion in 1974 on domestic programs. The rest were
deployed outside the respective countries, as shown in the
right-hand side of Table V. The left-hand side shows the
accumulated reserves, amounting to over $72 billion as
of Dec. 31, 1975. It should be noted that deployment of
funds outside the country declined in 1975 to $34 billion,
partly because of higher investment domestically, but also
because the revenue was less than expected and the prices
of these investments were increased drastically in the
meantime. Given the size of foreign investment by OPEC
and the composition of that investment, it is hard to expect any positive impact of this newly created wealth on
economic development of the LDC oil producers. In fact,
we may argue that most of OPEC investments in the industrialized countries are economically unjustified, politically compromising, and in the long run contrary to the
national economic interests of the countries they origi-
nated in. They also sustain the asymmetrical pattern of
interdependence with the DC consumers.

OPEC members, especially the Middle East countries,
have embarked on large programs of education, health, and
welfare for their citizens. Schools have been built in
large numbers; clinics and hospitals have been established,
sometimes in places where there are neither doctors nor
patients, Roads have been built though there may be
neither people nor goods to transport over them. However,
much of the local expenditure allocated to development projects has been concentrated in industries such as petrochemicals, cement factories, steel mills, food processing

TABLE V

OPEC SURPLUS DISPOSITION

Middle East:	Held as Foreign Reserves, Dec. 1975 (Billions)		Estimated Deployment of Investable Surpluses of all OPEC, Billion	
		In U.S.:	1974	1975
Algeria	1,353	Govt. and agency		
Iran	8,697	securities	6	3.5
Iraq	2,272	Bank Deposits	4	.5
Kuwait	14,000	Other*	1	2.6
Libya	2,195		11	6.5
Qatar	2,000			
Saudi Arabia	23,319	In U.K.		
U.A.E.	2,000			
	56,291	Govt. Stocks	.9	.4
Other Countries:		Treasury Bills	2.7	.9
		Sterling Deposits	1.7	.2
Ecuador	286	Other sterling		
Gabon	146	inv.	.7	.3
Indonesia	586	Other foreign		
Nigeria	5,795	currency borrow-		
Venezuela	8,861	ing	1.2	.2
	15,654		7.2	2.0
TOTAL	71,945	In Eurocurrency Markets:		
		In U.K.	13.8	4.1
		In other		
		Countries	9.0	5.0
		Intern.Organ.	3.5	4.0
		Other*	11.9	12.4
			38.2	25.5
		TOTAL	56.4	34.0
		TOTAL OPEC OIL REVENUE	100.7	99.6**

*Includes equities and other property, bilateral commitments, and loans to developing countries.

**New York Times International Econ. Survey, Jan. 25, 1976, p. 28. Source for other data: OAPEC Bulletin, Jan. 1977, pp. 28-29.

and agricultural development. In addition, large sums of money have been spent on the installation of tele-communication systems, the establishment of shipping lines, and the building of plastics factories. Construction has in all cases been an important factor in absorbing capital, both in housing and business projects.

The list may be long and detailed. Nevertheless, a large percentage of the oil proceeds has been expended on non-productive programs, or outside the national economies. Among the former we find a bulging expenditure program devoted to defense, even though there is no apparent or potential enemy. Kuwait, Saudi Arabia and Iran have spent more than 25 percent of their annual state budgets in 1974 on defense. Saudi Arabia reduced its relative expenditure on defense in 1975 to 10 percent of the larger budget, while Iran increased its share to 28 percent. Neither allocation can be justified on developmental grounds.[32] Whether it may be justified on defense grounds is also debatable; in fact it is easy to argue that the defense expenditure is induced by mythological enemies created by outside influences, including those of the arms producers.

One may also question the efficiency of expenditure on certain construction projects, steel mills, and other non-viable programs which sustain asymmetric interdependence, while contributing little to the needed structural change in the economy. While describing investment by the Arabs, the following observation applies to all OPEC:

> The paucity of contracts for plants producing machinery, electrical goods, scientific equipment and transportation equipment underlies the non-industrialized nature of most of the region. Such industries require skilled workers and large sophisticated, affluent markets. It may well be decades, for instance, before plants are established to produce the machinery and equipment for the region's growing petrochemical industry. Although autos are assembled in a number of countries and buses are assembled in Iran, Algeria and Lebanon, there are not supportive industries to supply parts to the assembly plants. On the other hand, a beginning is being made in Morocco, Egypt, Lebanon, Iraq and Iran, where contracts have been let for the construction of plants to produce tires, batteries, valves and miscellaneous auto parts.[33]

However, only two or the countries that are showing a beginning are oil producers; the rest are dependent on imports of machinery, rather than on making it for their industries.

These observations lead to the following conclusions: The LDC resource producers use a small percentage of their resources domestically; they have continued and sometimes succeeded in adjusting prices to their benefit; they have utilized the newly acquired wealth in ways that will not reduce their dependence, nor will it make their interdependence viable. Therefore, to develop their economies and to reduce their dependence and create stability, they need to adopt new policies, or options as suggested above.

New approaches or initiatives have been proposed for Saudi Arabia as an oil producer, presumably by oil producers as follows: "The Downstream Operations Initiative" would give Saudi Arabia certain economic privileges in the United States in return for secure oil supplies; presumably the same initiative could be applied to other parties. The "Oil for Industry" initiative would promote exchange of oil for industrial machinery and technological expertise to permit fair conditions for development and competition. "The Inter-Regional Development Initiative" would channel surplus capital into capital-starved countries in the region to promote inter-regional development.[34]

These initiatives, however, are not much different from the policies used in recent years, in varying degrees of emphasis on one initiative or the other. What is lacking is a serious effort to reduce to asymmetry of dependence and vulnerability of the LDC resource producers. The option that seems most appropriate, though probably the most difficult, is Option 5b, as illustrated above in Figure 1.

Will the developing resource producers be able to implement structural change as proposed in Option 5b of Table IV, namely to reduce the supply of raw material and increase the supply of processed derivatives without price control? Will they advance resource conversion and plan their utilization policy to be fully coordinated with their output policy?

No doubt they can, but whether they will or not depends on their commitment to development, their ability to recruit the complementary inputs, and their readiness to give up some of the power that seems to have been generated by their monopoly over the resource supply.

It has been suggested that developing countries go through four stages in the process of industrialization: from an open economy with production and export of raw material, to a closed economy with easy import substitution, to a closed economy with difficult import substitution, and finally to the phase of diversified export of manufactured goods with an open economy and industrialization.[35] Our proposal simply accelerates these stages by focusing on the conversion and domestic utilization of the strategic resources to promote diversification of exports. As illustrated in the case of Iran, there is no reason why the LDC resource producers cannot achieve this viable interdependence with the consumers of their products.

FOOTNOTES

*I wish to thank Andrzej Brzeski, Peter Lindert, Anasta-
sios Papthansis, Barnard Seligman, John Elliott and
John Shilling for helpful comments on earlier versions
of this paper.

[1]United Nations document A/Res/3202(S-VI) in Dept. of
State, Selected Documents, No.1, Aug. 1975.

[2]D.C.M. Platt, "Further Objections to the Imperialism
of Free Trade," Economic History Review, 2nd ser.
XXVI, #1, Feb. 1973, and bibliography in it, es-
pecially Bernard Semmel, The Rise Of Free Trade
Imperialism: Classical Political Economy, The
Empire of Free Trade and Imperialism, 1750-1850,
Camb, 1970.

[3]H. Chenery and M. Syrquin, Patterns of Development,
1950-1970, Oxford University Press, 1975, Fig. 5,
p. 36 and p. 90.

[4]Some suggest that mercantilism is reappearing in new
and possibly dangerous forms; H.G. Johnson, "Mercantilism: Past, Present and Future," in a volume
by the same author as editor, The New Mercantilism,
Basil Blackwell, Oxford, 1974, pp. 1-19.

[5]Albert Hirschman, National Power and the Structure of
Foreign Trade, Berkeley, University of California
Press, 1945, pp. 14-15.

[6]For more detail, Ibid., p. 17 ff.

[7]For a survey and critique of various theories of trade
and development, see Jorge Salazar-Carrillo, Oil
in the Development of Venezuela, New York: Praeger,
1976, Ch.2.

[8]Klaus Knorr, The Power of Nations, New York: Basic
Books, 1975 esp. Ch. 3.

[9]Kenneth N. Waltz, "The Myth of National Interdependence,"
in Charles Kindleberger, ed., The International
Corporation, Camb.: MIT Press, 1970, pp. 222-3.

[10]Klaus Knorr, Power of Nations, p. 216.

[11]It should be noted that the smaller countries such as
Kuwait and Qatar cannot hope to become industrial

economies in the sense of this analysis unless they integrate themselves with other economies in the region.

[12]If biased, this estimate would be against our hypotheses and hence may strengthen the conclusions if confirmed. Data are from U.N. Statistical Papers, Series J, World Energy Supplies, 1976.

[13]The relationship between manufactured exports and employment has been recognized, though its measurement has remained imprecise. A rough estimate may be found in W.G. Tyler, "Manufactured Exports and Employment Creation in Developing Countries: Some Empirical Evidence," Economic Development and Cultural Change, 24(2), Jan. 1976, p. 363.

[14]Fereidun Fesharaki, Development of The Iranian Oil Industry, Praeger, 1976, Ch. 6.

[15]Interdependence, as this relationship is known in the literature, between less developed and developed countries has been attacked as a mechanism which keeps the less developed in that position "exchanging raw materials and foodstuffs for manufactured products from the capitalist nations." Klaus Knorr, Power of Nations, p. 234; See also Sanjaya Lall, "Is 'Dependence' a Useful Concept in Analysing Underdevelopment?" World Development, 3, #11, 12, 1973, pp. 799-810.

[16]Klaus Knorr, Power and Wealth, New York: Basic Books, 1973, p. 3 ff.

[17]For various attempts to measure power see my Economic History and The Social Sciences, Problems of Methodology, Berkeley: University of California Press, 1971, pp. 271-3; for measurement of vulnerability in a microeconomic framework, Martin Shubik, Strategy and Economic Structure, summarized in Bruce M. Russett, ed., Economic Theories of International Politics, Markham Publishing Co., 1968, pp. 148-70.

[18]For a general discussion of the determinants of power see Klaus Knorr, Power and Wealth, Ch. 4, on which most of the following few paragraphs are based.

[19]Kenneth Boulding, Conflict and Defense, Harper Torchbook, 1963, p. 58.

[20]Import of luxury and consumer goods may be curtailed without serious harm to the economy. Assumption #3

286

however, may be challenged in the context of a
market economy.

[21]Howard R. Alker, Jr., Lincoln P. Bloomfield, and
Nazli Choucri, Analyzing Global Interdependence,
MIT Center for International Studies, C/74-27,
Nov. 1974, vol. 1, p. 109; Yuan-Li Wu, Raw Material
Supply in a Multipolar World, N.Y.: Crane, Russek
and Co., 1973, p. 12.

[22]S.H. Schurr and Bruce C. Netschert et al., Energy
in the American Economy, 1850-1975, John Hopkins
Press, 1962, p. 1.

[23]OECD, Statistics of Energy, selected volumes.

[24]UN, Growth and Stagnation in the European Economy,
Geneva, 1954; B.R. Mitchell, European Historical
Statistics, Colombia University Press, 1975;
Statistisches Jaherbuch for Das Deuteche Reich,
selected volumes.

[25]Alker et al., vol. 1, pp. 117-23.

[26]World Economic Interdependence and Trade in Commodities,
Command Document, London: Her Majesty's Stationery
Office, 1975.

[27]UN, World Energy Supplies, 1976, op. cit.

[28]The most recent attempt to promote agreements has been
the UNCTAD Conference held in Nairobi in the Spring
of 1976; 18 commodities were on the list for possible stabilization during 1978. In the meantime,
a fund would be created to stockpile surpluses and
help to stabilize prices. Wall Street Journal, July,
19, 1976, p. 14.

[29]The latest effort in this regard has been a confidential
memo from former U.S. Treasury Secretary Simon to
the U.S. President urging a four-measure policy of
getting tough with Iran as a means of combatting the
power of OPEC. "Washington Merry-Go-Round", Sacra-
mento Bee, Sept. 21, 1976.

[30]The split on prices within OPEC which has resulted in
a two-price system illustrates the point well.

[31]One could argue that as long as they receive the revenues they needed, they should be able to develop
by using these funds as they saw fit. Unfortunately

tradition, economic conditions, technology, and
the international market structure render this
argument superfluous. The fact is that they
have not used these funds as they might have.

[32]Middle East Economic Digest, Feb. 7, 1975, p. 5.

[33]Bertrand P. Boucher and Harbans Singh, "Plow-Back:
The Use of Arab Money," Aramco World Magazine,
Sept.-Oct. 1975, p. 23. It should be noticed
that the authors are quite sympathetic to what
is happening in the Arab world.

[34]Michael Field, A Hundred Million Dollars a Day,
London: Sidgwick and Jackson, 1975, pp. 66-69.

[35]Dudley Seers, "The Stages of Economic Development
of a Primary Producer in the Middle of the Twentieth Century," Economic Bull. of Ghana, 7, #4,
1963, pp. 57-69.

APPENDIX: DIAGRAMATIC EXPOSITION OF VIABLE INTERDEPENDENCE

The thrust of the above discussion has been that economics and politics are intertwined in the assessment of interdependence through strategic resources. The grounds for this premise are that control of resources commands power and entails vulnerability and nations try to minimize their vulnerability and maximize their power according to the situation. In the relationship between developing and developed countries, it may be rational to reduce vulnerability even at the cost of losing power, at least in the short run. Processing or conversion of strategic resources lead in that direction. The following diagrams are an attempt to show the interaction between economics and politics, both in substance and in method, with the expectation that rigor and clarity would follow.

Measurement of Conversion

A product is considered converted or processed if it is transformed from its primary or raw material form, as measured by the value added to it, relative to the highest possible value added to it as a marketable finished product, as shown in Figure A1.

Value added is measured on the vertical axis in money terms; processing of conversion is measured on the horizontal axis in percentage terms. Maximum value added $Vm=Vf-Vr$, where Vf is the value of the finished product, and Vr is the value of the raw material. Vm represents 100 percent conversion. Thus, any degree of processing of commodity X may be represented as Vx which is a percentage of Vm. For example, if a fully processed pound of cotton equals $10 and a semi-finished pound equals $7, given the same raw material value.

Resource Use, Power, and Vulnerability

Production and export of the raw strategic resource are measured on the horizontal axis of the right-hand side of Figure A2. Power, as a positive,

FIGURE A 1

RELATION BETWEEN VALUE ADDING AND RESOURCE CONVERSION

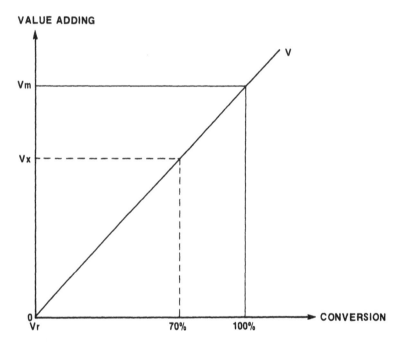

$$C_x = \frac{Vx}{Vf - Vr} = \frac{Vx}{Vm}$$

Where: C = Conversion
       Vf = Value of finished product
       Vr = Value of raw material
       Vx = Value added to commodity x
       Vm = Maximum value added

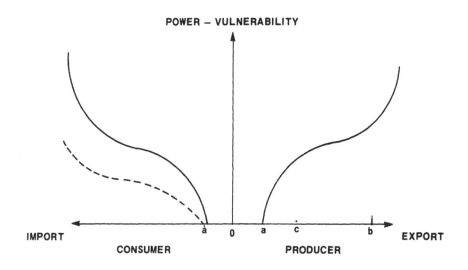

FIGURE A 2

RESOURCE EXCHANGE, POWER AND VULNERABILITY

POWER — VULNERABILITY

IMPORT

CONSUMER

PRODUCER

EXPORT

and vulnerability, as a negative, are measured on the vertical axis for the producer country. Beginning at the origin, the producer-exporter country would have no power until it has controlled a certain segment of the resource output and export Oa. The magnitude of that segment will depend on the number of producers and the country's share of that market. If the country is the only producer and exporter, the intercept Oa would virtually vanish and power would begin to rise as soon as production begins. As the country begins to export a resource, its power and its dependence (vulnerability) on the resource increase, at a high but decreasing rate up to a certain level, b, at which both power and vulnerability (dependence) begin to increase at an increasing rate. The acquisition of power up to b is due to the shock impact of entry into the market. The changing rates are reflections of the ability of the exporter country to capitalize on the momentum created by its newly acquired power position, and on how dependent on the resource the consumer country tends to be. The slower rate, between c and b, indicates that within a certain range an increase or a decrease in export of the strategic raw resource would have only a limited effect. Beyond b, however, the producer begins to have full power and to influence others by control of the resource. But at that point the exporter also becomes highly dependent on the sale of the resource and hence, vulnerable.

On the left-hand side of Figure A2, the power and dependence of the consumer (importer) are shown as functions of the control of the demand for the strategic resource. If the exporter and the importer are of equal size, wealth, technology, and determination and ability to back their decisions with military power, the two functions, on the right and on the left, would be mere reflections of each other. If, however, one or the other has a smaller share of the above characteristics, say the importer, that country's power function would be flatter and thus would reflect less power than that of the exporter country, as in the segmented curve. The loss of power, however, does not represent a decrease in vulnerability. On the contrary, it may represent an increase in vulnerability, according to how dependent the country is on the resource which must be shown on a separate diagram. This brings us to the following hypothesis: *The power of one country, producer or consumer of a strategic resource, reflects the strength or weakness of the other country, consumer or producer; however, a country's vulnerability is a reflection of its own dependence on the resource, either for revenue or in the production process,* as in Figure A3.

292

FIGURE A 3

BASES OF POWER AND VULNERABILITY

X's SIGNIFICANCE IN COUNTRY A

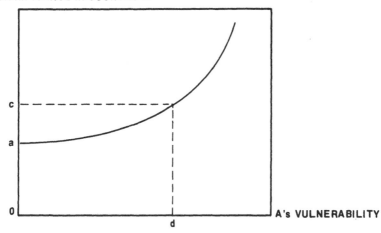

A's VULNERABILITY

B's ABILITY TO RESIST

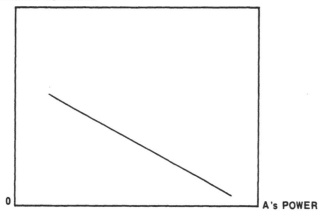

A's POWER

293

In the upper half of Figure A3, A's vulnerability is a function of the significance of resource X in A's economy. Vulnerability begins to be felt as the significance of X rises, vulnerability increases at an increasing rate, reaching a point of danger, Oc, on the vertical axis, corresponding to Od on the horizontal axis. This happens when interruption in the supply of the resource X would virtually cripple the economy.

In the lower half of Figure A3, A's power is shown as a function of B's invulnerability of ability to resist. As B's invulnerability rises, A's power declines in a one-sided relationship of dependence.

The implications of these relations are as follows: *A country's vulnerability can be reduced by reducing the significance of the resource in its relations with other countries. On the other hand, the power of a country in its relation with another can be curtailed only if the other country reduces its vulnerability or ability to resist.* Goodwill and self-restraint are considered too fragile as sources of a stable relationship.

Most producers of strategic resources export a part of the output in raw form and process or convert the rest into semi-finished or finished goods. Therefore, we should expect that interdependence with other countries would vary according to the resource utilization pattern, as represented in Figure A4.

The right-hand side of Figure A4 represents the situation in which conversion proceeds until all the resource supply has been converted into processed inputs or finished products with no trade involved. Beginning with no conversion but with trade, the producer has power and vulnerability as was shown in Figure A2 above. As conversion expands, both power and vulnerability decline because the producer would have less power over the consumer through loss of control over the supply, and because the economy would tend toward self-sufficiency and hence less vulnerability. In the extreme case, this leads to isolationism.

On the left side of Figure A4, the consumer country, in contrast, begins the relationship with power and vulnerability, but the power declines as more conversion takes place and less import of the raw material is possible. As conversion reaches a high level, close to self-sufficiency of the producer isolationist, the consumer country loses power through loss of control over demand. However, vulnerability of the consumer may rise sharply, as shown by the segmented curve, depending on the structural dependence

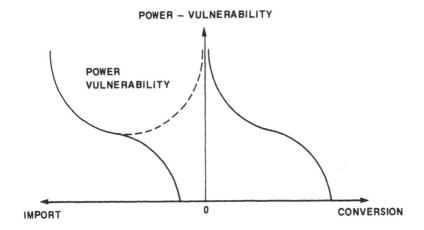

FIGURE A 4

RESOURCE CONVERSION—NO TRADE

POWER — VULNERABILITY

POWER
VULNERABILITY

IMPORT

0

CONVERSION

of that economy on the resource and its power-determining characteristics.

Given that no country would want to be totally isolated, trade may proceed on the basis of converted goods. If the producer of the resource converts and exports and the consumer expands the demand for the converted resource, as the supply of the raw material declines, dual dependence will be created, as shown in Figure A5. With no conversion, trade in raw material generates high power and vulnerability for both parties. The amount of export and import is implied. However, as conversion advances, the import of converted resources is shown to increase with a gradual loss of power and vulnerability, up to a point beyond which the control over demand for the converted resources becomes an important source of power. Hence, a high rate of conversion and export (import for the consumer) is virtually as unstable as the export with no conversion (import for consumer). The main difference is that in the process of conversion, the resource producer country will have developed its economy, advanced its technology, raised its level of income and provided employment for its labor force. To avoid instability and vulnerability, therefore, the producer country should seek a rate of conversion and a mix of raw material and converted resource export basket that are viable and consistent with healthy interdependence.

Figures A6a, b show the relationship that may result from combining the impact of conversion and trade (or no trade) on the producer and consumer of the resource. In Figure A6a, we show conversion and the tendency toward self-sufficiency or isolationism. The two curves intersect at a point, such as S, where both producer and consumer may be satisfied with the degree of conversion and trade. Beyond S on the conversion scale, isolationism becomes serious and unhealthy, and below S dependence and power render the situation unstable. However, the point S may be difficult to maintain since there are no forces to bring either country back to that point once a change has taken place. One would therefore think of a range within which conversion and power oscillate depending on the short run politics of the two countries; S_1-S_2 represents that range.

The conversion-trade policy may be more applicable and realistic. The curves shown in Figure A6b in which both producer and consumer of the strategic resource are represented, and range S_1-S_2 is the range in which a

FIGURE A 5

RESOURCE CONVERSION—TRADE

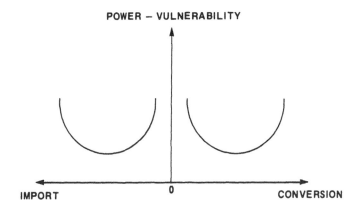

POWER — VULNERABILITY

IMPORT   0   CONVERSION

CONSUMER   PRODUCER
FINISHED GOODS   CONVERSION—TRADE

INTERDEPENDENCE BETWEEN RESOURCE PRODUCER AND CONSUMER

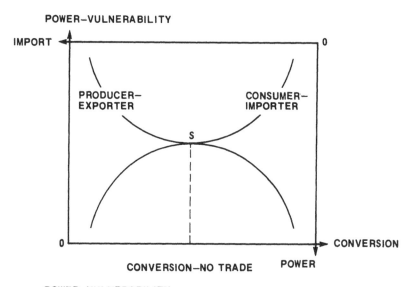

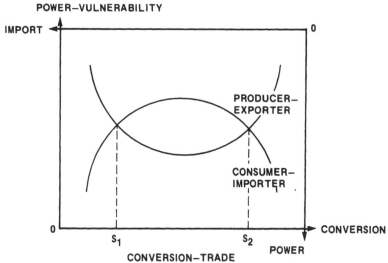

stable viable interdependence may exist. Prior to the intersection of the power-vulnerability curves at S_1, both countries are highly powerful and highly vulnerable and hence feel threatened. Beyond S_1, the power and vulnerability begin to decrease and the two countries become less interdependent and isolationist and hence less in threat of annihilating each other. However, as conversion and trade continue to expand, the converter-exporter country begins to command a monopoly power, and vulnerability, beyond S_2. The consumer-importer country also begins to command monopsony power in that segment. Therefore, they are again in an unstable threatening situation. The only stable range is between S_1 and S_2 in which neither dependence nor power and vulnerability are at an extreme level.

In that range both countries convert and neither country would have reason to move to more dual dependence where either little or total conversion would prevail. This range allows for trade, development of the economy of both to be capable of processing, and would make it possible for both economies to benefit from the resource in raising income, advancing technology, and maintaining a relatively high level of employment. Conversion and trade, in this case, would be viable in that they allow each country to specialize in the production of commodities derived from the resource and trade them with the other and thus both would have a more differentiated basket of trade commodities than under other forms of interdependence. Figure A7 represents a simplified impact model based on viable interdependence.

In Figure A7, the conversion-trade relationship is coordinated with value adding in the resource producer country, and in turn to the impact as indicated by development, employment, and technology. By regarding value adding as a function of conversion, we can estimate the impact of conversion in the viable range S_1-S_2 as Va_1-Va_2 on the value added axis. That is, value adding within that range would leave an impact on the resource producer country between M_1 and M_2 to render that economy self sustaining, with sufficient power and little enough vulnerability to want to stay there; hence the viable interdependence.

Viable interdependence, therefore, is a function of the structural change in both economies associated in a dual dependence relationship. The change would reduce the gap between the two parties in technology, income levels, and vulnerability. The new structure would make it unnecessary for one party to depend on the goodwill

FIGURE A 7

GENERALIZED IMPACT OF RESOURCE UTILIZATION

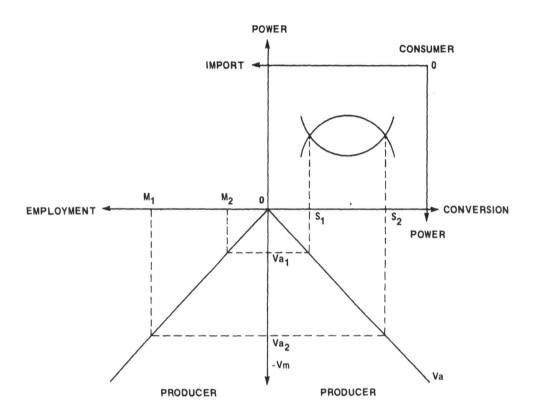

of the other, since it would make it less beneficial for either party to manipulate its power position, given the resistance or invulnerability of the other. The main questions that need to be asked are: How to determine the range S_1-S_2 for the producer and consumer of the resource, and what pattern of diversification should the structural change aim at? These are empirical questions; a preliminary attempt to find answers has been made above in the text. However, more thorough research is needed before precise determination of the range can be made.

IX
INTERNATIONAL POWER AND THE DISTRIBUTION OF WORLD WEALTH

Dagobert L. Brito
Ohio State University

Michael D. Intriligator
University of California, Los Angeles

INTRODUCTION

This paper presents an overview of a theory of power
and the international distribution of rights and resources
that we are developing in collaboration with J. David
Richardson of the University of Wisconsin, Madison. It
summarizes work to date and discusses planned future developments. We believe that such a theory is needed since
events of the recent past have made it increasingly clear
that the distribution of wealth among nations and the distribution of the gains from trade is a function not only
of markets and initial resources, as in the classical
theory of international trade, but also of the power of
the nations involved. One such event is the creation and
maintenance of a successful cartel by the oil-producing
countries. This cartel was able to use an embargo and
the threat of future embargoes to shift the distribution
of economic rents from the production and consumption of
petroleum. This display of economic power has served
as an example to other producers of primary products and
has caused them to consider the possibility of similar
actions to shift the distribution of the gains from trade.
Another such event is the emergence of various groups of
developing nations with demands for a new international
economic order. A third is detente with its implication
for trade between East and West.

Several future developments underscore the importance
of understanding the role of force in changing or maintaining the distribution of wealth among nations. The
first is the increase in world population and the fact
that a disproportionate share of this increase is occurring in the less wealthy countries. This predicted population increase and its concentration in poor nations
may lead to greater demands for a change in the distribu-

tion of the world's wealth. A second development which
highlights the importance of these questions is the proliferation of nuclear weapons and strategic delivery
systems. It is possible that in the future third world
nations may be able to make credible nuclear threats
perhaps against developed nations and perhaps against
one another in their attempts to alter the distribution
of the world's wealth. A third development is the question of rights to economic exploitation of the seas.

The relationship of a nation's power in its various
forms to its share of the world's wealth is becoming a
question of increasing practical as well as of theoretical
interest. Addressing these problems in a theoretical context is a natural continuation of the work that we have
been doing both on mathematical models of armaments races
(Brito and Intriligator) and on the role of power in bilateral trade (Brito and Richardson). In our research
on arms races it has become clear that is was necessary
to explain within the context of the model why the countries involved held weapons. We have been working on a
general equilibrium model in which force or the threat
of force played a role in the allocation of resources.
It is the evolution of this research which has led to
our interest in the more general question of the role
of power in the distribution of wealth.

This is a question that on the whole has been ignored
by economists. There are perhaps two reasons for this
neglect. First, force does not fit in the existing para-
digms of exchange, and second there is a feeling that
force is a malignant element in the process of exchange.
The result has been a feeling among economists that such
behavior is a political, rather than an economic phenomenon.

But political scientists have also generally failed
to address this issue. A principal example is the failure of previous research on arms races to specify the
basic cause of conflict and thus why nations choose to
hold weapons. In most of these models the arms race exists
in a vacuum with no reference to the role of power. Its
only connection with the rest of the world is the resource
cost imposed by acquiring and maintaining weapons.

The problem of rationalizing the holding of armaments
was not a serious one with the prenuclear age. A formal
theory of war is not required to understand intuitively
how nations use conventional weapons. If a nation wants
something controlled by another nation, the first nation
can use conventional forces to take it unless the second
nation has the force to protect its rights. Strategic

304

nuclear weapons, however, cannot be used like conventional weapons to acquire and protect rights directly. In the early 1950s United States superiority in strategic nuclear weapons enabled it to counter a conventional Soviet threat in western Europe. The use of strategic nuclear weapons in such asymmetric cases is reasonably clear. Conceptual difficulties occur, however, when both countries have comparable strategic nuclear forces. Since those weapons have an almost unthinkable potential to cause damage, there is a real question in the symmetric case about the reason for the existence of nuclear weapons. One manifestation of this problem is the current debate over the proper role of nuclear weapons.

Our previous work on arms races has led us to an appreciation of the importance of understanding the role of threats. We have also come to realize that the role of threats applies not only to arms races but to other economic and political phenomena such as international trade and the balance of power. Our fundamental research objective, which had previously been confined to the analysis of arms races, has broadened into that of developing a general equilibrium model in which power plays an integral role in the allocation process.

The balance of this paper is divided as follows: Section II summarizes the results of our past research and describes the general equilibrium model which we are developing. Section III of the paper gives a more detailed description of the problems that we plan to address and sketches how we propose to attack these problems. Section IV presents conclusions.

A SUMMARY OF WORK TO DATE

Our work to date consists of the development and synthesis of several models which represent component parts of the larger general equilibrium model. The complete model consists of three interacting components. The first is a nuclear war model, which determines strategies and outcomes of what would happen if there were various types of wars among the nuclear powers. The second is a model of an arms race, based, in part, on the potential outcomes determined by the nuclear war model. The third is a bargaining model in which weapons influence the allocation of rights to resources at certain crisis points.

By way of summary, Figure 1 illustrates the various interactions among the constituent models that are part

305

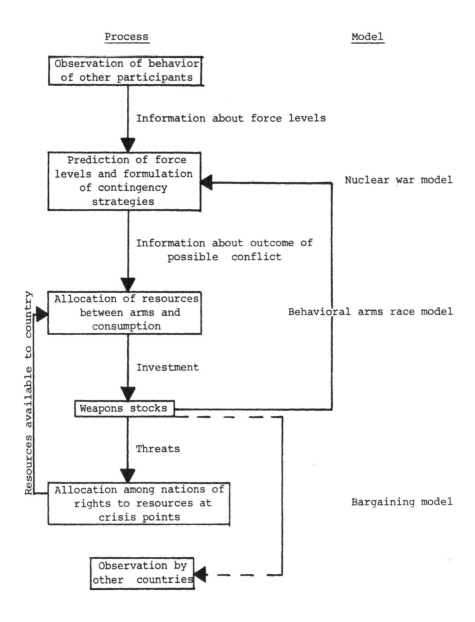

Process   Model

Observation of behavior
of other participants

Information about force levels

Prediction of force
levels and formulation   ◄─────── Nuclear war model
of contingency
strategies

Information about outcome of
possible conflict

Allocation of resources
between arms and   Behavioral arms race model
consumption

Investment

Weapons stocks

Threats

Allocation among nations of
rights to resources at   Bargaining model
crisis points

Resources available to country

Observation by
other countries

FIGURE 1

INTERRELATIONS AMONG THE MODELS

306

of our theoretical framework. It starts with observations
by each nation of the behavior of other participants, in
which nations may have different perceptions of one another. This information is used to predict future force
levels and to formulate contingent military strategies,
using the nuclear war model. These predictions and strategies influence the allocation of resources between arms
and consumption, as represented in the behavioral arms
race model. The resulting choices of arms acquisition,
together with existing levels and rates of obsolesence,
determine levels of weapons stocks. These levels have
three influences. First, they influence the observations
by other countries; second, they influence the formulation
of contingency strategies; and third, they influence the
allocation of rights in the bargaining model by affecting
the threat point. Finally the rights to resources influence the allocation of resources between arms and consumption.

The nuclear war model is an extension of previous
models which have been used to analyze two-nation conflicts (summarized in Intriligator and Brito (1976)).
See also Intriligator (1967, 1968, 1975) Brito and Intriligator (1973, 1974), and Kupperman and Smith (1972, 1976).
This model, which is based upon game theoretic concepts
in a dynamic setting, treats alternative alliance structures. It provides an important input for the arms race
model. Specifically it determines the threat point in
the bargaining component of the arms race model below.

The behavioral arms race model is also an extension
of previous models which have treated a bipolar world
(Brito (1972), Brito and Intriligator (1976b)). It is
formulated as a differential game of arms accumulation
in which each country attempts to maximize a criterion
function, e.g., the discounted utility of all future
consumption levels, conditional on the behavior of each
of the other countries.

The bargaining model is a nonzero sum game played at
certain crisis points at which rights to resources are
redistributed among the participating countries. This
allocation depends both on the existing allocation of
resources and the military power derived from the holding
of weapons. This game reflects the essential features
of brinksmanship by allowing each country to increase the
probability that it will obtain its demands, but only at
the cost of increasing the probability of its going to
war. (For details of this process see Brito and Intriligator (1976a)).

Having formulated the interactions among nations in acquiring weapons and at crisis points, the next step is to discuss the solution concepts we intend to employ. While some authors (e.g., Simaan and Cruz (1975) and Zinnes and Gillespie (1975)) have suggested use of the Nash equilibrium solution concept (not to be confused with the Nash solution of the bargaining problem) for the differential game of arms accumulation, we feel that this concept is not appropriate to the problem of arms acquisition. Such a solution concept requires that each country know the objective functions of all countries, which is hardly realistic. It also requires that each country have access to a common data set and process data in the same way, which is also quite unrealistic. We have therefore proposed an alternative solution concept in which, at each point in time, each participant in the arms race uses information about past current investment in armaments in order to predict the other participant's behavior conditional on its own investment is arms. These predictions are continually reestimated as new information is acquired.

The solution concept for the nonzero sum game played at the crisis points is based on our work on the bargaining problem (see Brito, Buoncristiani, and Intriligator (1975)). In this new approach to the bargaining problem a solution concept is formulated in which the final allocation depends on both the status quo and the threat point. Here the final allocation involves a reallocation of resources, the status quo refers to the existing allocation prior to the crisis, and the threat point involves the potential outcome of a nuclear war (as in the nuclear war model) using existing levels of weapons and a specific alliance structure.

THE LONG RANGE GOAL

The long range goal of this research is the development of a theory of the dynamics of international conflict based on postulates about economic behavior. As discussed in Section II, we have progressed to the point where we have developed a simple general equilibrium model in which power plays a role in the allocation of rights among nations. We plan both to extend the simple model we have already developed and to apply this model to several areas. Specifically we plan to address the following problem areas:

a. Strategic aspects of trade.
b. The balance of power and the timing of crises.
c. Nuclear proliferation.

Strategic Aspects of Trade

Economic analysis and academic commentary on international economic issues have often suffered from their failure to recognize the political conflict which is implicit in international economic policy-making. Many of the concepts that are familiar from international politics and military gaming have precise analogs in international economics--balance, fairness, retaliation, reciprocity, concession. And the important problem of how nations choose between consumption and accumulation of commodity and financial reserves is very similar in character to the problem of how they choose between consumption and weapons stockpiles.

As a result, it seems useful to employ some of the theoretical constructs that have been developed in our work on arms race models to address such familiar international economic issues as: determining the terms of trade, exchange rates, policies toward exports and imports, official reserves, commodity buffer stocks, and technology transfer. We propose to address a world composed of blocs of countries, a characterization that is appropriate for many real conflicts (e.g., between oil producers and oil consumers, developed and developing nations, and dollar and common-European-currency blocs). Interaction between the blocs should have aspects of both conflict and cooperation. Bargaining might take place periodically over variables that link the blocs economically and over which the blocs have interdependent control (e.g., exchange rates, commodity-price indexing formulas). These variables are generically described by the letter e.

The model employed consisted of two countries, each assumed to have a linearly homogenous, twice-differentiable production function.

Each country was assumed initially to have a fixed endowment of the rights to the flows, say x_i^0, y_i^0. There was assumed to be one key currency, M, serving all the purposes that money normally serves. It was the unit of account in which goods prices were measured. It was the medium through which x and y were exchanged for each other. And it was a store of value in its role as "reserves" or "official reserves." M was treated as a claim on country 1's output. When held by a resident of country 2, it was thus more descriptively a claim on country's 1 exportable, x, and the price of x in terms of M was assumed equal to 1. These assumptions permitted an alternative interpretation of M as a world stock of commodities with economic value, e.g., wheat or oil.

309

Both countries were assumed to be able to "sell" M out of stocks which they hold ("reserves"). Such M sales were normally made to purchase goods. Stocks of M could be negative for a given country, implying debtor status. Three behavioral assumptions were used to choose the model. The first is the familiar assumption of maximizing behavior:

(A1) There is an authority in each country that seeks to maximize the present value of consumption at each point in time.

The second assumption recalls the discussion of prediction in the bargaining context above.

(A2) At each point in time the ith country forms predictions of the jth country's control behavior for all future time periods. Such predictions are formed rationally, in the sense that they are based on both (i) observed behavior of the jth country in the past, in the future, and on (ii) the action that the predicting country itself intends to take toward its own control variable. When equilibria are generated by such predictions, they are self-fulfilling.

A third assumption parallels arms-control negotiations:

(A3) At a countable number of points in future time T: T=1,....; the controlling authorities in each country meet to negotiate the value of e, the interdependently determined variables (exchange rates, etc.). If negotiations do not break down (meaning if threats need never be carried out), then during the entire interval T,T+1 , the value of e remains fixed at what was agreed at time T. The negotiations process was assumed to be described by the solution concept in Brito, Buoncristiani and Intriligator (1975).

Some of the more important conclusions of this research were the following: (1) Reserve accumulations, whether of commodities or currency, improve a country's terms of trade, and therefore its share of world consumption and world wealth. Therefore, (2) there is a theoretical justification for mercantilism, i.e., for countries to seek balance-of-payments surpluses in order to build national wealth. (3) The model suggests that there is a theoretical justification for resource-exhaustion and stockpiling policies, i.e., for countries to accumulate and hold stocks of storable commodities such as oil. (4) There is also an analytical defense for the widespread

intuitive belief that international monetary systems
based on national reserve currencies are stable only
as long as those countries' balances of payments are
in balance. (5) Prediction-formation behavior and
the accuracy of forecasts have central roles in the
question of existence and dynamic stability of equilibria in international exchange of the type we describe.

Although these results are suggestive, the model
used is very primitive. We plan to expand the model
so that production, exchange, and monetary components
interact in a less restrictive fashion, and in a way
that brings us closer to conventional model specifica-
tion in international economics. The central theme in
this expanded model will be the relationship between
a nation's power and its share of the gains from international exchange. In particular, we plan to include:

(1) a fuller description of alternative payoffs
that are the outcomes of cooperation and conflict in
international economic policy-making;

(2) a more complete description of alternative
threats available to the various sides in the conflict
situations we intend to examine, leading to a "threat
set", with a probability measure defined on it;

(3) the development of a behaviorally-based rationale for the use of threats in international economic
policy-making, and an elaboration of their role in it;

(4) a loosening of the restrictive dimensionality
of our previous work to include at least a commodity
money that is not rigidly linked to another commodity,
and possibly also to include tri-lateral and multilateral international economic conflict;

(5) consideration of the suspected important ways
in which our conclusions will be modified when one
commodity is an exhaustible resource;

(6) consideration of the same when one commodity
is a public good ("technology" is what we have in mind,
along with the current conflict between developed and
developing nations over the terms of international
technology transfer); and

(7) elimination of the dynamic indeterminacy of
our earlier work through techniques developed in the
Brito-Intriligator approach to adaptive differential
games.

311

Among the issues we believe we can address with this model are: the advantages or disadvantages of a country's currency being held as a reserve currency; the impact of stockpiling on the terms of trade and national welfare; the national gains and losses from terms-of-trade index- ing and other commodity-price schemes being proposed currently by developing countries; optimal strategies for and toward blocs of producers of primary products and exhaustible resources; optimal pricing of technology and preservation of its advantage; and acceptable rules for international economic bargaining that reduce re- course to threats and consequent instability.

The Balance of Power and the Timing of Crises

In our work to date we have assumed that negotiations over the distribution of rights occur at known intervals. This is a simplifying assumption which should be dropped because it masks many important aspects of the problem. The timing of the negotiations over the redistribution of rights and the crises that may accompany these negotia- tions should be an endogeneous element of the model. To model this process requires that we in some way model the concept of the balance of power. Modeling this concept is a problem which eluded political scientists for a long time. We propose to model this problem following some suggestions of the work of Zinnes, Gillespie and Tahim (1976). However, it is our belief that the reason poli- tical scientists have had such difficulty in trying to model the balance of power is that they have tried to do so in a vacuum. We feel that the concept of the ba- lance of power has meaning only in relation to a particu- lar distribution of rights. Thus one could say that the power relation between a small nation and a large nation is stable if their shares of the distribution of rights are consistent with their respective national power. To illustrate, consider the case of Germany in the latter half of the nineteenth century and early twentieth. The various German states were unified into a nation later than the other major European powers. The German colo- nial empire was therefore smaller relative to its nation- al power than that of other colonial powers. German foreign policy during this period can be interpreted as an attempt to redress this imbalance. To model this pro- cess requires some theory that relates a nation's power and its existing allocation of rights to its equilibrium allocation of rights. It is reasonable to assume that crises and redistributions occur when there is a large imbalance in these relations. One can then view an arms race as an attempt to manipulate one of these factors.

312

The work we have done on bargaining provides a theoretical structure in which this problem can be addressed.

The determination of the crises points can be analyzed as an endogenous component of the general equilibrium model, using the structure of our approach to the bargaining problem. In particular, each side, over time, changes its perception of the threat point. When either side perceives that the threat point, given the existing (status quo) allocation, implies a new final allocation that represents an improvement to it, given the transactions costs involved, it will initiate a crisis. Thus the timing of crises depends on perceptions of both the threat point and the transactions cost. Analytically, this formulation can be represented as a zone around the existing allocation within which, given the transactions cost, neither side will initiate a crisis. This zone can be interpreted as a balance of power situation. We plan to analyze in detail both the nature of the zone of balance of power and its implications for crisis initiation.

Nuclear Proliferation

The problem of nuclear proliferation has traditionally been addressed by three groups of analysts with widely different approaches. One group has used formal models, based, in part, on the Richardson tradition. The second group has used a case-by-case approach to the problem, treating behavioral, technical, and political aspects involved in the acquisition of nuclear weapons by individual nations. The third group has been concerned with the legal and institutional aspects of proliferation.

Our objective is that of analyzing the problem of proliferation within the context of a general equilibrium model which formally treats the underlying behavioral and institutional issues and thus combines certain elements of all three previous approaches to this problem. This approach will allow us to analyze the effects of proliferation not only on military/strategic factors but also on economic factors, specifically the global distribution of wealth. The acquisition of nuclear weapons is a major manifestation of the potential power nations may use in influencing this global distribution. As new nuclear nations emerge, the relationships between the global distribution of power and the global distribution of wealth will be disturbed. This imbalance may, using the conjectured extensions of the bargaining model and the balance of power concept as outlined above, lead to crises and possible changes in the distribution of wealth. The main theoretical difficulty we see in this context is

313

that of extending the bargaining problem to the multi-nation case. We probably will not be able to analyze the general case in which alliance structures can change rapidly (e.g. recent development in the Middle East), but we believe we can treat the special case in which these structures change slowly over time (e.g. NATO-Warsaw Pact). Further it may be that most of the interesting transfers will be between members of the same coalition.

Among the specific questions we plan to address are whether there exist equilibrium levels for nuclear weapons and for the distribution of wealth and whether such distributions are stable.

CONCLUSIONS

The work we have done in the past on economic models of arms races has led to study the role of power and its influence on the global distribution of wealth. This is a problem that has practical as well as theoretical interest. From a theoretical perspective it addresses the role of power in the allocative process in an explicit theoretical framework that includes components such as bargaining and learning behavior. From a practical perspective it has implications for issues such as bilateral trade agreements, cartel behavior, the structure of the international monetary system, and nuclear proliferation.

BIBLIOGRAPHY

Abelson, R. (1963) "A Derivation of Richardson's Equations," Journal of Conflict Resolution, VII, No. 1, pp. 13-15.

Bader, W. (1968), The United States and the Spread of Nuclear Weapons, New York: Pegasus.

Boskey, B. and M. Willrich, Eds. (1970), Nuclear Proliferation: Prospects for Control, New York: Dunnellen Co.

Boulding, K.E. (1961), Conflict and Defense, Boston: Harper and Row.

Brito, D. L. (1972), "A Dynamic Model of an Armaments Race," International Economic Review, Vol. 13, No.2.

Brito, D. L., A. M. Buoncristiani, and M.D. Intriligator (1975), "A New Approach to the Nash Bargaining Problem," Econometrica, forthcoming.

Brito, D. L. and M. D. Intriligator (1972), "A General Equilibrium Model of the Stability of an Armaments Race," Proceedings of VI Asilomar Conference on Circuits and Systems Theory, November 1972.

_____ (1973), "Some Applications of the Maximum Principle to the Problem of an Armaments Race," Proceedings of the Fourth Modeling and Simulation Conference, University of Pittsburgh, April 1973.

_____ (1976a), "Strategic Weapons and the Allocation of International Rights" in Mathematical Systems in International Relations Research, Gillespie and Zinnes eds. New York: Praeger.

_____ (1976b), "Nuclear Proliferation and the Stability of Armaments Race," Journal of Peace Science, forthcoming.

Brito, D. L. and J. David Richardson, "Money Power and Bilateral Trade," paper presented at Econometric Society Winter Meetings, December 1975.

Brodie, B. (1954), Strategy in the Missile Age, Princeton: Princeton University Press.

315

_____ (1966), <u>Escalation and the Nuclear Option</u>, Princeton: Princeton University Press.

_____ (1973), <u>War and Politics</u>, New York: Macmillan.

Caspary, W. (1967), "Richardson's Model of Arms Race: Description, Critique and an Alternative Model, <u>International Studies Quarterly</u>, XI.

Carter, L. J. (1975), "Strategic Arms Limitation(II): 'Leveling VP' to Symmetry," <u>Science</u>, 21, February 1975.

Ellsberg, D. (1961), "Economics and National Security," <u>American Economic Review</u>, May 1961.

Fischer, G. (1972) <u>The Non Proliferation of Nuclear Weapons</u> (translated from the 1969 French edition), New York: St. Martin's.

Gillespie, J.V., and D.A. Zinnes (1975), "Progressions in Mathematical Models of International Conflict," <u>Synthese</u>.

Ilke, F. C. (1973), "Can Nuclear Deterrence Last out the Century?", <u>Foreign Affairs</u>, 51.

Intriligator, M. (1964), "Some Simple Models of Arms Races," <u>General Systems Yearbook</u>, IX.

_____ (1967), <u>Strategy in a Missile War: Targets and Rates of Fire</u>, Los Angeles, University of California, Los Angeles, Security Studies Project.

_____ (1968), "The Debate over Missile Strategy: Targets and Rates of Fire," <u>Orbis</u>, Vol. XI, No. 4, Winter.

_____ (1975), "Strategic Considerations in the Richardson Model of Arms Races," <u>Journal of Political Economy</u>, 83:339-53.

Intriligator, M. D. and D. L. Brito (1976), "Strategy, Arms Races, and Arms Control," in J. V. Gillespie and D. A. Zinnes, Eds., <u>Mathematical Systems in International Relations Research</u>, New York: Praeger.

_____ ,"Formal Models of Arms Races," <u>Journal of Peace Science</u>, forthcoming.

Kissinger, H. (1957), <u>Nuclear Weapons and Foreign Policy</u>, New York: Houghton Mifflin.

_____ (1960), The Necessity for Choice, London: Chatto and Windus. Kupperman, R. H., R. M. Behr, and T. P. Jones, Jr. (1974), "The Deterrence Continuum," Orbis, 18.

Kupperman, R. H. and H. A. Smith (1972), "Strategies of Mutual Deterrence," Science, 176:18-23.

_____ (1976), "Deterrent Stability and Strategic Warfare" in J. V. Gillespie and D. A. Zinnes, Eds., Mathematical Systems in International Relations Research, New York: Praeger.

McGuire, M C. (1965), Secrecy and the Arms Race, Cambridge, Harvard University Press.

Morgenstern, O. (1959), The Question of National Defense, New York: Random House.

Nitze, P. H. (1976), "Assuring Strategic Stability in an Era of Detente," Foreign Affairs, 54.

Pfaltzgraff, R. L.,Jr., Ed., (1974), Contrasting Approaches to Strategic Arms Control, Lexington: Lexington Books.

Quester, G. H. (1973), The Politics of Nuclear Proliferation, Baltimore: Johns Hopkins Press.

Rapoport, A. (1957), "Lewis Fry Richardson's Mathematical Theory of War," Journal of Conflict Resolution, Vol.1, No. 3

_____ (1961), Fights, Games and Debates, Ann Arbor: University of Michigan Press.

Richardson, L. F. (1960), Arms and Insecurity, Chicago: The Boxwood Press.

Rathjens, G. W. (1969), "The Dynamics of the Arms Race," Scientific American, April 1969.

Saaty, T. L. (1968), Mathematical Models of Arms Control and Disarmament, New York: John Wiley and Sons, 1968.

Schelling, T. C. (1960), The Strategy of Conflict, London: The Oxford University Press.

_____ (1966), Arms and Influence, New Haven: Yale University Press. Simaan, M. and J. B. Cruz, Jr. (1975), "Formulation of Richardson's Model of Arms Race From a Differential Game Viewpoint," Review of Economic Studies, 42:67-77.

_____ (1976), "Equilibrium Concepts for Arms Race Problems," in J.V. Gillespie and D. A. Zinnes, Eds., Mathematical Systems in International Relations Research, New York: Praeger.

Smoker, Paul (1963a), "A Mathematical Study of the Present Arms Race," General Systems Yearbook, VIII.

_____ (1963b), "A Pilot Study of the Present Arms Race," General Systems Yearbook, VIII.

_____ (1964), "Fear in Arms Races: A Mathematical Study," Journal of Peace Research, Vol. 1.

_____ (1965), "Trade, Defense and the Richardson Theory of Arms Races: A Seven Nation Study," Journal of Peace Research, Vol. II.

_____ (1967a), "Nation State Escalation and International Integration," Journal of Peace Research, Vol. VI, No. 1.

_____ (1967b), "The Arms Race as an Open and Closed System," Peace Research Society: Papers, VII (Chicago Conference).

Stockholm International Peace Research Institute (1974), Nuclear Proliferation Problems, Cambridge, Mass.: MIT Press.

_____ (1975), Preventing Nuclear Weapon Proliferation Stockholm.

The American Assembly (1966),"A World of Nuclear Powers?", Englewood Cliffs: Prentice Hall, Inc.

Willrich, M. (1969), Non-Proliferation Treaty: Framework for Nuclear Arms Control, Charlottesville, Va.: Michie Co.

Wohlstetter, A. (1964), "The Delicate Balance of Terror," Foreign Affairs, January, 1964.

Zinnes, D. A., J. V. Gillespie and G. S. Tahim, "A Model of a 'Chimera': The Balance of Power Revisited," manuscript.

X
INTERNATIONAL INSTITUTIONS AND INTERNATIONAL PROGRESS

John C. Pattison
Ontario Economic Council

Michele Fratianni
Indiana University

INTRODUCTION

Events since the late 1960s have called into question or tested the basic axioms which provided the potential for postwar gains from international specialization and integration.[1] Also many observers expect that international developments could provide many of the economic challenges of the next decade. These would include the indebtedness of many nations, protectionism, the exercise of commodity power, exchange rate instability and the coordination of economic policies among nations. If these were inter-regional issues within a nation, the political process would attempt to formulate corrective policies and implement them within the framework of a constitution and legal system. Internationally, the lack of a government to enforce agreement, property rights and to resolve disputes has been restrictive from the point of view of global development. Therefore, attention must be turned to international organizations.

As justification for looking at these institutions, consider the following points. First, because of the lack of a world economic constitution there is, and perhaps always has been, widespread disenchantment with international bodies. For example, Gardner (1974, 557) has noted that "Nobody now takes a major issue to ECOSOC, UNCTAD, GATT, IMF or OECD with much hope for a constructive result." Kindleberger (1970, 12) has stated that "The economist is inclined to...suggest that international organizations are rather like children's parties with prizes for everyone, no matter who wins the game." The Economist (January 12, 1976, 81) ran a story entitled, "Do we need an IMF?" Triffin (1976, 59) is concerned that "the unprincipled decision to increase international liquidity by 'restituting' a part of the IMF's gold without any pretence of first establishing a need for increased liquidity is a graphic demonstration of just how far the ideal of purposive international management has been eroded." Even Keynes has pronounced on the subject (quoted in Gardner 1972, 33):

There is scarcely any enduringly successful
experience of an international body which
has fulfilled the hopes of its progenitors.
Either an institution has become diverted
to an instrument of a limited group, or it
has been a puppet of sawdust through which
the breath of life does not blow.

Second, appeals for a new international economic
order call for the world economy to satisfy many of the
same goals that have been set for developed countries.
In particular, income redistribution is frequently mentioned. Yet there is no international equivalence to
the political and constitutional framework within which
income and wealth transfers are determined domestically.

Economists have moved away from the assumption that
national governments maximize a social welfare function
or the common good and from looking at each issue with
ad hoc hypothesizing. Theory has moved to assumptions
of maximizing self-interest. In contrast much of the
international economic literature is basically without
institutions or accords the "system" praise or blame
without behavioral analysis. Students of international
politics often do better on observation but get lower
marks on analysis.

In earlier papers we looked at the economic analysis appearing to underlie the work of one international
organization and explored the implications of a crude
model of theory of clubs for international organizations
in general.[2] These shed some light on particular aspects of the structure of the market in which international organizations work. It is our intention here to
develop the criteria appropriate to an analysis of international organizations. These will then be contrasted
with the existing economic literature, and policies for
reform will be discussed in this framework.

Although international political factors and interest group behavior are referred to occasionally either
directly or obliquely, there is an inherent economic
bias in much of the following discussion.[3] On the other
hand the paper by Tuma presents an analytical format
for dealing effectively with some power-interdependence
factors in international economics.

In the next section we develop some of the criteria
relevant to an understanding of international organizations' roles in the world economy. They provide insight
either on the roles, development or functioning of international economic organizations or guidance for focusing

on policy alternatives of suggestions for reform which
are discussed later in the paper.

THEORY OF CLUBS

The international economy has as many clubs as most
countries have trade associations, service clubs, etc.
Only a small number, perhaps ten to twenty clubs, are
of particular interest.

The economic theory of clubs as developed by
Buchanan (1965) and Ng (1973, 1974) has limitations for
the analysis of many international organizations. For
one, the assumption that non-members can be excluded is
valid only for some clubs such as GATT or customs unions.
The Olson (1965) model is both simpler and more interesting. According to this model, for an individual country
the optimum amount of cooperation is obtained where the
share of the gain going to the country multiplied by the
marginal increase in benefits for the group as a whole
equals the marginal costs. On the other hand, for the
whole club, the optimum extent of international cooperation will occur where marginal costs and benefits are
equalized. If exclusion of non-members is not possible
there is a strong likelihood that once the country with
the largest share commences its cooperative policy program, the benefits will accrue to all. No longer will
there be an incentive for other potential members to
participate, hence there can be a problem of free riding.[4] Before discussing some critical aspects of this
model, some simple implications will be mentioned.

First, market shares or relative pay-offs to individual countries are critical as they determine both
the likelihood of leadership by a major country, and
the possibility of free riding. Evidence points to
increasing atomism and less concentration in the international system. Not only has the growth rate of historically major countries declined (such as the United
States and the United Kingdom) but the strong growth
rates of many European nations and Japan have reduced
the relative size of the pay-offs to for example, the U.S.
Some simple numbers can illustrate the relative decline in
the U.S. share. As a share in the GNP of OECD members,
the U.S. has declined from 59 percent in 1953 to less than
40 percent in 1976. Japan has risen over the same period
from three to about 14 percent. Germany, France and many
other countries have also gained relatively.

321

As a share in world trade, the United States has also lost ground. The EEC has over twice the U.S. share of world exports. Germany and the United States are about equal in trade shares at the present time.

This theory suggests that the United States would have had an incentive to lead post-war international cooperation but by the early 1970s, the economic incentive to lead would have been vastly reduced. This is basically consistent with the post-war history from the Marshall Plan, GATT rounds of bargaining and finally the vents of August 1971, when the United States, finally and officially, threw out the remnants of the rules of the previous twenty years.

Most observers would categorize the role of the United States in the context of post-war economic cooperation in the above fashion without the use of an explicit model. Mundell (1972, 99) found it "inevitable" that the dominant country would influence the IMF. Gardner (1972, 99) noted that because none of the other countries "was big enough to be decisive, they did not assume the same responsibility that the United States had done for 'saving the system'." This is very close to the analysis of the Olson model. In terms of post-war economic history Marina Whitman (1974, 541) has pointed out that, "During the first decade or so after Bretton Woods, it was the United States, rather than the IMF, that made the bulk of loans to member countries."

The decline in the U.S. weight in the world reflects international monetary events as well as "real" factors. The non-reserve currency countries took little action to remedy the international disequilibrium. Their small and often numerically similar weights made cooperative action difficult to mobilize. In the end, considering its weight in the world economy, it was left to the United States to take action.

Another implication is that the larger the number of members of any club, the smaller the weights or shares of individual members simply as a matter of arithmetic and hence the less the likelihood that real cooperation (rather than merely following decisive leadership) would be forthcoming. This suggests that large clubs will be less effective. Certainly the increasing trend towards smaller clubs such as the Group of Ten, Group of Five, and perhaps even regional trade groupings suggests that they have a greater expected productivity for members. In any event the costs of decision making and management appear to increase as an increasing function of the number of members because of the need for multiple simultaneous interpretation, translation of documents, and so forth.

In more pragmatic terms the marginal change in GNP for members from moving beyond the group of five for most economic clubs is minimal. The group of five contains almost 80 percent of the GNP of the OECD area. For many types of questions, decision making is complicated with high costs and minimal returns by moving to larger clubs. Marginal contributions for a number of clubs are given in Fratianni and Pattison (1976c).

Richard Cooper (1975) has raised the issue of whether international organizations should exist to provide a sense of participation for nations, big or small, relevant or irrelevant. He recognizes that this will often reduce the efficiency with which essential tasks are tackled. The IMF and World Bank arrest the undesirable aspects of having well over 100 members by having multi-country representatives gear down the voting to 20 representatives.

One of the more intriguing aspects of the Olson model is that economic history since the period of industrialization has provided an oligopoly structure of nations which has tended to provide at least one country with a pay-off from cooperation. As the world becomes more atomistic, international economic cooperation becomes less likely in this model.

Another aspect which is fundamental is that of measuring the costs and benefits of club membership in order to maximize net benefits. Indeed not only is it difficult to measure these variables but the arguments involved in each function are far from clear.

Some early economic studies regarded the costs of membership as the dollar fees or costs borne by each member. However, to make sense of international economic cooperation in or out of formal clubs, the cost to individual members must include the implicit political and bureaucratic costs of formulating or changing a policy, a loss of sovereignty or nationalism, or an element of explicit real cooperation, transfers, loans, etc., such as central bank swap arrangements.

Measuring benefits is similarly difficult. For forum organizations, such as the OECD, free riding should mean that it is cheaper for countries to be free riders and pay for the publications rather than a share of the

expensive economic research and overhead expenses. In
fact these organizations provide a wide range of services including diplomatic point-scoring as an adjunct
to other foreign policy initiatives, advertisements for
government programs and policies in addition to the
services of economic research and consultation which
are usually considered. One interesting example of
economic failure or stalemate combined with diplomatic
success in international monetary reform is given by
Kindleberger (1976, 26).

To pursue the club analysis further, there is a
danger that the clubs, even though they are owned by
the members, will levy fees or costs on members until
there is an equivalence between marginal costs and
benefits for members. Marginal benefits (according to
popular and professional opinion) appear to be small,
positive by declining and the marginal costs of current
initiatives are rising. The total membership costs of
international organizations appear to be at least one
billion dollars a year.

ORGANIZATIONAL STRUCTURE AND THE THEORY OF INFORMATION

International organizations have grown in number
as well as in size over the period when their performance declined.[5] Recently several new bodies have been
started (such as the International Energy Agency). As
many observers have suggested that the number and size
of these groups should be rationalized, the obvious
question is by how much and where. Stated more positively, what is a desirable structure for a set of
international organizations. The functions of the
OECD, GATT, IMF, Bank for International Settlements,
etc., overlap for a great many purposes. Essentially
similar international studies are conducted for each
issue by every country as well as in groups such as the
European Community, EFTA, and so forth. This is supplemented by University and private research. The amount
of duplication is very great even among international
organizations, although the memberships differ. To a
large extent, duplication occurs because different clubs
cater to different interest groups, hence the analyses
are either not trusted or not of adequate coverage with
respect to issues, data and so forth.

Overlapping in certain functions could be easily
reformed. For instance, there is no need for duplication
in statistics. The United Nations and its specialized
agencies should centralize this function. The membership

of the OECD is both arbitrary and heterogeneous neither of which gives proper country coverage. Where atomistic competition is a characteristic of an industry such as agriculture or primary commodities there is little scope for economic cooperation aside from coordinating statistics and scientific research. Since agriculture is both atomistic and international cooperation simply does not occur it is difficult to justify having four major international economic organizations involved. Atomism, on the other hand, does provide the justification for international governmental intervention to support scientific research since individual producers will not be able to capture all of the benefits.

If these organizations were like governments one could suggest that each should tackle a sufficient number of functions so that "trade" and bargaining could resolve conflicting interests. In reality this is not a valid approach for at least two reasons. First, these groups usually must rely on the goodwill of members, as they have no coercive power. Their ability to produce and deliver a settlement over a number of issues is questionable to say the least. Second, most issues within these organizations are handled by separate committees where delegates have no authority for compromise in other jurisdictions. Presumably permanent delegations can bargain in the background but there is little evidence that such dickering can sway ministries in home countries.

The overlapping of function by international economic bodies can be looked upon favorably as competition to supply information to governments. One reason is that the cost may be worth paying to minimize information loss and distortion. This loss increases exponentially with the number of levels of the hierarchy, the share of the total information transmitted and entropy losses. Since international organizations are very hierarchical with no direct connection to national policymakers, that is information travels via diplomatic channels in turgid reports and via regular and ad hoc meetings of civil servants of varying seniorities, the information loss is likely to be high.

Although the theory of information has been developing for some time, its application to questions such as ours has been minor. Information theory has some insights to offer. Uncertainty in a system is maximized if the probability of each of n events actually occurring is $1/n$ (Theil, 25). In this case knowledge of what event occurred supplies a large amount of information. Given the large shares in the world economy -- both trade and GNP -- taken up by a small number of countries, the prob-

ability of given events occurring is greater than 1/n.
However, with the international oligopoly of major
economic powers being gradually eroded, the amount
of uncertainty in the international economy is increasing. This point is enhanced under flexible exchange
rates. It follows that the potential information gain
from international economic organizations is also increasing.

Another point to consider is 'what type of information is desirable?' When forecasts and outcomes are
statistically independent, a forecast has an information
content of zero and a potentially negative gain in information (Theil, 31). Clearly, where individual countries
can influence the forecasts of an international organization, as in the case of the OECD, any serious customer
should question the value of the policy making services
(forecasts) he is purchasing (see either Fratianni and
Pattison (1976b) or Business Week, April 26, 1976, page
92).

Another aspect is that there is no information gain
for a no change forecast because of the large realization
frequency which is likely to occur (Theil, 13). This,
plus the above point suggests the need for an assessment
of the forecasts of organizations such as the OECD.
Smyth and Ash (1975) have compared OECD half-yearly forecasts from 1967 to 1973 and found that not only were
they inferior to native forecasts, for example no change
in the balance of payments would have been more accurate,
but the forecasts did not improve over time. Goldstein
(1977) reached a similar view for the period from 1974
I through 1975 II.[6] To be charitable, the paper by Nugent
and Otani illustrates the many problems facing such organizations as the OECD in analyzing a major segment of
the international economy.

Theory also suggests that the time horizon of the
forecasting group must be longer than the speed of adjustment of the economies to adjust to policy changes. If the
horizon is shorter than the speed of response the information content is minimal. There is clearly also an aggregation problem to consider.

Another approach to the theory of organization is
essentially game theoretic. A basic requirement is the
knowledge of "who does what in response to what information." This highlights the basic weakness of international
organizations - at least the ones with many members. In
response to events with a high information content, many
groups merely conduct studies, having no ability to react
to events in a constructive way. The IMF of the BIS may

alter the course of events (e.g. setting different intervention levels for currencies). Usually one or more of
the major countries are forced to initiate policies even
if this is not the optimum solution.

A payoff function is a matrix which shows how the
outcome depends upon decisions of other participants and
external developments. Information and coordination is
useful in this context if the payoff matrix indicates
that actions by individuals are complementary. This may
seem obvious but international organizations have devoted
few resources to exploring the strength and timing of responses of countries to policy actions or events in other
countries. In reality this is an important and complex
problem. The simultaneous recognition of unemployment or
inflation and policy responses by individual governments
could easily lead to pronounced worldwide cycles because
of international linkages and feedbacks. The increasing
covariance in the cyclical economic activity of industrialized countries is a dramatic testimonial to simultaneous
decisions to deflate or reflate in key decision making
centers. Although interdependence is recognized and ap-
plauded as the raison d'etre for these groups, they have
shown little interest in exploring the theory or the empirical nature of such relationships.

While no hard rules can be formulated, the theory
of information suggests empirical studies and criteria
by which to appraise the nature of information generated
by international organizations. The microeconomics show
these groups to be costly so that duplication and overlapping to compete in the supply of information is likely to be expensive.

Public Finance Considerations

Questions concerning the economics and policies of
international organizations are often questions of the
optimal structure of government to accomplish given ends.
Consequently, looking at the issues raised in the context
of decentralized local governments in turn offers some
clues as to the issues in the international sphere. Rothenburg (1972) denotes four criteria for the evaluation of
political jusrisdictions in line with goals of efficiency
in output and given value judgments about income redistribution.

First, since majority rule imposes political external diseconomies on minorities, these will be minimized
where the voting community is homogeneous, that is political jurisdictions will tend to be smaller. Developments

in Quebec are an example.

Second, consider the existence of spillovers across jurisdictions. Parts of the total population affected by actions of one jurisdiction have no direct political influence on the active party. The effect of German pollution on the Netherlands, or the interdependence of business cycles are two of a large number of examples. These would suggest a larger jurisdiction. Third, the cost minimization of the provision of public goods suggests larger units.

Fourth, if the world system desires a goal of income distribution to be implemented, the criteria of maximal consensus and homogeneity will be inconsistent. Rothenburg argues that optimal heterogeneity will be required for "socially desired" redistributions, hence larger jurisdictions.

There are a great many implications to be drawn. Obviously clubs such as the OECD were formed to promote homogeneity and consensus at least in contrast to fora which include LDC's, tropical countries etc. The role of spillovers accords with the fact that for many economic issues, national jurisdictions are too small. Many national events, tasks and policies have spillovers. On the third point many public goods should be provided to and paid for by a wider group. Fourth, it is obvious that world income redistribution is a non-starter with no world political authority.

Hartle and Bird (1972) look at the demand for local political autonomy in terms of maximizing the present value of utility from consumption, the stock of real or financial assets as well as the stock of the intangible asset status (which yields prestige) and the stock of self-respect (which yields pride). Within this framework, to merge with other geographic groups could provide either capital gains or losses in terms of prestige according to the perception of the other groups. Information plays a useful role in this informal model. Information to the effect that other groups have better characteristics produces a windfall loss. This is consistent with the move of the third world to establish their own press service. Hartle and Bird (1972, 453) feel that policies to reduce "information flows between units with some differences in shared values will tend to increase nationalism or localism, while any policy increasing such flows will reduce it." They recommend policies to stress common values in the larger unit, encourage respect and foster knowledge of other subunits.

Education, communications media and personal contact are important.

Agency Growth and Survival

As mentioned earlier, one of the more interesting phenomena of recent years has been the emergence of new agencies and the expansion of existing bodies. To some extent this has been a result of increasing international interdependence and to some extent a recognition of the economies to be reaped from the production of international as opposed to purely domestic research and policy development information.

On the other hand there is much that can be explained by an analysis similar to that of Wilson (1961) or Kaufman (1976) and an associated literature. The philosophy behind this analysis is that agencies do not respond passively to demands made in the best interest of the international community but rather that there is an incentive system under which both client governments and international organizations interplay.

On the other hand following the analysis of Wilson (1961), agencies have a supply of incentives from which they may reward members. This includes committees, research work, extensive international travel. In turn member governments use these incentives to reward their own employees and political friends.[7] The continuing growth in the supply of incentives leads to the stability of the leadership of these groups as they can continue to essentially reward their clients with the clients' own resources. A reduction in the supply of incentives or patronage can very well lead to changes in leadership for international organizations. However, much as Wilson noted that within a city, certain municipal wards object to patronage - within the international community, certain countries object to the use of patronage by organizations in order to properly encourage the functioning and independence of these groups.

Kaufman (1976) pointed out many of the same features. This explains why the clientele of international organizations are often the most ardent defenders of these bodies even when their deficiencies are well known. With respect to the growth of agencies, it is a fact that new ideas for cooperation will likely receive more attention in newly formed bodies rather than being added to the workload of already overburdened organizations. Logrolling is also a factor as discussed briefly in Fratianni and Pattison (1976c). The deaths of existing organizations are even less frequent than those recorded

329

for U.S. government organizations by Kaufman.

Some obvious implications emerge. If birth control
or rationalization for government organizations is desirable, greater thought will have to be given to many of
the factors discussed in this paper. On the one hand it
is very obvious that there could be great costs foregone
in the absence of a mechanism for the protection of property rights or the resolution of conflicts. Competition
among agencies can lead to improved policy making. On
the other hand we have seen very conclusively an overlapping of jurisdictions in recent years with no measurable
improvement in policies. Also, it is our opinion that
there are grave impediments to the functioning of agencies in an international economic order. Unless statesmen
can come to grips with the issues of how to bind members
to an organization where world welfare has some prospect
of being improved, the growth of international organizations is merely a placebo.

The Role of Economic Theory

It is obviously important for any group which provides advice on economic policy to understand economic
theory. In particular the interdependence of targets,
indicators and instruments and the assignment of instruments to targets are fundamental. The side effects, for
example, income distribution, exchange rate or balance
of payments implications etc. must be understood. Hence
any policy advisor must have explicitly or implicitly
a theoretical framework with which to analyze economic
problems and policies.

On the side of policy agencies, Brunner has suggested that (1972, 7):

> policy makers find it advisable to raise
> the public's cost of information bearing
> on the precise nature and consequences of
> their activities...a "bureau's" rational
> preference (is) for vague, inchoate and
> malleably suggestive ideas.

It seems however that the actual behaviour of bureaux
will depend upon their function. One important distinction is that between a forum and a service organization.[8]
The former provides a framework for discussion, consultation and perhaps conducts research tasks for a number
of governments. Service organizations conduct more concrete activities. Fratianni and Pattison (1976b) have

330

suggested that eclecticism is a preferred strategy with respect to economic theory and analysis for a forum organization. By being eclectic an international organization can avoid antagonizing members, and escape from trying to compare and discriminate among alternative policies which would pose problems for the client governments. Eclecticism also permits the blame for bad or ineffective policies to be shifted without reflecting badly upon the work of the group. A service organization, on the other hand, needs a firm theoretical framework in order to accomplish its given tasks properly. Also a concrete analytical framework can prevent questions of international favor and discrimination among member countries if the methodology is known to members.

In an earlier paper we found the "Economics of the OECD" (a forum organization) wanting. For example, in the monetary studies series the OECD adopted the analytic methods used by the central banks of the countries involved even when they were known to be of dubious value and had been publicly criticized. Further support for this assertion can be found in that article.

Since we have not examined a service organization in our previous work let us stop to consider briefly the International Monetary Fund, the most important example of a service organization.

In contrast to forum organizations such as the OECD, the International Monetary Fund has occasionally been in the forefront of economic developments, for example in the analysis of the monetary approach to the balance of payments. Sidney Alexander's 1952 paper in the IMF Staff Papers was one of the early strands in the criticism of the elasticity approach to devaluation. Alexander introduced the real balance effect into the analysis and pioneered the absorption approach (that is, if one ignores the writings of Isaac Gervaise in 1720).

This work developed into an analytical framework for analysis by the Fund notably by J.J. Polak in articles in 1957 and 1960, and received some attention in the "change in policy orientation adopted by the British government under pressure from the International Monetary Fund after the failure of the devaluation of 1967 to produce the expected improvement in the British balance of payments" (Johnson, 1972a, 229).

It is also the case that economic theory has often been used as a tool to enact changes in the policies of international organizations. For example, Mikesell (1972) has noted how the World Bank's lending policies were criticized in the 1950s by the use of an explicit growth model, where capital was a major determinant of the growth rate. In the view of the critics the role of the Bank was to bridge the gap between the level of investment consistent with the target growth rate and the amount available from domestic sources. Hence the Bank's bankable project loan orientation was criticized in favor of a more liberal approach.

Finally, almost the whole population of international organizations have been individually criticized for, either supporting capitalism and imperialism, or for being Marxist. The title of Teresa Hayter's book concerning the World Bank and the IMF, Aid as Imperialism (1971) speaks for itself. Brunner (1976) has analyzed the New International Economic Order as an attempt by UN members to use that institution for the promotion of socialism. The obvious point is that the institutions involved each serve a market. The IMF, World Bank, OECD etc. are the creatures of capitalist countries and hence are obliged to respect the economic systems of the members. On the other hand, Brunner recognizes that "A majority of members of the UN" (1972, 6) are promoting socialism -- hence it would be suprising if the UN leaders were not sensitive to the wishes of a majority of its members. Here the voting system - one member, one vote, irrespective of size, economic output, population etc. - is the cause of this development.

NATIONALISM

There is not much in the economics of nationalism that is of direct relevance here. Johnson (1968) surveys some of the literature and makes many useful comments, for example (p. 9):

> One would expect to find nationalist sentiment strongest where the individuals concerned are most vulnerable to competition from foreign culture or from foreign economic activities: conversely, one would expect to find that nations that are leading culturally and economically will tend to be internationalist and cosmopolitan in outlook because this would tend to extend the market area for their cultural and economic products. These expectations accord broadly with experience.

The literature on international trade theory also offers insights into optimum policies to improve national self interest. Application to tariffs, industrial policy (e.g. OECD work) custom union issues etc. is straight-forward and will not be pursued here.

The role of nationalism in the context of international institutions is a more difficult question. In the above paragraph it is assumed that countries act in an unconstrained manner in their self interest. Within institutions, what are the constraints, and what has been the experience?

The longer run constraint is the danger of damaging the prestige and authority of the international organization. On the side of the institution itself this is reduced by the natural desire to accommodate the national clients who pay for the institution. In another dimension, marginal amounts of 'national interest' can be traded for alternative policies in bargaining for position (usually implicitly, rather than explicitly) within international bodies.

Much depends upon the judgment and backbone of each institution. Small countries have less scope for nationalistic tendencies within many international organizations simply because their budgets (and other implicit weights which organizations attach to members) are often low enough to disregard. Hence, in contrast to the view expressed in the section concerning the theory of clubs (that small countries are in the diplomatically unenviable position of being unable or unlikely to initiate cooperative initiatives) they are fairly obvious targets for the implementation of policies within an institution.

Scott (1974) indicates that nationalism must be an important constraint. "A Cosmopolitan Optimum" to be reached by the calculus of economics cannot be attained: (p. 15) "In international bargaining, each country looks after itself." Even in this situation there is a sizeable role for international surveillance, short-run notification, and establishment of conventions to reduce the costs of nationalism in the international community.

In practice no international body has been free of national interference. With respect to the IMF,

333

Bernstein (1972) has noted that occasions exist when "countries press their national interests in the Executive Board, sometimes with an exaggerated idea of how important the issue really is." Stern (1972, 104) has noted "the importance of national (and regional) sovereignty can be illustrated by the cleavages between the U.S. and Western Europe...in periodic meetings and decisions...in the Group of Ten and in meetings of central bankers in Basel."

One observable element of nationalism has been the tendency of nations to argue on the basis of a principle at one particular point of time and then change when this is no longer in the national interest. Bernstein (1972, 65) has noted:

> The European members of the Executive Board, for example, favored a liberal policy on drawings in the early years of the Fund, while the United States favored a very conservative policy. More recently, the reverse has applied. The United States once supported the policy that newly-mined gold should not be sold in premium markets because it deprives the monetary system of reserves. Now the United States supports the policy that newly-mined gold should be sold in premium markets and not acquired by the Fund or by central banks.

Personnel policy has been influenced by national interests and the desire to place nationals in senior positions. Certain posts in the IMF, World Bank, OECD, etc. have systematically gone to certain nations. Just as important, nations have used international organizations to serve the national interest by dumping unwanted officials on these bodies. Every institution has those from national administrations who have been both rewarded and simultaneously sent to pasture by being sent to these groups (e.g. James, 1971, 62). This appears to be one of the more common forms of abuse in the national interest.

Economic History

One point of note which emerges from a consideration of economic history is that, against the background of an environment which is not favorable to institutional forms of international cooperation, the role of individuals is crucial for both failures and successes. For example, Gardner (1972) has pointed out that if Hull, rather than Morganthau, had been Roosevelt's neighbor, the postwar world might have seen an International Trade Organization rather than the IMF. The role of Keynes and others can also be seen in particular negotiations and developments. Clarke's study <u>Central Bank Cooperation 1924-31</u> (1967) contains much useful information which highlights the crucial role of individual initiative among senior civil servants from a small number of countries.

In the same book, Benjamin Strong, Governor of the Federal Reserve Bank of New York, was seen to reflect a preference for dealing with one issue at a time rather than in a forum with "all countries at once" (page 41). It also appeared that, in contrast to the present time, central bank cooperation was only a "fair weather instrument" (page 72). The importance of nationalism has always been a factor for international organizations. Strong informed a senior League of Nations official that "neither the League nor any group meeting under its auspices was in a position to advise central banks on policy and that, in particular, any advice to the Federal Research would be very badly received in America" (Clarke, 1967, 38). It is also amusing that Strong felt that "it was expecting entirely too much of human nature to think that representatives of the central banks of a great many nations having differences of language, customs, beliefs and financial and political needs could sit down and agree on anything at all" (Clarke, 40). Clarke observed that there was a failure during this period to understand the interdependence of international economic problems -"danger spots were recognized individually, no one viewed them as parts of a single problem" (page 142).

Clarke (1973) has also looked at attempts to reconstruct the international monetary system in the 1920s and the 1930s. He found that international monetary reconstruction was over-whelmed by national policies, that pressures on decision makers at international conferences were short term in nature.

Mundell (1972), looking over two centuries of international monetary economics, found that the Bretton Woods system was unique. Only two other periods existed with a stable monetary order (An order...is a framework of laws, conventions, regulations, and mores that establish the setting of the system and the understanding of the environment by the participants in it (Mundell, 92)). These were the Roman-Byzantine era and the gold standard of the 19th century. The Roman era was not voluntary but imperialistic. The gold standard evolved, it was not created.

Consequently from the point of view of history, the postwar period of cooperation, that one can date from the Bretton Woods meeting, was unique. It achieved greater success than in any earlier period. The interdependence of economic life was elevated to a far higher place in the priorities of policy makers. But history also indicates that what cooperation did take place was fragile and the role of individuals in assuming responsibility for cooperation was central to any success.[10] At the present time, the institutionalization of cooperation makes the visible signs more apparent but there is little concrete evidence of success in influencing policy - actions taken would often have been taken in the best interest of the country in any event.

Institutions and Reform

The above discussion suggests relevant factors for the analysis of international institutions. It is now appropriate to contrast these factors with the literature on the reform of the international economic system. Much of this literature has consisted simply of a look at international monetary reform. Since this is central to many of the other areas, proposals for international monetary reform will provide much of the material for this section. We believe that, although there are more general points involved, an analysis of the GATT, WHO, etc. would require far more specialized and detailed attention.

Various writers such as Whitman (1974) or Bergsten (1975) have set out three alternatives for the future of international economic relations: an automatic self disciplining system such as the gold standard; the hegemony of a major power either to resolve conflict or to make its targets consistent with the remaining countries; or finally the confluence of national goals. With respect to the latter there is no reason to expect the market to make national economic targets consistent. Whitman's alternative (1974, 540) is for a "supranational-institution, which would substitute some mixture of rules and discretionary judgment for automaticity in de-

veloping consistent compromises among member countries."
A fourth alternative could be a serious breakdown in
international economic relations.

Whitman came down on the side of the United States
resuming its role as the nth country to stabilize the
international monetary system, and questioned whether,
in fact, the U.S. had abandoned this role. This was
not accepted uncritically by her discussants. With
respect to the role of international institutions there
are two points to note concerning her analysis. First,
she recognized that the U.S. could not undertake an
unlimited commitment to absorb current account deficits
and this role would have to be delimited by multilateral
negotiation. Second, although the use of supranational
authority was raised as an alternative there was no
discussion of how such an authority could work. Prag-
matically taking political and legal factors into account, Whitman felt that reform will be "informal,
piecemeal, evolutionary" (page 583) rather than by efforts to build a comprehensive formal constitution.

Whitman also reviewed alternative proposals for
reform. The United States proposal implied the need
for stronger international institutions. Yet this is
in contrast to the, at best, ambivalent U.S. attitude
towards existing bodies. The United States felt that
international decision making would only work if carried out by national representatives of high stature
and influence (Whitman, 546).

Harry Johnson (1972c) has suggested that the major
problem of reform is not deciding upon the mechanics
of a system to replace the dollar standard but a change
towards greater responsibility towards the world economy
as a complete system by the major countries. As suggested in the earlier sections there is a tendency for
countries to only support international efforts when
these are in their short term best interests. The presence of large numbers of institutions has permitted the
development of 'forum shopping' by governments to find
the institution which is most favorable to the national
position at issue.

While considering the role of the U.S. in reform
proposals, it is worthwhile to note that both Whitman
and Johnson, and a wide range of others have agreed
that a return to price stability in the United States
is a necessary precondition for reform. While the rate
of U.S. inflation has not declined to that reached by
Germany or Switzerland it is certainly below the OECD

337

average (if that is a meaningful statistic).

The Committee of Twenty of the International Monetary Fund (1974, 7) preferred the supranational option "based on cooperation and consultation within the framework of a strengthened International Monetary Fund." The tasks would not only include surveillance, cooperation and the job of making national targets consistent but also the active management of international liquidity.

One of the aspects of the Outline of Reform that should be commented on is the pledge to the effect that members signing would not introduce or expand trade or other current account restrictions (IMF, 1974, 23). This is an inevitable although inadequate attempt to tie together some of the functions of the GATT. The GATT not be outdone, set up in 1975 a special Group of 18 to follow trade developments, forestall monetary disturbances and coordinate policy with the International Monetary Fund.

In overlooking the literature there is not much recognition of the fact that the system of international organizations is out of control and that analytical issues related to the functioning of this system are at least as important as, for example, a theoretical understanding of how the international monetary system should work. One exception is Richard Gardner, whose 1974 Foreign Affairs article was a formidable indictment of the structure of these organizations. Gardner felt that a major hope was in disaggregation to decentralized institutions with select restricted membership to deal with problems on a case-by-case basis. He also recognized the necessity to rationalize this development in the context of a large and proliferating number of bodies. Since Gardner's article was published, governments have usually chosen to initiate new bodies rather than go through the time consuming process of adapting existing bodies.

Gardner also pinpointed the major structural problems of "how to equilibrate voting power, not just with national sovereignty but with responsibility for implementing decisions" (page 570). As the United Nations current voting arrangements stand, a small share of the UN populations can have a two-thirds majority and outvote major countries who have a responsibility for implementing an issue which may have no effect on those small countries which can control the vote.

338

The Jamaica agreement on international monetary
reform did legitimize floating exchange rates and
appeared to increase the responsibility of the International Monetary Fund to survey and police the
behavior of members. Since the criteria for such
Fund activities were not themselves spelled out---
indeed they involve many critical areas on the frontiers of theoretical and empirical research -- it
will be of more than passing interest to see how the
Fund acquits itself.

Report of the Trilateral Commission

The recent Trilateral Commission report on The
Reform of International Institutions (with Bergsten,
Berthoin and Mushakoji as rapporteurs) deserves attention. It is well informed on both economic and
political issues. (While we allow ourselves the
luxury of an economic view of the world we are under
no illusions that economics is sufficient over the
short run of the political horizon). In line with
the earlier set of options the Commission comes down
in favor of the supranational option and hence has
to face the issues raised in our paper.

The Trilateral Commission makes a number of general points, of which we are in general agreement.
In particular, functionally specific organizations,
such as the IMF, or GATT, perform better than multi-
purpose bodies such as the OECD. They also highlight
the necessity of consistent, decisive leadership and
its current absence. The report stresses that "all
important actors must be involved" (page 7), yet
we are concerned that this criteria be supplemented
by consideration of efficiency and effectiveness.
It is a simple fact that beyond a small number of
members, say the Group of Ten or Working Party Number
Three of the OECD, the performance of international
institutions declines rapidly and the payoff from
additional members is marginal, unless weighted voting
or other forms of representation can be employed.

The report recommends the establishment of a GATT
for investment and the extension of GATT rules to
prevent export controls. It recommends proposals to
strengthen and enhance the existing structure of bodies, as well as to bring new nations into the "inner
circles of international decision making." It is suggested that Iran, Brazil and Mexico should join the
OECD. Saudi Arabia might be invited to meetings of

339

the Group of Ten. The extension of multi-country representatives, as in the IMF, to other bodies is recommended.
While the reader can see that we have reservations about
some points, the Trilateral Commission's Report is one
of the more practical and sensible documents to read
to come to grips with current problems and issues.

The Club of Rome Report

The Nobel Laureate, Jan Tinbergen (1976) has just
prepared a report on the international order for the
Club of Rome. This monumental report leaves no international problem untouched and relies upon a massive
restructuring of institutions, domestic political processes, goodwill and charity to remedy international
economic problems. The report is concerned with power,
leverage and solidarity without considering their development, stability or ultimate consequences. In distinctions to the differing sizes of political jurisdictions mentioned in Section 2.3, the Club of Rome finds
that large jurisdictions are best because externalities
are minimized. International organizations are to be
the agent for the restructuring of the international
economic order.

There can be no doubt that the world economy faces
serious difficulties for the years ahead. The Club of
Rome's Report puts together a discussion of many issues
that have not received adequate study. However, unless
attention is paid to the economics and politics of international organizations, it is difficult to see how much
progress can be made no matter how admirable the basic
intentions.

CONCLUSIONS

The current status of international institutions
has developed haphazardly. It does not represent a
proper correspondence between the systematic needs of
the world economy and institutional capability, neither
in terms of the allocation of tasks to organizations,
nor of nations as members to these bodies. Indeed it
would be remarkable if such a development had occured.

Programs for reform are difficult to formulate
because of many of the conflicting tendencies mentioned
in this paper. If we were to make any recommendations
they would be that an economic analysis of the following
two broad areas is missing and is required. First, the

microeconomics of how an institution can work is needed, that is attract the optimal number of members and deliver the product. Equity, efficiency and so forth can be a part of this. The second need is for an understanding of how to run an international body: voting, budgets, staffing, the incentive system, etc. The economics of most international organizations have never been subjected to proper scrutiny, and their operational effectiveness has suffered as a consequence.

Finally additional progress will be difficult to achieve in improving international economic progress through institutional forms of cooperation unless the major nations accept greater responsibility towards both the concept and the mechanics of the world economy as an integrated system. One contribution of the existing international economic bodies is the keeping alive of this ideal.

This paper is the responsibility of the authors and not their respective institutions. The authors wish to thank Tony Culyer, Nake Kamrany, John Shilling and Elias Tuma for comments on an earlier draft.

[1]This is not to say that either the distribution of the benefits nor the burden of responsibility falls evenly on all constituents.

[2]The first refers to Fratianni and Pattison "The Economics of the OECD" (1976b) the second is "The Economics of International Organizations" (1976c). Some further thoughts on the subject are contained in "When it pays to cooperate" (1976a).

[3]We do not regard this as a deficiency for focussing on longer term issues. On the other hand many political factors impacting on short run economic events do need more careful economic attention: the diplomacy of trade conflicts, international monetary events, policy coordination and so forth.

[4]Note that to move questions of Pareto optimality in the analysis of clubs, for example, looking at the impact on non-members, is a much more difficult and interesting task (see Ng. 1974). It is also necessary to point out that this analysis assumes the usual convexities and well behaved functional properties that are beloved by economists.

[5]This statement is supported both by the statements of observers mentioned in the first section as well as by an itemization of events in recent years. The latter would include protectionism by a growing number of countries, failure to coordinate policies (where such mechanisms do exist), competitive exchange rate changes, and so forth. This is in clear distinction to the liberalization dating from the return to currency convertibility in 1958.

[6]These analyses are in no way invalidated by the unsubstantiated suggestion that the organizations are sufficiently successful at influencing policy

that the results are altered. For one thing the time lags in response to policy changes are generally longer than the forecasting horizon.

[7]International clubs offer attractive trips to domestic civil servants. Most of these are strong supporters of international organizations, particularly the OECD in Paris, GATT, UNCTAD, etc. in Geneva, or FAO in Rome. This analysis also explains, although not very satisfactorily, the paradox that the United States administration is known not to be favorably disposed to the IMF in Washington even though it is, beyond any doubt, the most efficient and satisfactory international organization.

[8]John Shilling has suggested that a distinction which is at least as important is that between groups which are financially independent and those which are not.

[9]A cynic might say that they were bound to be correct sooner or later.

[10]This comes out forcefully in Charles Coombs' (1976) review of his years at the New York Federal Reserve Bank, where he was responsible for U.S. Treasury and Federal Reserve System operations in Foreign currencies and in gold from 1961 to 1975.

REFERENCES

Acheson, A. L. et al. (1972) Bretton Woods Revisited, University of Toronto Press, Toronto and Buffalo.

Bergsten, C. F. (1975) Toward a New International Economic Order, D.C. Heath and Company, Toronto and London.

Bergsten, C. F., G. Berthoin and M. Mushakoji (1976) The Reform of International Institutions, Trilateral Commission, New York, Tokyo and Paris.

Bernstein, E. M. et al. (1976) Reflections on Jamaica, International Finance Section, Princeton University.

Bernstein, E. M. (1972) "The Evolution of the International Monetary Fund", in Acheson et al., Bretton Woods Revisited.

Brunner, K., (1972) "The Ambiguous Rationality of Economic Policy", Journal of Money, Credit and Banking, February, 3-12.

Buchanan, J. (1975) "An Economic Theory of Clubs", Economica, February, 1-14.

Clarke, S.V.O. (1967) Central Bank Cooperation 1927-1931, Federal Reserve Bank of New York, New York.

Clarke, S.V.O. (1973) The Reconstruction of the International Monetary System, International Finance Section, Princeton University.

Coombs, C. A. (1976) The Arena of International Finance, John Wiley and Sons, New York.

Cooper, R. N. (1975) "Prolegomena to the Choice of an International Monetary System", in Bergstein and Krause, World Politics and International Economics, Brookings Institution, Washington.

Fratianni, M. and J. C. Pattison (1976a) "When it Pays to Cooperate", The Banker, August, 891-894.

_____, (1976b) "The Economics of the OECD" in Brunner and Meltzer (ed.) Institutions Policies and Economic Performance. North Holland. Also published as a supplement to the Journal of Monetary Economics.

344

_____, (1976c) "The Economics of International Organizations", mimeo.

Gardner, R. N. (1972) "The Political Setting", in Acheson et al., Bretton Woods Revisited.

_____,(1974) "The Hard Road to World Order", Foreign Affairs, April, 556-576.

Goldstein, H. N. (1977) 'Review of OECD Economic Outlook, 18'. Journal of Money, Credit and Banking, February, 117-122.

Hartle, D. and R. M. Bird (1972) "The Demand for Local Political Autonomy: An Individualistic Theory", Conflict Resolution.

Hayter, T. (1971) Aid as Imperialism, Penguin Books, Harmondsworth, England.

International Monetary Fund (1974) International Monetary Reform Documents of the Committee of Twenty, Washington.

James, R. J. (1971) "The Evolving Concept of the International Civil Service", in Jordon (ed.) International Administration, Oxford University Press, London, New York and Toronto.

Johnson, H. G. (1967) "A Theoretical Model of Economic Nationalism in New and Developing States", in H.G. Johnson (ed.) Economic Nationalism in Old and New States, Chicago.

_____, (1972a) Further Essays in Monetary Economics, Allen and Unwin, London.

_____, (1972b) "A General Commentary" in Acheson et al., Bretton Woods Revisited.

_____, (1972c) "Political Economy Aspects of International Monetary Reform", Journal of International Economics, September, 401-423.

Kaufman, H. (1976) Are Government Organizations Immortal? Brookings Institution, Washington.

Kindleberger, C. P. (1970) Power and Money, Macmillan, London and New York.

345

Kindleberger, C. P. (1976) "The Exchange Stability
    Issue at Rambouillet and Jamaica", in Bernstein
    et al. Reflections on Jamaica.

Mikesell, R. (1972) "The Emergence of the World Banks
    as a Development Institution", in Acheson et al.
    Bretton Woods Revisited.

Mundell, R. A. (1972) "The Future of the International
    Financial System", in Acheson et al. Bretton
    Woods Revisited.

Ng, Y-K, (1973) "The Economic Theory of Clubs": Pareto
    Optimality Conditions", Economica, August, 291-
    298.

Ng, Y-K, (1974) "The Economic Theory of Clubs: Optimal
    Tax/Subsidy", Economica, August 308-321.

Nugent, J. and I. Otani (1976) "Stagflation in the
    World Economy", Paper prepared for the Conference
    on Major International Economic Issues, University
    of Southern California, December.

Olson, M. (1965) The Logic of Collective Action, Harvard
    University Press, Cambridge, Massachusetts.

Rothenberg, J. (172) "Local Decentralization and the
    Theory of Optimal Government", in Edel and Roth-
    enberg, Readings in Urban Economics, Macmillan,
    New York.

Scott, A. (1974) "Economic Aspects of Transfrontier
    Pollution and Balance of Trade: OECD Performance"
    Economic Journal, June, 361-364.

Stern, R. M. (1972) "Commentary" in Acheson et al.
    Bretton Woods Revisited.

Theil, H. (1967) Economics and Information Theory,
    North-Holland, Amsterdam.

Tinbergen, J. (Coordinator) (1976) Reshaping the Inter-
    national Order, E. P. Dutton and Company, New York.

Tuma, E. (1976) "Strategic Resources and Viable Inter-
    dependence", Paper Prepared for the Conference on
    Major International Economic Issues, University
    of Southern California, December.